NIGE TASSELL

The Bottom Corner

Hope, Glory and Non-League Football

YELLOW JERSEY PRESS
LONDON

1 3 5 7 9 10 8 6 4 2

Yellow Jersey Press, an imprint of Vintage
20 Vauxhall Bridge Road
London SW1V 2SA

Yellow Jersey Press is part of the Penguin Random House group of companies
whose addresses can be found at global.penguinrandomhouse.com

Penguin
Random House
UK

Copyright © Nige Tassell 2016

First published by Yellow Jersey Press in trade paperback in 2016
First published by Yellow Jersey Press in paperback in 2017

www.vintage-books.co.uk

A CIP catalogue record for this book is available from the British Library

ISBN 9780224100601

Printed and bound by Clays Ltd, St Ives plc

Penguin Random House is committed to a sustainable future
for our business, our readers and our planet. This book is made
from Forest Stewardship Council® certified paper.

MIX
Paper from
responsible sources
FSC
www.fsc.org   FSC® C018179

To Jane,
the first name on the team sheet

Contents

1

AUGUST

Sleeping giants and summer lawns

With expert fingers, Steve Laker delicately pulls a wad of football cards from their cellophane sheath. The cards date from the early 1970s and, in their original plastic wrapping, would have been accompanied by a hard, yellow strip of bubble gum. The gum, tasteless and inedible, would have been discarded as soon as the packet was opened. The cards were the real treasure, the faces of footballing icons gazing straight back into the eyes of the beholder.

Laker flicks through the pile with the dexterity of a Monte Carlo croupier, a new player revealed on each turn of a card. These are faces familiar to any student of FA Cup football who's of a certain age. Here's Charlie Cooke, the Chelsea winger whose chip supplied Peter Osgood's equaliser in the 1970 final replay. There's Allan 'Sniffer' Clarke, scorer of the only goal in 1972 when Leeds prevented Arsenal leaving Wembley with the trophy for a second successive season. And here's a young Peter Mellor, a shot taken of the Fulham goalkeeper two or three years before he gifted West Ham both goals in the '75 final.

Laker is hoping that some of this FA Cup magic will rub off on his fingertips. On this particular Friday afternoon, he's at work in his day job as a cigarette-card dealer; downstairs from his office is a warehouse packed with five million such cards. But tomorrow he'll be donning his tracksuit as the manager of Bishop Sutton, a team from a one-shop Somerset village embarking on their latest FA Cup adventure. It may be mid-August, but for those clubs at levels nine and ten of English football's pyramid, tomorrow is a red-letter day – the Extra Preliminary Round of the world's oldest cup competition.

There is every indication that Bishop Sutton's FA Cup adventure this year will be a short one – say, ninety minutes plus stoppages. Despite winning the Toolstation Western League Premier Division just a couple of years back, they finished last season on a nineteen-match losing streak. Along with a lorryload of 5-0 and 6-0 thumpings, their porous defence conceded double figures on three occasions, 13-0, 11-0, 11-1 – the stuff of mismatched schoolboy football. Relegation became a nailed-on certainty as early as Christmas. After seventeen consecutive seasons in the same division, they slipped down to the tenth tier, finishing fourteen points adrift of the nearest team and desperately hoping that no one noticed a goal difference of -109.

Despite the drop down a division, those poor performances have continued into the new season. Two matches, two home defeats. They haven't won a competitive game since last November; they haven't even scored in one since March. In the top ten tiers of English club football, no other team is as out of form as them. Bishop Sutton occupy the bottom corner. Yet Steve Laker isn't a manager nervously looking over his shoulder, expecting his chairman's patience to have finally evaporated, a metaphorical P45 close to hand. While some might suggest the cold hard facts are inescapable, impossible to argue against, there are extenuating circumstances.

After winning the league title in 2013, Bishop Sutton's modest ground needed upgrading to meet the requirements of the Southern League. Without the funds to enact these, the club was denied promotion. Once the news came through, the make-up of the club changed overnight. 'There was a mass exodus of players and management staff all at once,' Laker explains, 'leaving the club in the situation where they had to bring in a squad from Bath University, along with two members of staff from there as managers. They did well and kept the club in the Premier Division. The following season, one of the managers got a job with Southampton's academy and the other said he couldn't fully give his time to Bishop Sutton because of university commitments, so he stepped down. As soon as those two went, players started drifting away.'

At that point, Laker – who as a youngster was attached to one of Plymouth Argyle's satellite academies before playing several years at county league level – was persuaded to leave his position as assistant manager at Bridgwater Town and head inland to the Chew Valley. 'When I came on board, I was left with just two players mid-season. The university players were great, but they weren't regular enough. University students aren't back until September and then they disappear for Christmas. It could be as many as ten games that they miss.

'I needed a squad of players who were going to be there week in, week out. I tried to bring in any Tom, Dick and Harry just to finish the season. We had to sign people at the absolute last minute just to get a team out. I'll put my hands up – some of them simply weren't good enough. But you get heavily fined if you can't fulfil a fixture. I think it's close to £1,000. I had ten games left, so potentially that's up to £10,000. That would have crippled the club. My personal goal for the rest of that season wasn't results. It was to fulfil our fixtures. We managed to do that, but unfortunately it was at the cost of a place in the Premier Division.'

In rebuilding the team, Laker – at the age of just thirty-one – is rebuilding the club. This is an outfit from a small village, where the bare bones of the first team are, through his signings, slowly gaining flesh. There's no set-up stretching through the age groups here, no reserve teams; just an under-18s side that one of the first-teamers looks after. The progress – or otherwise – of the first team determines the fate of the whole club. And, extenuating circumstances or not, the pressure will surely build on Laker over the next month or two if there's no tangible improvement on the pitch. A Premier League or Championship manager might be under the round-the-clock scrutiny of fans and media, but, with his well-upholstered current account able to cushion any downturn in his professional fortunes, he can flick the switch to 'off' whenever he chooses, able to skip gaily off the merry-go-round and escape into an extended sabbatical or early retirement. The actual *survival* of a football club is not weighing heavy on his shoulders. It is on Steve Laker's. Real pressure.

Tomorrow, the FA Cup will provide a distraction from the league form, a chance for Bishop Sutton to undertake a piece of giant-killing, however modest. Their opponents are Street, from one division above. But a small slice of glory isn't what's really on offer. Laker takes a sip of his lukewarm coffee and offers an earnest appraisal. 'The FA Cup is potentially a bloodline for a lot of clubs. I think it's something like eighteen hundred quid if you get through the Extra Preliminary Round. It's vital for immediate income.

'At Toolstation level, especially in the Premier Division, a lot of clubs pay their players. And some of them pay decent money – anything up to £100 per match. But, quite frankly, we're not in a position to pay players. I'd love to be able to, but I worked out that, to pay sixteen lads just ten pounds a game, it'd cost six and a half grand a season.' This frustration at not even being able to cover his players' petrol money comes in the same month in which Cristiano Ronaldo not only bought his agent an entire Greek island as a wedding gift, but also reportedly installed a £20,000 waxwork of himself in his Madrid home. 'We ask players to play for the love of the club and the love of football. We don't ask them to pay subs, but they get the referee, they get the linesmen, they play under floodlights during the week ... And they're playing in the FA Cup.'

With no budget to pay players, bolstering his squad

with talent that can cope at this level of football becomes a tough ask. Laker's priority is to stabilise the club, end this season mid-table and entice more players come next summer. 'Everybody around the league knows that we are a team that's crumbled. Also, there's such a large volume of teams in and around the Bristol area playing Western League or Southern League football. We're all fighting over the same players.'

Despite promising his wife that, after a draining season, he'd take a couple of months away from football during the summer, Laker spent June and July on the prowl for new players. 'I haven't stopped. It's gone right through from last season to this one.' And not only has his summer been written off, each week during the season is entirely dominated by football matters, whether it's talking several times a day to his chairman, filing player registrations, checking on his players' availability for the weekend, taking training sessions, writing match reports for the programme or undertaking admin for the website. 'Officially, it's training twice a week and a Saturday match. Unofficially, I'm probably doing as much as a Conference manager does.' As if to prove a point, his phone explodes into life. A glance at the caller's name. 'Yup, that's a football call.'

Laker's frank words about the realpolitik of non-league football finances and the real worth of the FA Cup to teams at this level have been refreshing, but his keen, sharp, brown eyes can't hide a sense of excitement about tomorrow's game, especially as he never played in the competition himself. 'On the surface I'm calm, but only because I can't show the excitement that's underneath.' He definitely thinks his young charges have a chance against Street come three o'clock tomorrow. 'Last season we drew with them and lost to them. We know them well and we know they've got some quality players.' He deftly slides the football cards back into their protective sleeve. 'But it's all down to the ninety minutes. It's eleven versus eleven.'

* * *

When the third goal goes in, Steve Laker spins 180 degrees to slam his palm into the roof of the dugout, before theatrically extending his arms to an unspecified deity in the sky. We're ten minutes into the second half, but Street are effectively already into the next round. Bishop Sutton's modest dreams – of on-the-pitch FA Cup glory and of an injection into the club's coffers – have been dashed for another twelve months.

It all started promisingly enough this afternoon with the sunshine – after two grey days of downpours – flavouring the air with optimism here at Lakeview, Bishop Sutton's home ground. The weather makes everything even more idyllic, the view across to the hills on the other side of the Chew Valley equalled by very few football stadia. Hedge trimmers buzz in adjacent gardens, accompanied by shrieks and splashes from trampolines and paddling pools. Oohs and aahs drift across from the cricket pitch on the other side of the hedge as either a dropped catch or a failed stumping uses up one of the batsman's lives. Dragonflies dance on the air, while a pair of swallows bank and weave, taking impossibly sharp turns as if tracing the pitch's white lines. Afternoons like this were surely the inspiration for the title of Joni Mitchell's 1975 album *The Hissing Of Summer Lawns*.

The club's own summer lawn looks in fine fettle, even if the immaculately mown stripes on the Lakeview turf serve to emphasise the sharp slope from penalty spot to goalmouth at the nearside end (insert your own 'level playing field' joke here). Just beyond the touchline, a clump of exotic fungi is a reminder of the many damp days endured so far this summer. Today's weather, though, is certainly far removed from the conditions often endured when the big boys join the competition in the Third Round in early January – the FA Cup of deep mid-winter, of sticky pitches, of clag and clod.

For those teams for whom the competition is synonymous with August (and September if they're lucky), this afternoon is one of the highlights of the season. This weekend, 367 other clubs share Bishop Sutton's dreams, clubs whose names are simultaneously prosaic and strangely evocative – the likes of Shepshed Dynamo, Penistone Church, Billingham Synthonia and West Allotment Celtic, with their raggle-taggle teams of factory workers and plumbers, firefighters and postmen. Come quarter to five, their dreams will either, like Bishop Sutton's, be mourned from the bottom of a pint glass in the club bar or, like Street's, stay alive until at least the next round, disappointment deferred for now.

This is my first-ever experience of the earliest stage of the FA Cup, an occasion also regularly ignored by the media, the obligatory Road to Wembley coverage only usually kicking into gear once the forty-eight clubs from League One and League Two enter the competition in what's patronisingly referred to as the First Round Proper. This year is slightly different on account of Northumberland club Ashington, the boyhood team of Jack and Bobby Charlton, being currently managed by former England fast bowler Steve Harmison. He receives the kind of coverage denied all others at the same league level, extensive photo opportunities to get up close and personal with the trophy. For a man who once bowled out Australia in an Ashes Test with two runs to spare, Harmison's team leaves it equally late against Albion Sports this afternoon, sneaking an equaliser in the fourth minute of stoppage time to earn a trip to Bradford for the replay the following Wednesday.

In the Bishop Sutton programme, among those vital paid adverts from estate agents, builders' merchants and TV repair men, a page of player profiles introduces the squad. I read the descriptions – 'a great communicator', 'a towering midfielder with lots of skill', 'he comfortably plays where he's asked without hesitation' – and try to match them to the players currently warming up. All neat haircuts and light summer tans, they look confident going through their sharp one-touch drills and set-ups while some bland, generic R&B plays tinnily from a phone tossed down on the turf.

There are other suggestions that a surprise might be on the cards. As the teams line up, nervous looks play on the faces of some of the Street team. 'Let's fucking put this to bed early doors,' one of their senior players barks, possibly wary that the hosts' summer acquisitions might have reinvented and rejuvenated them, that they are no longer the whipping boys of last season. Indeed, the ferocity with which a tight offside decision in the first thirty seconds is met by the Street dugout ('You're an absolute disgrace, linesman!') suggests that such wariness extends to the visitors' management team, too.

Bishop Sutton do have the better of the early exchanges. Hope is offered in the first few minutes by a fizzing thirty-yard effort that zips just past the Street goal, its speedy passage towards those trampolining kids only halted by the bonnet of a Honda Accord in the car park. While the ball's being retrieved from some stinging nettles, I notice that, despite the clement weather, two spectators are watching the action from the front seats of a Vauxhall Astra parked directly behind the goal Bishop Sutton are attacking. They must be home supporters, well aware that their team's recent scoring record (490 goal-free minutes and counting) puts their car in little danger.

Indeed, that early shot is as good as it will get this afternoon for the home side. By the interval, Street are two goals to the good; they've also had a couple of disallowed efforts and have hit the woodwork twice. The half-time whistle is greeted by stony silence from the home support. They've got used to saving their breath round here over the last few months and the game isn't discussed in the club bar during the break. Instead the conversation, between those watching the half-time scores on the TV set in the corner, is dominated by a discussion of how much weight Garth Crooks has put on of late. Or Girth Crooks, as one wag puts it.

Garth's certainly had his lunch today, but I've held off as I fancied, at my first match of the new season and after a summer of salads, gorging on some typical football fare. A hot pie or a bag of chips. Perhaps a burger nicely blackened at the edges. But here in the club bar, a former prefab school classroom with a rudimentary skittles alley along the side, there's no smell of frying onions, no squirt of the ketchup bottle. No hot food at all. I wander out of the ground back to the main road in the hope that the village's Indian takeaway has dispensed with commercial sense and decided to open on this quiet Saturday afternoon. Munching on a reheated onion bhaji on the touchline would do the trick. But no. The game will be long finished before they open their doors, so it's back to the club bar to peruse its modest selection of crisps and chocolate. At least the beer's cheap. And there's no queue.

The ease with which you can get a drink confirms the poor attendance today; it's announced later that just forty-three souls have paid their way, a third down on last week's gate. No wonder they haven't fired up the chip fryer. If you were feeling generous, you could float the notion that this afternoon's derby between Yeovil and Bristol Rovers has spirited fans away from Lakeview. But it's most likely that the locals fear, just two games into the new campaign, that the rot of last season still festers.

The local population certainly hasn't shown its support for the day the FA Cup came to the village. The bunting's not been hung from the lamp posts. In fact, the only evidence that the match is even on is a single sign opposite the club's blink-and-you'll-miss-it entrance down a narrow lane. You get the sense that the neighbouring cricket team, playing at a lower level than the football team and thus less in need of players of a decent calibre from outside the village limits, is more connected to the village. There's not a single Bishop Sutton native in the starting XI on the footballing side of the hedge. All have been shipped in from outside, mostly Bristol, a dozen miles to the north. It's a situation mildly analogous with almost all professional sides – the local area unrepresented in teams made up of have-boots-and-will-travel-to-sign-the-fattest-contract mercenaries. Except, of course, there's no cash luring these players down to Bishop Sutton.

The supporters who are here, spaced evenly around the pitch's perimeter, don't form a unified mass. Indeed, the cheers that greet each Street goal this afternoon suggest that at least half of those forty-three attendees are away fans. You'd have thought that, with most of the Bishop Sutton players making their debuts in the competition, wives, girlfriends and other family members might have turned out. But they've largely stayed away, too.

One family showing their support is that of Josh Dakwa, Bishop Sutton's nippy right-winger. His father Kojo – along with Josh's sister and niece – are here from Bristol for what is only his son's second appearance for the team. Leaning on the pitch's perimeter fence for the second half, Kojo spies me taking notes and asks if I'm a scout, mainly out of curiosity but possibly also out of mild hope that I'm here in the service of a team a division or two further up the league ranks.

As Street maintain their superiority and calmly extend their lead, Kojo and I let ourselves be entertained by the cabaret turn that is Bishop Sutton's goalkeeper. Undeniably an effective shot-stopper (his penalty save is but one of several fine stops during the second half), he is also the angriest goalkeeper I've ever watched, unleashing frequent gushes of industrial vernacular that would make even the saltiest seadog blush. Rather strangely, the twentysomething referee is ignoring the string of c-bombs the keeper's dropping. 'They're making me look shit,' he loudly complains to no one in particular about his own defence as the net ripples and bulges with another Street goal.

If I were a scout I'd certainly be scribbling some positive notes about one of those Bishop Sutton defenders, a young lad called George Thorne who, despite being just four months past his seventeenth birthday, puts in a mature, level-headed performance. Certainly his robust, immaculately timed challenges have the sparse crowd purring their approval. Circumstances might have dictated that Steve Laker be reliant on youth as he rebuilds the side, but Thorne has certainly been a wise signing, a player destined to spend his Saturday afternoons further up the pyramid, playing a better grade of football.

By the final whistle, Street have scored six without reply, their savvy centre-forward 'Scouse' securing his hat-trick near the end. He's exactly the kind of experienced striker Bishop Sutton are crying out for. Blindly optimistic types might point out the result could have been worse. A combination of the woodwork, the linesman's flag and various parts of the potty-mouthed goalie's anatomy prevented the score from reaching the double figures that were all too familiar last season.

Those zigzagging swallows escort the players off, the birds soon to leave these shores, missing the potential humiliations yet to come for the home team through autumn and winter. The awkward silence is pierced by a successful appeal from the cricket match. In the bar afterwards, the local supporters sigh in the way they've grown accustomed to and again allow themselves to be distracted by the results coming through on *Final Score*. While the young ref gets cross-examined by the eighty-something Bishop Sutton old guard, the victorious side emerge from the changing rooms, visibly relieved that a possible banana skin has been avoided and that they're into the hat for the next round.

Final Score has long since finished by the time the home team emerge, subjected to an autopsy in the dressing room, picking over the bones of a defeat that could easily have been heavier. A repeat episode of *Pointless* is halfway through as they slump at the table to receive their wages – chips and double sausage in a polystyrene tray, sustenance cruelly denied us spectators at half-time.

Ever the optimist, Steve Laker doesn't appear too battered by the experience, his resolve as firm as it was the previous afternoon back in his office. There are heavier defeats in the cup this weekend – FC Liverpool put nine past Chadderton, while Coleshill Town went two better at home to Ellesmere Rangers. Laker's still in his job, too, unlike Ashford United's manager, who received his marching orders after their own cup exit.

During the following week – a week when Chelsea pinch Barcelona's Pedro from right under Manchester United's nose – Laker does likewise and spirits a striker away from another rival team. One step closer to where the manager wants to be. Onward and upward. Yes, there's another goal-free defeat midweek, but hope is very close at hand. Four days later comes that rare commodity, an item as collectable as Laker's cigarette cards: a Bishop Sutton goal.

It's only a shame that Wincanton Town score six in return.

* * *

If you can judge a football club's prospects by the mood of its car-park attendants, then good times are just around the corner for Tranmere Rovers. Or perhaps the joviality is because, on this battleship-grey August Bank Holiday Monday, the workers are possibly earning time and a half. Either way, there's a palpable buzz here at Prenton Park ahead of today's match against Kidderminster Harriers. Fanzine sellers are upbeat, while young autograph hunters in brand-new, ridiculously luminous away kits cheerily hover around the players' entrance with clipboards at the ready.

They could certainly use some good news round here. The past two seasons, both of which ended in relegation, were the seal on years of neglect and underachievement. The ultimate humiliation came last season when Tranmere lost their Football League status after a full ninety-four years. They are now Tranmere Rovers of the Conference – or, as we should be calling it after it was rebadged over the summer, the Vanarama National League. New realities abound in Rovers' recalibrated world, where they're now forced to rub shoulders with the likes of Boreham Wood and Welling United and Braintree Town. With facilities that several Championship teams would envy, not to mention home attendances more than five times the size of those of some other Conference sides, Tranmere are now a seriously oversized fish in a modest pond. But they need to learn how to survive in these different waters. And quick.

As recently as two and a half years ago, Tranmere sat atop League One, looking in decent nick for a return to the familiar environs of the Championship. The second tier was their home during the most glorious years of their history. Under the avuncular guidance of Johnny King (a man immortalised in bronze by the main gate), they loudly rapped on the door of the then sparkly new Premier League during the 1990s, appearing in three consecutive play-offs but never quite making it to the top table. The managerial reins were then handed to John Aldridge, himself paid tribute to by having a supporters' bar named after him here at Prenton Park. Aldridge turned them into a cup side of some note. As well as a Wembley appearance in the 2000 final of the then Worthington Cup, his players also claimed the scalps of a succession of Premier League sides on their way to three FA Cup quarter-finals in just five seasons.

Since the days of the two Johns, the revolving door of the manager's office has barely stopped spinning. The club is now on its eleventh boss in fourteen seasons. One of the shortest reigns was that of John Barnes, who, having amassed all of three wins during his fourteen matches in charge, suffered the ignominy of being replaced by the team physio.

The current manager is Gary Brabin, a man with substantial experience in the fifth tier who was brought in over the summer by owner Mark Palios, himself a comparatively new presence at Tranmere. He and his wife Nicola took over the club at the end of the 2013–14 season after the first of those two relegations. At the time, the couple were buying a Football League club. Twelve months on, they're now the owners of a non-league club. But the Palioses aren't shirking the challenges. They're not about to cut their losses and run.

A Birkenhead boy of Greek descent, Palios was a tigerish midfielder for Tranmere for nine seasons during two spells in the 1970s and early 1980s. Since his playing days, he's been hugely successful in the City, running business regeneration operations for PricewaterhouseCoopers and turning around the fortunes of a range of organisations, among them the Royal Opera House and the Kirov Ballet. But he's most famously known as the one-time chief executive of the Football Association, a tenure that showed he doesn't hold back from making the toughest decisions, whether rescuing the grossly overspending

Wembley rebuild or issuing Rio Ferdinand with an eight-month ban for a missed drugs test.

Turning around Tranmere's fortunes is his latest project and, after years of minimal investment from previous regimes, his plans seem to have the backing of fans and officials alike. With his neat silver hair and calm, authoritative demeanour, he has the air of an airline pilot or consultant surgeon as he glides along the back corridors of Prenton Park. He receives nods of acknowledgement and approval from the club's grandees, as well as the close attention of stewards and hospitality staff. 'Good afternoon, Mr Palios.' 'Good journey here, Mr Palios?' 'Three points today, Mr Palios?'

Ninety minutes before kick-off, we settle into seats in the main stand, the ground currently empty aside from a stewards' briefing to our right and a fox scuttling up and down the steps of the away end to our left. It's here that Palios reveals his reasons for taking on what many might see as a hopeless cause.

'I came here in April 2014 and the club was mired in scandals. The manager had been sacked for betting and players who had been associated with the club had been arrested for spot-fixing. The club hadn't been invested in for quite some time. The owner, Peter Johnson, gave it his best years but wanted to sell. You sensed there had been a terminal decline. On the final day of the 2013–14 season, Nicky and I were driving through France, listening to the last game against Bradford. With ten minutes to go, we were safe, still in League One. Then we conceded and Notts County scored.

'I don't know whether Peter would have put cash in again, but he was going to have to do something significant. There was a structural loss of about £1 million. The first thing I did was to make sure we had enough breathing space to fix the problem. So the deal I did with Peter gave us two years to fix the profit-and-loss account.'

Although, as any chairman with a large financial stake at risk would be, Palios is clearly disappointed at slipping out of the Football League, he's far from panicking. 'I went on radio and TV that day, saying "It is devastating today, but not disastrous tomorrow." You prepare for the worst but hope for the best. We've budgeted for not necessarily going up this year, but that doesn't mean we don't have the ambition to go up. That's a totally different thing. But we wouldn't have done anything different this close season than we would have done had we stayed up.

'One of our advantages is that we have a large gate for the lower leagues. And there is a correlation between what you spend and where you end. My view is that if we have a top-third budget in every league we play in that I can support as break-even – and we've some way to go to get there – then we should be there or thereabouts in the play-offs, keeping the fans interested every season.

'Sensible business would keep away from football clubs because it's just too hard. One of the more frustrating things is the gap between what you do in business and what goes on on the pitch. It's an art, not a science. In business, I can go and buy a new machine that will cost me x. I know what x is. It will cost me y to run it. I know what y is. We produce z units. I know what z is and

I know what I can sell them for. You can't do that with players. The art form conflicts with the economics. But that's part of the beauty.'

Mark Palios, his eyes widening as he gazes around Prenton Park, clearly contemplating the potential that needs unlocking, is undeniably a dreamer. It's just that those dreams need to be based on unstinting economic discipline. He's at ease balancing the two – 'I don't have a difficulty making the transition from the boardroom to the boot room,' he smiles. But having a chairman who's as literate about football as he is about business might appear to put Gary Brabin on shaky ground. Palios has, after all, already seen two managers depart during his twelve months back at the club.

'The manager here is unfortunate because I played over four hundred games in the Football League and I ran the FA. But I don't interfere. I don't want to influence his decisions on a micro level. Over a period of time, of course, you do get your views across and if I see things I just don't agree with, it's my prerogative to tell him. But I will never ever tell him who to sign. I will never ever tell him who he should play. And I will never ever tell him how to play.'

Even if he wanted to interfere in team affairs, Palios already has a long enough to-do list. He fires off a barrage of initiatives to boost the club's solvency ('we make a loss three hundred and forty days a year because there's no income but you still have the overheads'), although the issue of the club's academy remains a thorny one. If Tranmere were to remain in non-league football beyond this season, their academy funding would be dramatically cut.

Plus, the advent of the Elite Player Performance Plan – created with the intention of upping the fortunes of the national side by improving the quality of home-grown talent – allows Premier League clubs to help themselves, at genuine knock-down prices, to the prize crop of lower-league academies. Under the terms of the Premier League-authored plan, a top-flight club could sign a promising youngster for as little as £3,000 forty-eight hours after expressing an interest in that player. Several lower-league clubs have subsequently shut their academies, citing the plan as part of the reason for the closures. For Tranmere, a club that in the past has survived financially by selling its young talent at an opportune moment in their careers, it may mean being reliant on sifting through the reject bins of bigger clubs to find the stars of tomorrow rather than developing their own.

Palios confides in me details of his intentions for the stadium, plans that will lower the blood pressure of any fans who may have been concerned that, to ease the cash worries, the huge Prenton Park site might be sold for housing and a new soulless arena built out near the M53. Plenty of other clubs have gone down that route. Instead, Palios wants Tranmere to remain at the beating heart of the Birkenhead community. He's loving being back. 'It's great to be with real football people,' he smiles. 'Sometimes, when you operate at the top end, some of the people you meet in international football have either lost the reason why they're in it or are in it for the wrong reasons. We were at Altrincham on Saturday and they are rock-solid. Just like people were in League Two last season. We went down and everybody was very sympathetic and understood our pain. It was just a nice environment to be in. For me, it's far more fulfilling being here than being at the top level of the game.'

Before he departs to press the flesh with sponsors and hospitality guests, Palios recounts with great affection the time he spent with the travelling support at the fateful game in Plymouth last April that confirmed Tranmere's disappearance from the Football League. 'I'm still humbled by that day. They were fantastic, thanking me and Nicky for being there. It was an embarrassing and very strange experience, but it also filled me with hope.' The blackest day in the club's history, yet the Tranmere faithful were already renewing their vows. Such is their devotion that, even though season ticket prices were increased for this first year of non-league football, sales have far eclipsed those of that single season in League Two.

I head back outside. The Kidderminster Harriers bus has taken a wrong turn into the car park – unsurprising as the teams have probably never played each other before – and is frantically reversing, all beeps and shouted directions. There's likely to be a big Bank Holiday crowd this afternoon, but that huge car park will be far from full. And that's the beauty of Prenton Park's location. This is a ground in a heavily residential area, the row of houses opposite presumably the retreats of Tranmere obsessives able to emerge from their front doors at 2.54 pm and still be in their favourite stand, burger in hand, by kick-off. And if they did that, they'd avoid the delights of the 'fanzone' which, on this afternoon's evidence, appears to be little more than two inflatable goals and an over-chatty DJ playing 'Uptown Funk' to an unpopulated corner of the car park.

I take a stroll around the block. Football grounds are made to be walked to, after all. The 100 yards from car to turnstile just doesn't do it. I think back to my favourite season of non-league football, that of 1991–92, my final year at university, when Colchester United achieved the Conference/FA Trophy double. Even though the 4A bus could deposit me right outside the entrance to Layer Road, I perversely chose to get off in the town centre and walk the rest of the way, even in the rain. For it was in those twenty minutes that you could almost taste the expectancy, where you could ascertain the collective mindset of your fellow fans. Were they surfing on an irresistible wave of optimism or gripped by an impending, bowel-wobbling sense of doom?

It was also as part of this pedestrian caravan that I could eavesdrop on club gossip. This might be whether the ageing player-manager would – despite a series of lumpy, unproductive personal performances – continue to pick himself as centre-forward and penalty-taker as he desperately attempted to reach his target of 100 career goals. Or it might be hearing which player was last seen being poured into a taxi just thirty-six hours earlier in a state of severely advanced refreshment.

As I stroll along Borough Road back towards the ground, Tranmere's white-shirted brigade grows in number at each road junction, the optimism shown in the length and strength of their stride. Hope has been renewed, despite recent disappointing results. Such hope, such loyalty, seems a tad curious when, at least in the view of Ryan Ferguson, columnist for the long-running fanzine *Give Us An R*, Tranmere remain 'a star-crossed football club that perpetually finds new and ever more painful ways to kick its fans in the gut'.

I meet Ferguson outside the pub over the road, where he offers the diagnosis of someone inextricably tied to Tranmere since the age of six. 'It's been a very testing time,' he shrugs, nursing a pint of orange juice after having overdone it after the Altrincham game two days ago. Hollow laughter shades his words. 'You're supposed to come to football for entertainment, not torture. There was no philosophy underlining the club until the Palioses arrived. We used more than fifty players that season, one loanee after another. There was no continuity in the side from one week until the next, no cohesive style of play.'

Amid all the comings and goings over those twelve months, Ferguson did welcome one particular departure. 'Everyone was pleased to get rid of Peter Johnson, to be honest. He did save the club back in the 1980s when it was on the brink of extinction, but he put the club up for sale in 2002 and reduced expenditure to a bare minimum. From trying to compete for promotion, the expectations dropped to just trying to survive day to day, hence the loanees. So when the Palioses arrived, it was refreshing. They were very open with the fans and showed them their plans. They've got the vision and passion and wherewithal to actually go through with it, rather than just offering showcase gestures to appease the fans.'

Ferguson, like thousands of others, is adjusting to his new existence as a fan of a non-league side. 'It still stings. But it's still Tranmere. We're all looking at each other going "We'll only be here for a season." But no team has won the Conference title in their first season after relegation since 1990. It's a tall order, but I think we deserve it. We've not had a promotion or won a cup since 1991.

'Reaching the play-offs has to be the bare minimum. But this team's got to create a winning culture. You need in the region of eighty-five or ninety points, so how many defeats can you afford? Five? Six? We've already had two. We're already eight points adrift of the leaders. Eight points at any time of the season is a lot.' The fact that Bristol Rovers returned to the Football League at the first attempt last season, via the play-offs, certainly offers a scintilla of hope to the most jaded Tranmere fan.

And as jaded as Tranmere fans can get – understandable when analysing the brutal truth of the last few seasons – attendances at Prenton Park are, alongside those at Wrexham, easily the highest in non-league football. 'There's no other elite sports team representing the Wirral,' says Ferguson. 'It's a working-class part of the country and a lot of people feel disillusioned with politics, so they turn to Tranmere for a sense of community, a sense of pride, a sense of identity.'

There is something of the outsider in the collective psyche of the Wirral. A peninsula jutting into the Irish Sea, there's almost an island mentality about the place. Tranmere remains a proud club, one that refuses to be dazzled by the sunlight glinting off all that silverware on the other bank of the Mersey. Ferguson recalls a quote from Johnny King, one that likened Liverpool and Everton to ocean-going liners while seeing Tranmere as a deadly submarine. 'That strikes to the heart of what the club actually is, fighting in the shadows of the giants.'

Here in the fifth tier, though, Tranmere are now seen as the giant, the glory days when Aldridge and Pat Nevin and Jason Koumas ruled Prenton Park still within living memory, still marking them out as the scalp to claim. 'We're not used to being the big club, even though our Kop stand alone has a larger capacity than seven entire grounds in this division. It's a monument to the time when it was built, when the club was dreaming of the Premier League. But you don't win games for the size of your stand, do you?'

Back over the road and now within ten minutes of kick-off, that oversized Kop end, ridiculously dwarfing the adjacent Johnny King Stand, is filling up nicely as the loyalists say their little prayers in return for three points to get the season back on track. Life in the Conference did start well for Tranmere, with two wins from two, but their form has hit the rails since; a scoreless draw at

Braintree was trumped by a home defeat to newly promoted Boreham Wood, a team two divisions below them
three months previously. Such patchy results are set in
sharp relief by the form of the division's runaway leaders,
Forest Green Rovers, who have maximum points from
their first six games.

At first, Kidderminster don't offer much of a threat
and Tranmere are two goals to the good before the
half-hour mark. The ground is buzzing, the Bank Holiday crowd audibly appreciating the endeavour and
industry shown by certain players. Commitment to the
cause of getting out of this division at the first time of
asking is an attribute strongly applauded by this discern-
ing crowd.

Gary Brabin has made some astute signings over the
summer, targeting players who don't just have Conference experience but who have been part of teams who've
escaped back into the Football League. As Mark Palios
emphasised earlier, 'these players won't find it a shock in
this division. But if you've played your whole life in the
Football League, even in its lower reaches, when you're
playing in front of a gate of five hundred and a dog on a
Tuesday night in January, it's really difficult to motivate
yourself.'

With the Kop in fine voice, it's all smiles high up in
the main stand, if a little more restrained. This is
the territory of those who've forked out for hospitality
packages – mostly, I'm guessing, local entrepreneurs
accompanied by their wives, many of whom are dressed
if not to the nines, then at least to the sevens. For their

£50 a head, they get these prime seats, a three-course lunch and a fair chance of a five-minute address from the manager while the crème caramels are being served.

These seats are also the domain of those with closer connections to the club. Up here are several players currently either injured, suspended or on the fringes of the first-team squad. A few of them furtively play with their phones when they think no one can see them. This is also where the players' relatives sit. One of them – a man in late middle age, clearly thrilled that his daughter has married into football – is the most ani-mated person in the whole stand, offering positive appraisals of his son-in-law's performance to everyone within earshot.

When your team is enjoying a comfortable cushion, the half-time refreshments taste better and the half-time music sounds sweeter; today's selection makes full use of the musical heritage of their neighbours across the water. We get The La's, Echo & The Bunnymen and Frankie Goes To Hollywood – although quite why Tranmere come on to the pitch to the theme tune from *The Rockford Files* remains a mystery that only Jim Rockford himself could solve.

The second half renders that two-goal cushion not quite comfortable enough. With Tranmere failing to score a game-killing third, Brabin makes a substitution in the last ten minutes, taking off his target man and replacing him with a central defender. Within sixty sec-onds of changing the system, a defensive lapse on the left gifts Kidderminster a goal that's anything but a consola-tion. A soft stoppage-time equaliser sends the couple of

hundred travelling fans into raptures, before they taunt
the Koppites at the other end of the ground. 'You aren't
going up! You aren't going up!'

Ire and insults are aimed at Brabin who, stalking his
technical area during the final minutes, is in danger of
wearing a hole in the strip of astroturf in front of the
dugout. There's still enough time left for Tranmere to
both hit the post and blaze a gilt-edged chance over the
bar before the inevitable boo-fest on the final whistle,
drowning out the DJ's possibly ill-advised choice of the
theme from *Local Hero*. Disgruntled supporters file out
of the ground, a precious three-point haul having slipped
through their team's fingers. Among them is arguably
Tranmere's most famous supporter, Nigel Blackwell from
indie satirists Half Man Half Biscuit. As a Rovers loyalist
all his life (back in the mid-1980s, the band politely
declined a career-enhancing invitation to appear on *The
Tube* because it clashed with a home match against
Scunthorpe), he's perfectly qualified to place this latest
surrender in the context of Tranmere's modern history.
'Typical bloody Rovers, that,' he grumbles, before a hint
of the gallows humour he's had to develop in recent times
at Prenton Park. 'Still, it livened up the last ten minutes,
didn't it?' Another fan storms past us, unable to put such
a brave face on affairs. 'Change the player, not the formation. Fucking shocking.'

Still in the ground, the Kidderminster fans can
be heard celebrating like it was a cup final triumph,
their cheers and chants echoing around those large, now-
empty stands. Tranmere Rovers – the prize scalp, the

division's giant, the biggest name in non-league football –
have been cut down.

* * *

Some things don't matter.

Late equalisers and 6-0 reverses are temporary aberra-
tions, quickly forgiven if not easily forgotten. They are
bruises, nothing more, their pain diminishing by the
time the next match comes round. They don't last.

Other things do. On the weekend between Bishop Sutton's FA Cup exit and Tranmere's mild capitulation to
Kidderminster, a freak accident would rock – and unite –
non-league football. A vintage jet, performing aerial
stunts for the crowd at the Shoreham Airshow, plunged
out of the Sussex skies and onto the Saturday lunchtime
traffic driving along the A27, the main trunk road serving the south coast. An ordinary day, an ordinary road,
an extraordinary incident.

Among the eleven victims were two semi-professional
footballers on their way to their regular appointment lining up for Southern Combination Premier side Worthing
United. The players – goalkeeper Matt Grimstone and
midfielder Jacob Schilt, both twenty-three – were in the
same position as thousands of other players at that precise moment, football obsessives en route to their
matches, en route to the portion of the week that their
lives revolved around.

Every club, every football fan, knew these players.
They had lads just like them in their own team. The

solidarity of all levels of the non-league scene – shown in messages of support, the wearing of black armbands and the filling of collection buckets – was instant and unanimous.

For the players, fans and officials of Worthing United, this new season had been rendered meaningless, no one clear about how footballing matters could possibly continue. Theirs were dreams that had now departed.

2

SEPTEMBER

International men of mystery

At 8.34 pm, twenty minutes ahead of schedule, Philippine Airlines flight PR720 descends through the dark west London skies and, with the slightest of skids, touches down on the tarmac of Heathrow's south runway. Within half an hour, its cargo of businessfolk and extended families blearily make their way across the Terminal 4 concourse, dreaming of their beds as they shunt overburdened, misbehaving trolleys towards the taxi rank.

The man in seat 2A fits neither category; he wasn't away on business and is travelling alone. He wheels his trolley to the entrance of Café Rouge and orders a coffee, into which he tips two sachets of sugar in an attempt to counteract the effects of a fourteen-hour flight from Manila. Back in the Filipino capital, his face adorns giant billboards. Here, in the now-quiet surroundings of a British airport's arrivals hall, he is anonymous, unrecognised, unapproached.

His name is Rob Gier and he is the captain of the Philippines national football team. He is also the centre-back for Ascot United, currently occupying ninth place in the Uhlsport Hellenic League Premier Division.

The international breaks during a season don't normally affect the non-league world, save for, in the absence of Premier League and Championship matches, perhaps a few extra folk clicking through the turnstile of a local semi-pro side. But on this particular weekend, when a ninth-tier outfit like Ascot boasts a globe-trotting player in its ranks, they know they're going to be a man down when Saturday comes.

While he waits for his coffee to cool, Gier – looking remarkably fresh, thanks no doubt to the restorative powers of flying business class – revisits every twist and turn of his domestic career, explaining how he came to be inhabiting English football's lower reaches. He's now back at the club he used to play for as a kid, but he's been around the block a few times. Having been scouted by then Premier League Wimbledon at the age of thirteen, Gier went on to play around seventy-five matches for the Dons in the Championship before spending several seasons slipping and sliding on the lower slopes of the pyramid, desperate for a faltering career to find traction. In the process, he accumulated a CV typical of many journeyman players, one of seemingly ever-diminishing returns.

A two-season spell at Rushden & Diamonds was bittersweet. Gier was voted supporters' player of the year in his first season, the club was relegated to the Conference the next. His options weren't abundant; short-term spells at two other Conference sides, Cambridge United and Woking, followed. 'I flitted about for a bit. Not many people want to sign a centre-half who's just been relegated – and I was a small centre-half at that. In the lower leagues, everyone just looks at your size first. But I was always a player who read the game, rather than being a physical guy.' Indeed, of no more than average build, Gier has the physique of a creative midfielder rather than someone operating at the bloody heart of defence.

He had a successful try-out at left-back for another Conference club, Aldershot. That season was arguably his best ever, playing nearly fifty games as the Shots returned to the Football League, sweeping to the Conference title with a record-breaking points haul. But the champagne soon went flat. 'I was one of two players who didn't get a contract at the end of the season. That was a big kick in the bollocks. I'd done my graft in the Conference for a couple of years and worked hard to stay in the game. And it was a brilliant season. We did the double, totally dominating the league.' But the exit door still slammed shut behind him.

Gier – the son of an English father and a Filipino mother – managed to stay in the Conference with Grays Athletic, albeit commuting from Oxfordshire to Essex every day to train and play for a swiftly rotating procession of managers. 'It was a big mistake going there. The club was in turmoil. That really was the ugly side of Conference football. And I wasn't enjoying playing. I was drained by that point. But it just so happened that that coincided with my first call-up for the Philippines.

'My mother had kept on to me: "Contact the Philippines. Send your CV in." I didn't know if they even had a team. In the end, just to shut my mum up, I managed to find a contact on Facebook. "This is who I am. These are my details. Would you be interested?" I didn't hear anything for six months but, just as that time at Grays was coming to an end, the president of the Philippine Football Federation got in touch out of the blue. "We have a tournament coming up. Would you be interested in coming out? It's in the Maldives." "OK, let me have a think about that. A rainy day in Essex or a week in the Maldives? Yeah, OK!"'

With his Grays contract mutually terminated, Gier packed his bags for Manila for four weeks of pre-tournament preparation. 'At this time, we were one of the lowest-ranked teams in South East Asia. We were considered to be the whipping boys. The bigger South East Asia teams would see playing us as a chance to bump up their goal difference. The squad would probably get together perhaps once a year. And when I first went out, I was sleeping on someone's floor.'

After the tournament in the Maldives, Gier rethought his priorities. 'A mate of mine asked if I wanted to get involved with property development. And I did. I fancied a step away from the professional game. I'd been a pro for eleven or so years and was playing for the money, not for enjoyment. So I went into partnership with my mate and that was fine, but by the following Christmas another friend was bugging me to go and play for Ascot. And I fancied having a kickabout with my old mates. It was so nice to make a conscious choice to play football because I wanted to, not because I was going to get paid.'

He's been there ever since, a calm presence in the Ascot defence, four rungs down from his old stomping ground of the Conference. In the twenty-first-century football world, where loyalty to a salary-paying club comes before any pride in representing your country, Gier flipped the equation back to how it used to be. International football takes priority, having downgraded his club commitments to advance his prospects with the Philippines.

It was a mutually beneficial arrangement. Ascot secured the services of a player of true pedigree, while Gier was granted the opportunity to renew his love for the game. 'There was no commitment, no stress. If I didn't want to play one week because I had a wedding to go to or something, it was "No problem. We'll see you Thursday night at training instead." You'd have a competitive game, have a shout and a holler at the referee, and have a chat and a beer afterwards. So often in the pro game, you do your training, you get in the car and go home. There's no social side.

'Ascot's my release. I don't get paid. It costs me to travel to training and matches. I'm playing football for fun. It's what it's all about. And it's been great for me. Playing for Ascot means there are no problems with being available for matches or training camps outside the FIFA dates. When you combine all these tournaments and friendlies and camps together, you can be away for as much as six months of the year. I would never have been able to get that time off if I was playing for a bigger club.' And you can't blame him for prioritising World Cup qualifiers in exotic locales over muddy midweek encounters against the likes of Tuffley Rovers or Highmoor-Ibis.

'It's still a competitive league,' he defends. 'We're not having a beer at half-time or anything! There are still some really good players in that league. I've seen that throughout my career – so many good players who've fallen by the wayside just because of an injury or because of someone's opinion.' His experience at Aldershot, clearly still smarting six years on, puts him in the latter category. 'I don't think I ever got over the disappointment of not getting a new contract there,' he sighs, taking a sip of his now-cool-enough-to-drink coffee. 'One thing you learn in football is that you don't always get what you deserve. Fairness isn't always top of the agenda with a lot of football clubs and a lot of football managers.'

If the scars of life in the domestic leagues still retain a level of rawness, the tale of how his international career took flight must surely have accelerated the healing process. The 2010 Suzuki Cup proved to be the pinnacle of a life spent in football – an episode later dubbed as the Miracle of Hanoi. 'We qualified by the absolute skin of our teeth,' he reports, the mood suddenly lightening. 'It was the first time we'd qualified for the tournament proper, so that in itself was a huge achievement.'

But the dream didn't start and end with qualification. Having shared a 1-1 draw with the region's powerhouse Singapore in the first match ('We were such underdogs. No one gave us a hope in hell of even scoring'), they then beat hosts and holders Vietnam 2-0 'in front of 40,000 Vietnamese and zero Filipinos. We had just our kitman and our physio.' A good result against Cambodia set up a two-legged semi-final against Indonesia, but the home leg was to prove problematic. With the only pitch in Manila not fit for purpose, both matches had to be played in Jakarta. It was the equivalent of Ascot drawing Arsenal at home in the FA Cup and having to switch the tie to the Emirates as their ground, within Ascot Racecourse's acres, would be unable to cope with a match of such magnitude.

The atmosphere in Jakarta, playing before 90,000 highly passionate Indonesian fans, was intense. 'They were so loud. My centre-half partner was as close as you are now and we couldn't hear each other even at the tops of our voices.' Despite their narrow exit from the competition, they were front-page news on their return to Manila. 'From the moment we arrived back, football in the Philippines just exploded. Everyone wanted a piece of us. We couldn't go out as a team. We couldn't go to a shopping mall or get a coffee because we'd be mobbed. We were on every TV show, in every magazine. We were the hottest ticket in town.'

Since then, the footballing infrastructure has improved exponentially. 'The Miracle of Hanoi was the catalyst for everything. There's now the UFL, a professional league. There are now two main stadiums and lots more pitches around. My first training session out there was on a pitch at a college. It was just a dustbowl. There wasn't enough grass on it for a cow to graze on. So, for all the planets to align and for us to have done so well in 2010, it was a miracle, really.' There was also the small matter of an exhibition match against David Beckham's LA Galaxy. 'To be on the same pitch as Becks was unbelievable, but I pulled my calf after about five minutes. I was absolutely devastated. And it was a long ball over the top from him did it. That's my claim to fame. David Beckham pulled my calf.'

With a furtive glance at his watch, Gier politely checks that he's not going into too much detail – a roundabout way of asking whether he's boring me. It's anything but boring, the kind of cockles-warming fairy tale that could prick up the ears of a Hollywood producer. What's good enough for the Jamaican bobsleigh team would surely also be good enough for the footballing minnows of the Philippines, the rank outsiders who went from 0 to 60mph so speedily.

He's been the national captain since 2012 and works for the PFF off the pitch – compiling match reports, watching videos of upcoming opposition teams, trying to uncover other European-based Filipinos. Isn't the latter just a case of typing 'footballer born in Manila' into Google? My flippancy isn't ungrounded. It turns out that the Younghusband brothers, the national team's true poster boys, were found via Championship Manager. 'Some kid playing it found out they were Filipino and that's how they got involved with the national team.'

Aside from the on-pitch triumphs, Gier's international career has also allowed him to reconnect with his Filipino roots. When he was originally called up back in 2009, at the age of twenty-eight, it was the first time he'd been back to Manila since he was twelve. 'Your time is so limited in the pro game. You only really get June off, so I never got round to going back. But when I did go back, travelling from the airport just felt so familiar, so natural. I knew straight away it was the right decision. And it was a real eye-opener going there – learning about where my mum came from, the hardships she had, meeting my family again. It's not just been a big thing in my football career. It's had a big influence on my life in general.'

He drains his coffee, drags himself to his feet and releases the brake on his trolley. His dad's been patiently waiting for the last hour, parked up in a nearby lay-by ready to drive his son on the last leg back to Oxfordshire. It's a long way from Manila to Gier's home in Wallingford, but the frequent flying is never regarded as a bind, especially when it means he enjoys a life unlike that of any other non-league player.

The terminal's automatic exit doors open and he looks back over his shoulder. 'I get to travel the world and play football. What's better than that?'

* * *

There are many sounds that accompany non-league football. You can hear plenty of them tonight. The clunk and clang of an elderly turnstile. The sizzle of burgers on a griddle. The distorted voice of the loudspeaker, rendering the diligently compiled team announcements unintelligible. The collective grumble of the crowd: 'What did he say . . . ?'

Welcome to the poetically named Draycott Engineering Loop Meadow Stadium, home to Didcot Town of the Evo-Stik Southern League Division One South & West. It's a ground that doesn't appear to occupy a cherished place in the local community. No central location in the heart of things, this. Instead we're in the darkness on the edge of town, a ground reached only by navigating a warren of new-builds and speed bumps. Adding extra poetry to the location, in the distance the massive, squat chimneys of Didcot power station are back-lit by an angry, blood-red sunset. A twenty-one-cart goods train rumbles past on the nearby railway line.

We might be on the wrong side of the tracks, but it's still a heavenly, inviting prospect. A dry, chilly Tuesday night that draws us like moths to the floodlights' flame.

Tonight, the light jacket of summer has been swapped for something a little more insulating and the consumption of hot, sweet tea is mandatory. Autumn has already made itself very much at home. A pair of young female Didcot fans have wisely brought rugs, their legs encased in tartan as they burrow down into the front row of the main stand, cradling Thermoses of soup. Oxtail, if my nose is reliable. Elsewhere in the stand, just-from-the-fryer chips are hungrily and appreciatively munched, although one of the officials from tonight's visitors, Marlow, noisily bemoans the non-availability of fried onions for his burger.

This is midweek non-league football as it's always been – unvarnished, unsanitised and a million miles from the posturing and preening of the Champions League. Indeed, when tonight's half-time scores are called out, they ignore the latest news from Camp Nou or the

Allianz Arena. Instead we're only updated with the other scores from this particular division of the Southern League – how the unglamorous likes of Tiverton Town and Swindon Supermarine and AFC Totton are faring. They keep to their own round here.

The majority of the Loop Meadow crowd are men on the cusp of, or well into, pensionable age. For decades, most will have spent their Tuesday nights, and their Saturday afternoons, right here. The view stays the same; it's just the players that change. That's somehow reassuring. When play tonight gets underway, several of them still place faith in a timeless referee/spectacles jibe. Halfway through the first half, an already exasperated home fan hurls a terrifically old-school piece of abuse towards the flag-happy near-side linesman – 'You shithouse!' Not all the banter is trapped in amber, though. When Didcot's keeper slices a clearance straight onto the thudding steel roof of the main stand, one tech-savvy fan points out that he 'needs his GPS correcting'.

There's plenty of on-pitch entertainment, too. We get eight goals for our nine quid, Didcot claiming five of them. I miss at least three, though, as tonight I only have eyes for one man. I'm not following the play, instead scrutinising the off-the-ball movements of the visitors' holding midfielder with the freshly shorn mohawk. As at Bishop Sutton, I could easily be mistaken for a scout, the man sitting on his own with no apparent team affiliation, scribbling notes every couple of minutes. Like Rob Gier, the blue number four is another international playing in the Thames Valley at a level markedly below his natural talent.

Sam Bangura, of Marlow and Sierra Leone, moves across the turf with the assurance and composure of a player who's had time and care invested in him. And he has. Like Gier, Bangura was picked up in the early years of secondary school by a Premier League club – this time, Chelsea – in whose academy he spent his teenage years. But while Gier managed to break into the first team at Wimbledon, Bangura was released without once getting close to making the senior squad at Stamford Bridge. He's one of three ex-Premier League academy players on duty tonight; the other two spent their formative years at Southampton. All three stand out among the usual, more workman-like fare of the pyramid's eighth tier.

Bangura is impressive in a quiet, undemonstrative way, neat and tidy in the tackle but also given licence to spray the occasional Hoddle-esque, defence-splitting ball. Despite being only twenty, his on-field maturity, fitness and athleticism suggest he's playing well within himself, an elegant player who clearly belongs a few divisions higher. It's a long way from the national stadium in near-equatorial Freetown to the chill of a modest ground sponsored by a local engineering firm, where the lights in the gents aren't working and where there's a cement mixer parked behind one of the goals.

After Marlow's 5-3 defeat, Bangura explains how he got here. He was eight years old when his father moved the family over from war-ravaged Sierra Leone in 2003. The ten-year civil war had recently concluded. Growing up in peaceful Reading, young Sam became as football-obsessed as his classmates – 'I had to join in,' he says.

Until that point in his life, he'd barely kicked a ball. 'Sierra Leone is a nation that loves football, but when I was growing up there, you couldn't be outside much because of what was happening on the streets. You were either at school or you were being home-taught. That was about it. There wasn't any playing football. None of that.

'But I picked up the game quite quickly and joined a local team within two or three months. I got signed by Chelsea when I went to secondary school at eleven. A Reading scout was watching me at the time, but someone from Chelsea also came to watch our team. But there was no pressure from scouts watching me. Back then I didn't understand the structure of modern football. My manager said "Reading have come to see you". I thought Reading were just another Sunday team.' They weren't. Quite the opposite. Reading had just been promoted to the Premier League.

'Two days later, I went to Reading to play a trial and Chelsea were there again. They watched that game and then spoke to my parents, asking them if I'd like to sign. So I joined their academy and went there three days a week, on Tuesdays and Thursdays after school and on Saturdays. They slowly move you up the system. You miss one day of school. Then you miss two days. Then you start going to school up there.'

Despite the obvious cachet of being part of the chosen few at one of Europe's most successful teams so far this century, Chelsea's academy has proved to be a graveyard of ambition during the Roman Abramovich reign. Upgraded in 2005 at a reported cost of £30 million – and with annual running costs rumoured to be around the £8 million mark – it simply hasn't delivered. Or, more precisely, it hasn't been allowed to deliver. Turning an academy into a conveyor belt of future stars requires stability and that hens'-teeth-rare phenomenon: a manager given time and space to create a sense of tradition, a dynasty.

But the cheque book wins the day at Chelsea. A succession of first-team bosses – twelve in ten years, in fact, a stability-fracturing series of caretaker, short-term and permanent appointments – have relied on the contents of the owner's pockets to bring speedy success and a modicum of job security. No one is patient enough to turn graduate into superstar, especially when superstars are readily available for a fee comfortably covered by the loose change found down a Russian oligarch's sofa. The academy's last great success in transforming a teenager into a first-team stalwart was all the way back with John Terry. The only recent academy graduate to become a fixture of the first-team squad (but not the starting XI) has been the perpetual bench-warmer Ruben Loftus-Cheek.

The odds were therefore stacked against Sam Bangura, and the rest of his academy team-mates, being offered a professional contract. In 2014, after eight years at the club, he was released. 'It's tough, but you are made aware. The coaches will say "Only one of you in this team will make it. Maybe none of you will." Most of those drift on to League One or Two or non-league football, if they're still in the game at all.' Their talent stifled, their hopes extinguished, these young lads become landfill. Behind the shrug, though, Bangura seems protected by an in-built resilience, one that his contemporaries may have been short of when it came to coping with the splintering of teenage dreams. 'Most things I should be upset about don't hit me as they should because of what I've been through and what I've seen growing up. I'm just one of those people who moves on with life quite quickly. When I was released by Chelsea, I just got up on my feet and moved on.'

His contemporaries may have acted differently, ranting and raving when they got their cards. But, as he showed on the pitch tonight, there's a wise head on these twenty-year-old shoulders. Bangura isn't one for hyperbole or self-promotion. He's measured and considered. Every other sentence begins with 'To be fair . . .'

That process of moving on was made easier thanks to the call-up by the Sierra Leone FA, just as he was saying farewell to Stamford Bridge. The team boss – a twenty-something Ulsterman called Johnny McKinstry – had, as boss of the Sierra Leone under-21s, seen Bangura play at a tournament in Wales with the Chelsea academy. He liked what he saw, made a mental note and then, once promoted to managing the national side, made the call. Bangura was soon on his way back to the city of his birth and the prospect, after years of playing in scarcely attended youth matches, of walking out into the cauldron of the national stadium in Freetown.

'On the way to my first game against Tunisia, every shop was closed and the streets were packed. Everyone was following the coach, making noise all the way. It took us about half an hour to get off the coach as the little tunnel where they park it was full of people. That was when the pressure started to hit. The hotel had been quiet, but when we got onto the main road it was "Wow!"' Bangura doesn't need me to contrast it with the quiet residential streets surrounding the Loop Meadow.

Addressed by the president of the Sierra Leone FA in the dressing room, the fear factor didn't dissolve once Bangura was in his natural environment of the pitch. 'It was scary at first. Obviously I'd never been in front of a crowd that big before. I didn't know what to expect. But it makes you want to play more. You work harder with so many people watching. Johnny protected me from getting too much attention. He came along to most of the interviews I had to do. But we also helped him as much as he helped us. I was new and maybe six or seven other players were new. It was the first time for us all. And it was Johnny's first game too, so it worked out quite well. We were fighting for a spot in the team, trying to impress the new boss and the country, as was he. We all had something to prove. It all worked out.'

An away match against Cape Verde followed three days later, but of late things have been quieter for Bangura on the international front. A player without a club is hard to pick for his country. Dropping a long way down the pyramid might equip him with the nous and worldliness lacking in youth games but, following McKinstry's departure, it also takes Bangura off the radar of the new manager. Not that playing in the eighth tier is necessarily straightforward in itself. An international player with eight years' experience at Chelsea tends to attract attention, not to mention a pressure to dominate matches at this level. 'It's all eyes on you from the coaches and the players. You can't put a foot wrong.'

Bangura's LinkedIn profile – a particularly twenty-first-century method for a footballer to tout his wares – makes it clear that while he might be a regular in Marlow's starting line-up, he's 'free to leave the club at any stage if the right opportunity comes along'. So what shape does the 'right opportunity' take?

'I'd take it if it was at Conference South level. Yeah, I'd take that. Or higher, of course. Mark, the manager at Marlow, has quite a few connections and gets quite a few people to come and watch me. I'm training at Wycombe twice a week at the moment, too. They're happy with the way I play, but their worries were that I'd never played at men's level. It was the Wycombe manager who advised me to go to non-league for experience. All that you learn at Chelsea doesn't go out of the window . . . Well, to a certain degree it does.'

Every match for Marlow down here in the second tier of the Southern League, one infinitely more rough and tumble than those technically neat but ultimately meaningless academy matches, is one small step towards gaining sufficient experience to satisfy the recruitment team at a club like Wycombe. 'I've got quite a few teams keeping an eye on me, but they're all saying the same things. They all want to see me playing competitively against men week in, week out. That's what they want.' While he waits for offers, Bangura has set this season aside to notch up game-time, to gather the kind of experience that gives League clubs no reason not to sign up his services.

As level-headed as he is, Sam Bangura will still be susceptible to the fickle fortunes of football. He's negotiating a wobbly tightrope between hope and reality, when what he really wants is to be catapulted across that yawning void, to be fired back up the pyramid. He knows – from both his experience in the Chelsea academy and his disappearance from the Sierra Leone squad – that this is a sport with no guarantees. There's a distinct possibility that Bangura might get forgotten about down in the depths of the Southern League.

When he considers the trajectory of his career so far, does he regret that he listened to the overtures of Chelsea? Would he have had a greater chance of success if he'd signed for Reading instead? And what would his advice be to an eleven- or twelve-year-old in his position now? It appears that last question is more pertinent than I realise. 'My little brother's at Reading at the moment and the Chelsea coach is trying to get him over. I'm trying to give him advice based on my experience there, so that he can make up his own mind. I'll probably tell him to go with whatever he's comfortable with. I've got a few friends at Reading and they're complaining about not playing there either.'

And let's not forget that, without the blue of Chelsea, Sam Bangura would never had had the opportunity to slip into the green of Sierra Leone.

* * *

Barnsley, on a beautiful Indian summer evening in late September, is a rather blissful place to be. Certainly it is here at Shaw Lane, a buzzing, hillside sports club catering to the varied appetites of this corner of South Yorkshire, be it cricket, rugby, athletics or, of course, football.

Wisps of pipe smoke float up over the immaculate hedges of the bowling green, while, a little further on, the pleasant scent of a nearby bonfire adds extra spice to the evening air. Unathletic kids who look like they've come straight from a casting session for *Kes* – filmed just a mile or two north of here, incidentally – take several attempts to awkwardly scramble over a twenty-foot-high fence to get, rather incongruously, onto the running track that's otherwise padlocked out of reach.

On the 3G pitch on the far side of the car park, six- and seven-year-olds are taking their first lessons in tactics and technique. It being the early stages of a fresh season, parents make awkward conversation while the coaches gently encourage and cajole their nervous new charges. The reach of the global game is conspicuous in the choice of the kids' box-fresh football kits, but it's also pleasing to see the exact same number of cherry-red Barnsley FC shirts as there are Barcelona ones. A score draw between the two marketing departments.

Further up the hill, looking across the skyline of the town centre, is the club's full-size pitch, the home of their senior side – Shaw Lane Aquaforce. It's a handsome-looking ground, a large, level rectangle cut into the hillside, with a neat perimeter path leading to a pair of dugouts on the far side.

You can measure the health of a club from its dugouts. Most are a crumbling mess of peeling paint and broken seats, littered with the discarded detritus of the last match – empty Lucozade bottles, rotting banana skins, sodden shin-guard tapes. Shaw Lane's dugouts look like they're on loan from a well-heeled stadium in some glamorous European capital. Fashioned from sturdy transparent plastic, their full-height dimensions mean their occupants don't need the flexibility of a contortionist to use them. Along with the well-maintained stand, with its four rows of equally well-maintained seating, these dugouts suggest this to be a football club that's very much on the rise. And that suggestion would be right. For Shaw Lane Aquaforce, now of the Evo-Stik Northern Premier League Division One South, are on the hunt for their third promotion in as many seasons.

After an approving circuit of the pitch, I saunter back down the hill, a chill now frosting the air as mist begins to gather on the high Pennine peaks to the west. An ice-cream van optimistically rings its tune – *Doctor Zhivago*, it's always *Doctor Zhivago* – somewhere down in the town. The chalkboard outside the clubhouse advertises tomorrow evening's 'Italian Night' – £25 for a three-course meal, plus 'Italian Opera Music' from 'Female Sopranos'. Tonight, though, a one-sided Rugby World Cup match on the bar's TV is failing to hold the attention of the early-evening drinkers.

Beyond the bar, a series of display boards lining the corridor is of more interest, an extended salute to Barnsley's sporting heroes. There are plenty to choose from – pocket-sized cricket umpire Dickie Bird, Olympic sprinter Dorothy Hyman, Manchester United's Greenhoff brothers and a young, mustachioed Mick McCarthy, Worsbrough Bridge's most famous Irishman. Perhaps, if his goals help Shaw Lane Aquaforce to continue their run of successive promotions, these display boards will, in years to come, salute the young man whose Vauxhall Corsa has just pulled into the car park.

Adam Priestley has come straight from work and is still wearing the uniform of his employment – polo shirt, shorts and trainers. He's a PE teacher and cover supervisor at Morley Academy on the southern fringes of Leeds. This afternoon, he excitedly reports, he's been testing the school's newly acquired mountain bikes ahead of demonstrating them at an imminent parents' evening.

But it's not Adam Priestley the cyclist I'm interested in hearing about. It's not so much Adam Priestley the prolific marksman of the second tier of the Northern Premier League, either. It's Adam Priestley the international striker, the man who's surely the only player in the entire non-league pyramid who has lined up against the current holders of the World Cup.

For, despite his cheery Yorkshire accent, blond-haired Priestley has won eleven caps for UEFA's newest member country – Gibraltar. This meant, when the territory achieved full member status in 2013 and the draw for the Euro 2016 qualifiers was made, the not unattractive prospect of a pair of games against the superstars of Germany beckoned.

Priestley was born on the rock twenty-five years ago while his dad served in the RAF there. 'I've got a Gibraltar birth certificate as long as my arm,' he grins, taking his first sip of a pre-training orange juice. Again, as with Rob Gier, it was parental pressure that ignited international ambitions. 'Throughout my childhood, my dad had always hammered it home. "You were born in Gibraltar. You can play for Gibraltar." He seemed to know that sometime during my sporting lifetime the likelihood was that they would be accepted by UEFA. He knew I wasn't playing at a high-enough standard to get a call-up for England and I've always felt I had that connection with Gibraltar just because of my dad hammering that home – even though I'd never been back there since I was born.

'Someone messaged me on Twitter during my first season at Farsley and pointed me in the direction of the Gibraltar FA. In the first instance, they had home friendlies against Charlton and Hibs, which they invited me over for. I trained for four days with them but didn't expect to play. But I managed to get the last twenty-five minutes against Hibs and must have done all right as I got picked for the squad after that.'

The draw for Gibraltar's first Euro qualifying campaign had already been made before the 2014 World Cup, pairing them with Scotland, Ireland, Poland, Georgia . . . and Germany. It certainly gave the World Cup final extra spice in the Priestley household. 'I'd gone out for a meal and came home with about fifteen minutes of the match gone. I sat there in my front room with my dad, rooting for Germany. And when Götze scored that goal, I just thought "Oh my God, we're going to be playing against the world champions. The best team in the world." It was so surreal. Even sitting here now and thinking about it, how could it be that a normal guy like me, who works in a school in Morley and who lives in a little village in the middle of nowhere . . .' His voice breaks a little and his eyes twinkle some more as, even all these months later, the concept continues its orbit around his brain. 'How is it happening to me?'

Certainly the notion of playing in front of 42,000 spectators in Nuremberg is surely an alien concept for someone who plies his trade on this hillside pitch framed by advertisement hoardings for Barnsley Towbar Centre, Bretton Reed Smith bookkeepers and Costcutter. A bumpy, sub-zero pitch, where the shouts and catcalls of 150 or so brave souls are perfectly audible, has to be a world away from the sleekness of a top-class stadium. 'When you're warming up, you forget who you're playing against,' he reasons, running a hand through his side parting. 'Well, I do, at least. You're there to do a job to the best of your abilities. No matter if I'm playing ninety minutes, a hundred and twenty minutes or just five minutes at the end, my attitude and my mindset are always the same. I'll work as hard as I can, do whatever I can to score, win tackles, win the ball.

'It's more when you're in the changing room afterwards that it catches up with you, when you think "I've actually just done that, haven't I?" When we played the Germans in Faro [the Portuguese city hosts Gibraltar's home matches], we went into their changing room after-wards to chat to them. We were sat there talking, getting autographs, getting boots signed. That's when you think "Oh. My. God."' When the Gibraltar team travelled back from the corresponding fixture in Nuremberg, the shirt of midfielder Lars Bender was in Priestley's luggage.

'It's the way they move the ball around. I've played with good players who have a picture in their head of what to do before the ball comes to them. But these inter-nationals must have three, four, five different pictures of what they can do. You cut off one option and they've got others somewhere else. They're just so sharp in their thinking. They spend all day perfecting the art of foot-ball. I'm in a classroom teaching English.'

Where other internationals experience well-documented tug-of-wars between club and country, Priestley has a balancing act between *school* and country. 'The school has always been very supportive. It's good publicity for them. Parents of prospective students are quite shocked to find out about me. "This is Mr Priestley. He plays for Gibraltar."' It's cachet for Shaw Lane, too, along with getting a few extra paying folk through the turnstile. Priestley explains how, when he first started playing for Gibraltar, a group of young lads who'd seen him on TV began coming to every home game of his then club Farsley Celtic. 'They were like a mini fan club.'

Then there's the reaction of the opponent charged with marking someone who's played at the very highest level. 'One time, this lad was just on at me all through the first half, tripping me, nipping at me, all sorts. "You play international football, do you?" I scored two in the second half. "Go on, go on. Say something now." There have been times when you play against teams who've gone "Who's the player who plays international football?" "Well, that'll be me." It gets a little embarrassing.'

A prolific sharpshooter for both Garforth Town and Farsley before he joined Shaw Lane at the start of this season, Priestley's goals are almost always accompanied by an unfussy celebration reminiscent of Alan Shearer – wheeling away with head slightly ducked and a single arm raised. Modest and unshowy. While he could have stayed one of the main attractions at Farsley, the move to Shaw Lane is a marker of ambition. There's a longer drive down to Barnsley three times a week to play at the same level in the pyramid, but the sense of upward momentum around the place is palpable.

'I can't deal with looking back and thinking "If only I'd done that . . ." It's like when I was first invited over by Gibraltar. I had to pay for everything. I had to get a credit card so I could pay for my flight. But there was nothing that was going to stop me from going. I didn't want to be that person sat at home saying "What if I had gone?" Now I'd do anything to play for my country. I'd even sleep in a tent in the woods . . .'

In football, at whatever level, personal ambition and professional development are subject to the roll of the dice. As both Rob Gier and Sam Bangura can testify, players are at the mercy of circumstance, misfortune and, most markedly, the whims and peccadilloes of others. Injuries change the script; so do managers who might not like the cut of your jib as much as the previous one did. Players have to operate within these conditions. They don't get to forge their destinies alone. The playing field is rarely level.

At the moment, Adam Priestley is having to work around such conditions – for both club and country. The current Gibraltar manager has been leaving the striker out of the squad of late, concerned that – at the level of domestic football he's playing – fitness is an issue. 'It's difficult,' says the otherwise chirpy Priestley, sighing for the first time that evening. 'He sees that I only train twice a week with the club, but I actually train every day. I go to the gym. I'm outside every day for my job. It's frustrating. When I didn't get called up for the Poland and Ireland games, I was devastated, especially after how well I'd played against Germany.'

Coupled with that is the limited amount of game time he's been getting of late at Shaw Lane. 'I injured my hamstring against Germany, so spent pre-season trying to get myself back to top fitness. I've worked hard to get there, but early in the season I wasn't playing well. The other strikers started scoring so I got dropped to the bench. And they've continued to score since. It's unfortunate. The manager says I've been playing well when I've come on as sub, but the other lads are playing well and scoring. He's got no reason to change it.' The man who's shared a pitch – and held his own – with Müller and Özil and Schweinsteiger can't get into the first team of an eighth-tier club from South Yorkshire.

For all Priestley's smiles and positivity, you can read

between the lines. Having turned twenty-five last month, there is clear concern that, if he wants to play several leagues higher up, things need to happen soon. He's now the age that Jamie Vardy was when he made the jump from non-league to the professional ranks. Maybe Priestley's got a couple of years to reach a higher level before he hits his physical peak, but he's certainly too young to be adopting the world view of those who've gone over the crest of their career, the high points only visible in the rear-view mirror. Nevertheless, the tone and vernacular of the veteran does slip into Priestley's conversation at times. 'If I never played for Gibraltar again, I'll have eleven caps,' he prematurely reflects. 'And those are never going to be taken away from me.'

After this evening, though, Priestley doesn't have to wait too long for his chance to add more chapters to his footballing narrative. A few days later – while his international colleagues are stepping aboard a Tbilisi-bound plane for their penultimate Euro '16 qualifier – he's setting his Corsa's sat nav for the villages surrounding Huddersfield, specifically the home ground of Shelley FC. There, in a first-round tie of the Sheffield & Hallamshire Senior Cup, he'll help himself to a hat-trick, earning a starting position in the next league match against table-topping Stafford Rangers. Another goal in that game, this one a spectacular overhead kick, cements his place back in the side and takes Shaw Lane up to second place in the league. This season's hopes of promotion – and of an international recall somewhere in the middle distance – just had a little more air pumped into them.

While Priestley, Gier and Bangura – this trailblazing international brigade – keep their eyes on distant horizons, they constitute the tiniest minority. Elsewhere, the non-league world's gaze stays firmly on the local, on the immediate environs, on home. And there's one place where the notion of 'home' is stronger than anywhere else.

Destination Manchester.

3

OCTOBER

Love will tear us apart

The Curry Mile, the endless procession of exotic eateries that forms the spine of the south Manchester suburb of Rusholme, is an unlikely crucible of revolution. But it is just that – even if there's no blue plaque above the site of this particular insurrection, the Dildar curry house. Indeed, the Dildar is no longer there: 111 Wilmslow Road is now occupied by Kebabish, a restaurant promising 'the thrill of the grill'.

A little over ten years ago, over a fragrant feast of South Asian cuisine, a small handful of disaffected, increasingly hostile Manchester United fans were busy deconstructing the state of affairs at their beloved Old Trafford following the club's takeover by Florida billionaire Malcolm Glazer. They were getting more bitter by the day. By the hour, in fact. The mists obscuring the deal were beginning to clear, revealing the depth of debt the club was being plunged into to secure the takeover.

The despair at the numbers being touted provoked an extreme response. That evening, over the curry-house table, the idea of forming a fan-owned breakaway club was first mooted, a suggestion that impartial observers might have merely put down to the intake of successive pints of Kingfisher.

But this tiny germ, this seed of such an ambitious dream, wouldn't go away. It hadn't dissolved by the following morning, unlike the Alka-Seltzer in the bedside glass of water. Quite the opposite. It grew and grew – and very quickly. Two public meetings were held, at the Central Methodist Hall and the Manchester Apollo respectively, from which a steering group was swiftly commissioned. In July 2005, within just two months of that meal at Dildar, the new club was already playing its first friendly.

A decade on, FC United of Manchester can bask in its extraordinary success, the most impressive ascent by a fan-owned club yet seen aside from that of AFC Wimbledon. Having started that first season in the North-West Counties Football League Division Two, three back-to-back promotions saw the club fly up the pyramid at an unparalleled velocity, with every tackle, every shot roared on by an average home gate of between 3,000 and 4,000, numbers utterly alien to sub-Conference football. (Indeed, for their first-ever league game, a 5-2 victory away to Leek Town, 2,500 supporters descended on the Staffordshire club's ground. This was more than Leek's total home attendance for the entire previous season.)

Champions of the Northern Premier League Premier Division last season after four consecutive play-off disappointments, FC United have now reached a new altitude – that of the Conference North, just two steps off the Football League. Nosebleed time. But this on-pitch milestone has been dwarfed by an off-pitch achievement. They've recently been handed the keys to their very own stadium.

Broadhurst Park, in the north Manchester suburb of Moston, is something of a handsome beast, especially when bathed in the golden glow of a gorgeous early autumn evening. It certainly doesn't appear a hotbed of anger and dissent. Obscured from the road by a row of mature sycamores, it looks more like a newly completed tertiary college, all glass and wood cladding. The wood is significant; it resembles railway sleepers, an allusion to Manchester United's origins as Newton Heath, a club formed by local railway workers in 1878. The fact that Broadhurst Park is less than two miles from the suburb of Newton Heath but eight from Old Trafford is not insignificant, either. Keeping their distance.

Since forming, FC United have played the vast majority of their home games at Bury's Gigg Lane ground, a few miles to the north. On the occasions that their matches clashed with those of their landlords, they used the facilities at a range of local clubs – Altrincham, Radcliffe Borough, Hyde United, Stalybridge Celtic and Curzon Ashton. It was the equivalent of being a long-term fixture on your mate's sofa, but having to find another sofa when he had his girlfriend over. But those nomadic days are done with. They've got their own place now.

'Welcome to the Costa del Moston!' cries one of the club's officials, raising an arm to the spotless, perfectly blue sky. The synthetic fibres of the new 3G pitch shimmer in the sunshine, while the club's substantial haul of trophies dazzle in a window above the main entrance. In the car park, the man in the burger van is warming up his grills, while his colleague sets out the condiments on a red plastic table. Excitingly (for me, at least), these include three different varieties of mayonnaise. Another van – the excellently named Wrap Scallions, specialists in tortilla-based sustenance – carefully reverses into its designated space, managing to avoid the young lads busy pulling wheelies on their BMXs.

The hurt and mistrust that fuelled the club's formation is now conspicuously absent. Instead it's all bonhomie and smiles. Successive promotions have healed those wounds in double-quick time; no more do the faithful look back in anger towards Old Trafford. They've got their own highly successful club on which to channel their thoughts, on which to nail their allegiance.

On the way here, I went looking for what FC United ran away from. The Megastore at Old Trafford is a potent symbol of what the *Guardian*'s Barney Ronay describes as 'a sport that has turned itself inside out for television, marketing, profiteering owners and the rest'. The Megastore is an extraordinarily overpowering retail experience, an enterprise better equipped to quickly relieve you of your cash than your local Asda or Morrisons at their Saturday morning peak. You have to pass thirty-eight tills on your way out, thirty-eight ways to efficiently, and rather significantly, reduce your bank balance.

When he took over, Malcolm Glazer and his equally eager sons took the world's richest football club and, using huge loans to complete the process, overnight flipped it into the club saddled with the deepest debt. When they refinanced after just a year, the annual interest alone totalled £62 million; it was the mother of all mortgages. So perhaps such rampant commercialism is understandable. Those repayments aren't cheap. You certainly wouldn't be surprised if, in their transatlantic isolation, the Glazer family inspected the match-day takings of the various retail outlets around the ground before they glanced at the actual result of the game.

The Megastore is a cathedral of commerce, a tourist attraction that keeps the cash for those mortgage repayments spilling in on non-match-days. Nowhere does it feel tied to the city itself. Several of the sales assistants have accents that are closer to Berlin than Burnage, while around four-fifths of the customer base this afternoon are from the Far East. The longest queue is at the counter where your name can be branded onto the back of a United shirt. An extra £11.95 in exchange for a hollow sense of belonging, a shallow affinity bought and not earned. And as long as your name is no longer than the maximum ten letters allowed.

You'd hope that the descendants of whoever designed the original Manchester United badge are on some kind of percentage. Anything and everything wears the badge. Stationery sets, alarm clocks, golf tees, garden gnomes . . . I flick through the sale rail. The cheapest item of reduced stock – clothing that's both faulty and non-returnable, mark you – is a cool £55.

There's no megastore here at Broadhurst Park. The

retail experience isn't that sophisticated. The merchandise manager is currently wheeling a clothes rail across the car park from a shipping container. He's en route to one of the corners of the pitch. It's from there that he'll hawk his wares before pushing a hopefully lighter rail back again.

A couple of primary school-age lads, old-style autograph books tucked under their arms, wait patiently outside the main entrance for their favourite players to arrive for this evening's game against Worcester City. Their heroes are approachable heroes. Fans of Premier League clubs have to be content with a blurred glimpse of a player as he speeds in or out of the stadium car park in an unfathomably expensive sports car. At Broadhurst Park, the players have time for their young admirers. FC United's captain, Jerome Wright, gives one a hug and asks him how his week at school has been since he last saw him. Fortunately, the players are equally approachable to middle-aged men brandishing dictaphones. I follow Wright into the bowels of the new stadium and, retiring to the empty main stand, he explains the appeal of a club for whom he's the longest-serving player.

'This is going to sound cheesy, but it's a very special place to be. The type of lads we have, and their ability, and where they could be, proves how different this club is to most. A lot of the lads have been offered double or triple money to play at a higher level. I could name ten of the boys who've had offers from the Conference, where the money would be, for us, life-changing. But these boys chose to stay. Nearly everyone has had an opportunity to play elsewhere, but they all chose to stay.'

Wright is among those who've been offered higher-level football, but who instead is content to spend his day in a regular 9–5 job, working in the Wythenshawe head office of Timpson ('they do your keys and your shoes and your phones'). That salary pays the bills. The modest cash earned from semi-pro football is his pocket money. That's enough for him. After all, following one particular experience, Wright could never leave.

'I broke my arm two years ago. At the time I was doing fencing for work and I couldn't lift anything heavier than a two-litre bottle of milk, so I couldn't work for three months. It might sound over-exaggerated, but my whole world fell apart. Because I was self-employed, I lost my house. I couldn't drive so my car went – I couldn't afford it. But, behind the scenes, a small group of supporters organised a gig after a match. I'd been given a few weeks off because I was being a whingey sod, a mard-arse. Then the manager phoned up, insisting that I came to this one game and this party. There, they auctioned off signed boots and signed programmes and all the money went to me. I could finally pay my bills.'

The fans' benevolence confirmed that Wright couldn't be anything other than an FC United lifer, his reward leading the team out onto Broadhurst Park's already hallowed turf. 'I was here when the first spade went into the ground where the centre circle is,' he gushes. 'I was so excited. It was just grass. It was just a field.'

We gaze out towards the far side of the pitch where the

ladders are out. The faithful are hanging up their flags with statements of defiance and principle. '2 Uniteds, 1 Soul', says one; 'Makin' Friends, Not Millionaires', says another. The people up the ladders are the people who put Jerome Wright's life back on track. 'If any person involved at FC United ever needs a favour and they come to me, I'd jump up and do anything that needed doing. Anything.'

Below us on the touchline, casting a beady eye over the first players warming up on the pitch, is another man for whom FC United has significantly recalibrated his life. Karl Marginson has been the club's first-team manager since that initial friendly in July 2005. At the time, he was working as a van driver, his shifts beginning at 4 am as he delivered food supplies to nursing homes and schools. Once the working day was done, he could then apply his brain to building up this brand-new club.

'For the first two years, it was managing a football *team*. Then, when we started to realise what we could achieve and how far we could take things, it became more about managing a *club*. The drive and determination have been there since day one – not just from me, but from the steering group members, the board members, the supporters. Sacrifices have had to be made and I was fully prepared to do that.'

Marginson took up the FC United reins at the age of thirty-five after a playing career as a sturdy midfielder for a small handful of Football League clubs and a larger number of non-league sides in the North West. A dyed-in-the-wool Manchester United fan ('I still am, I still am'), he didn't sign up as a disaffected Stretford End regular. He was otherwise engaged on a Saturday, of course. 'I didn't have the opportunity to become disenfranchised because of my own footballing career. So it wasn't a massive turning away for myself like it was for quite a lot of our supporters.'

Nonetheless, Marginson – known by everyone around Broadhurst Park as 'Margi' – fully understood the cause, the reasons for the bitterness. He got it. And, once approached about the job, he was knocked out by the scale of the ambition. 'I went along to the steering group meeting and couldn't believe it. They were talking park-and-ride schemes and such like. It was mindblowing.' And, gazing around the meeting, Marginson knew he wasn't looking at the faces of wildly idealistic dreamers and hopeless fantasists. 'No, there was too much intelligence in that room. There was too much commitment. That was never really a question.'

Marginson hung up his van's keys after five years of juggling the double lives of delivery driver and football manager. Since then, he's been employed full-time by the club. His ten-year tenure is in marked contrast to the managerial merry-go-round over at Old Trafford in recent seasons, where David Moyes and Louis van Gaal have shown themselves ill equipped to fill a certain Glaswegian's shoes. The sands are increasingly shifting, not only under the feet of Premier League and Football League managers, but also those of non-league bosses. By Christmas, six Conference bosses will already have exited stage left.

As long as he avoids notching up the club's first-ever relegation, Marginson – lionised later this evening in the chants of the FC United faithful – will continue to be the occupant of the manager's office come the end of the season. Thanks to the club's structure, it would take more than an impatient, trigger-happy chairman to dispose of his services. A mid-table finish would probably satisfy everyone. Repeating the achievements of last season is unrealistic; that title-winning match remains a memory that Marginson holds more dear than any other from the last decade. 'The players and supporters were all together as one on the pitch. We are together. We are united. It's more than a football club. It's a belief.' A grin breaks out on that otherwise unreadable poker face. 'Obviously the fans shouldn't have been on the pitch, but . . .'

Then, right on cue, a group of visiting North Americans being given a guided tour around the new stadium encroach on the playing surface for a photo opportunity. A club official's voice is bellowing and undiplomatic. 'Get off the pitch! Get! Off! The! Pitch!'

If Marginson wasn't a particularly disaffected, disenfranchised Manchester United fan, there are thousands around Broadhurst Park who were. I'm off to meet one of the more vocal ones now. Accompanied by the wiry intro to The Smiths' 'What Difference Does It Make?' over the PA, I climb the steps of the main stand up to the press benches in the top row. Here sits Steve Bennett, known to everyone around the place as Swampy. Over the years, he's undertaken various roles at the club, but is best known as the match-day commentator for the club's own online radio station. With headphones clamped around his ears and just-glugged coffee racing through his veins, he runs through his final preparations. The Motson of Moston, if you will.

Tonight he's accompanied by Ian 'Burkey' Burke, BBC Radio Manchester's non-league reporter and unarguably the most chipper co-commentator in the land. Burkey has been busy on the internet this afternoon and has come brandishing a book he's compiled that contains the vital statistics of every person on the pitch. Should Swampy need to know the age, birthplace, shoe size or, quite possibly, favourite pizza topping of the Worcester City number six, Burkey has the answer at his fingertips.

Sitting next to Swampy, I discover it's a real treat to watch a match in the flesh with an inbuilt live commentary. I now understand those curious diehards who watch games with the earphone of a transistor radio – or, these days, an iPhone – screwed deep into their ear, listening to someone else's interpretation of a match that's going on right before their eyes. It helps that Swampy and Burkey make an amiable duo, both possessing a deep knowledge of non-league football and clear ideas on the way the game should be played and administered (Swampy is the most vociferous opponent of garishly coloured boots, for instance. I'm with him on that).

Alongside the plentiful left-wing allusions that are liberally scattered into the commentary, the pair also send themselves aloft on some surreal flights of fancy. No other football commentators make a sharp turn to ponder the history of the Bee Gees' childhood Manchester home, or to deduce which former breakfast TV presenter a certain player's hair most closely resembles (they both agree it's Anne Diamond). We're all the richer for these digressions. Think *Test Match Special* but with no cake and a Trotskyite subtext. And the odd porn-star reference. When the visiting right-back hits the turf dramatically, Swampy notes that 'he's gone down like Ron Jeremy'.

The soundtrack to an at-times feisty first half is the massed chorus of the St Mary's Road End, singing with all the passion that used to reverberate around the standing paddocks of Old Trafford before the fabled prawn sandwich brigade took occupancy. It's the kind of high-volume singing rarely heard in non-league. The FC United fans' uncontained pride at their new, permanent base – after seasons of hopscotching around Greater Manchester – means that one of their favourite songs now takes on extra poignancy. 'This is how it feels to be FC,' they chant, adapting Inspiral Carpets' most famous hit. 'This is how it feels to be home / This is how it feels when you don't sell your arse to a gnome.' While articulating their joy that their transformation from nomads to homeowners is complete, the song still can't resist a dig at the bearded billionaire whose takeover inadvertently shaped this destiny.

As well as the choral singing, and the odd blast of old-school hooter, FC United's sponsor-free, crimson kit also harks back to times past, a design intentionally redolent of Manchester United's late-1970s strip. That would have been the era when the main movers and shakers behind the scenes here at Broadhurst Park would have, as teenagers or younger, fallen in love with a team crammed with United legends like Gordon Hill and Stuart Pearson, Sammy McIlroy and Gordon McQueen. Clearly a case of rediscovering something they had lost.

The first half's two main incidents both involve former Coventry striker Lee Hughes, who's leading the Worcester line. The first sees him control the ball impeccably and curl it into the far corner for the opening goal. Twenty minutes later, he makes an early departure, having grappled one of the opposing midfielders and placed his hands around his throat before, seeing the approaching referee, quickly patting his opponent on the head as if he was play-acting. Nice try. Still a red card, though.

At half-time, while Hughes has his early bath and the queues form in the bar behind us, Swampy removes his headphones, ready to explain the inevitability of FC United's rise. 'There were enough people involved for us to really do something,' he says, rubbing his straggly beard. 'How that would transpire we weren't sure – whether it was going to be playing park football on a Sunday or playing in a semi-professional arena. It wasn't a case of "Can it happen?" It was "*When* can it happen?" "And what form will it take?"'

Although not among the diners at Dildar, Swampy was present at that first mass meeting. The forward momentum ever since has been irresistible, no time nor inclination for regret and retreat. 'I grew up with Manchester United. It's in my blood. It was in my heart and soul. But after the anti-Glazer campaign, which had been lost in all fairness, it was very hard to think of any reason why you'd like to go back to Old Trafford. You don't cross a picket line and that picket line's not been crossed ever since. And I can't see myself crossing it for any reason at all. A free ticket? Free hospitality at Old Trafford? Not for me any more.'

Aside from his time clutching the commentator's mic, Swampy has been heavily involved right across the club. 'I was the assistant in our treble-winning under-18s team,' he beams. 'At the coalface, on the pitch every Sunday afternoon.' As a community coach, he's also worked in prisons, young offenders' institutes, local play schemes and after-school clubs. Like Karl Marginson said earlier, FC United exist to be more than a football club. And it's this level of involvement, of making a difference in small incremental ways at the most grassroots of levels, which provides the personal satisfaction. 'It's something I would never have got anywhere else,' Swampy announces as the teams come back on. 'You don't get these kind of opportunities at Man Utd or Man City.' Then comes the first cliché from his mouth all evening. 'It's been a roller coaster of a ride.'

The headphones are back on for the second forty-five, a half that the home side dominates. It looks certain that they'll grab a point with four minutes left, but Sam Madeley puts the ball over from two yards out. Perhaps he was dazzled by his Swampy-baiting, Barbie-pink boots. Two minutes later, ten-man Worcester launch a swift counter-attack and it's 2-0. Game over.

The rampant ambition, the upward trajectory of progress, might have to take a breather this season. It's going to be a tough learning curve here in the Conference North, a season of consolidation. Tonight's opponents, who've been in the sixth tier for more than a decade, have shown them the canniness, the sporting nous, required for survival. This season, it'll simply be a case of settling both into this level of football and into their new stadium.

A quick bag of chips (adorned by all three varieties of mayonnaise) and I head the car back down the M6. I'm due to meet someone else whose eyes are also firmly planted on steering their club into uncharted territory.

* * *

'You've got to evolve. You can't freeze yourself in time because of tradition. You get left behind.'

Dale Vince carries dreams and aspirations every bit as ambitious as those of FC United. As the owner of Conference stalwarts Forest Green Rovers, he is surely the most progressive, most visionary chairman in non-league football.

It was following his dreams that got him to where he is today. A former new-age traveller who once lived in a decommissioned military vehicle, his drive to harness the planet's non-fossil natural resources is what has defined him. He is the founder and owner of Ecotricity, the country's first green energy company. Spot a sky-scraping wind turbine on your travels and it's almost certainly one of theirs. In the twenty years of their existence, the company's success has made Vince – in anyone's language, and certainly in the language of someone whose home was once a decommissioned military vehicle – a very rich man.

As he walks through the restaurant here at Forest Green's New Lawn stadium, on the outskirts of Nailsworth in Gloucestershire, Vince looks successful. He doesn't strut or swagger, but he does give off the aura of someone with a back story of achievement. If you knew no better, you might think he was a former pop star, someone whose band enjoyed plenty of hits in the 1980s, the royalties from which allow him to live a comfortable life for the rest of his days. He wears a pale-blue T-shirt, studded with reddish spangles, that looks reassuringly expensive, while a silver pendant winks in the energy-saving lights of the restaurant. His shoulder-length hair has recently been shorn at the sides, revealing a silver loop piercing the tragus of his left ear. This is not the look of an archetypal football club chairman.

Neither is this the usual story of a successful local entrepreneur – perhaps a sheet-metal magnate or a toilet-roll tycoon – emptying his bulging pockets to fulfil a childhood fantasy of running his own club. For starters, and despite being based in nearby Stroud, Vince had never visited the New Lawn before the club asked for help. Dipping a toe into the choppy, cash-dissolving waters of football was never on his agenda. But he's done so in a rather revolutionary way, as he explains in discreet, hushed tones.

'In early summer 2010, I read about how the club was in financial trouble and had been relegated, only to be reprieved by the bankruptcy of another club. Someone invited me to see what they were doing up here. It was a lovely place with lovely people. They said they only needed forty grand for cashflow to get through the summer and then everything would be fine. That was no problem to me. It just seemed worth saving – it's a big part of the community. I thought it would be the decent thing to do.

'But one thing led to another. They had no idea how much they really needed. Within three months, they were saying I should be chairman. I really didn't want that – I'm so busy. But it was a choice of walking away and seeing it fail or rolling your sleeves up and getting stuck in. And that's what we did. We spent the next couple of years putting an awful lot of work into the club. Not just me, but a lot of members of Ecotricity – IT, marketing, PR, finance . . . Just sorting out the books properly took twelve months before we knew where the club stood. There were a lot of historical debts, lots of undocumented stuff, turnstiles that didn't count numbers . . .

'The people who'd got the club into this league had done as much as they could, but it was a volunteer-run club in a league that had progressively become full-time and professional, as clubs kept dropping into it from the Football League. It was as far as you could take a club like this on a volunteer basis.'

Having thrown himself and his employees at the challenge, it wasn't a case of Vince sinking a few million into the business and seeing if the team could float to the surface. Instead, he saw a gilt-edged opportunity to think bigger, to use the club as a platform for his principles. 'One of the ways we've justified this big investment is by bringing our eco message into the football world, one that's relatively untouched by it. In life, there's no point preaching to the converted. One of the things we've learnt in all our years of doing this is that, if you're going to do a green version of something, then you've got to make it better than – or at least as good as – the conventional version. You have to wow people.' The pitch here is the world's first truly organic pitch and, yes, it does have that wow factor. From the restaurant's windows, the playing surface below, even in the slate-grey murk of the day, looks immaculate.

It's the same with the food provision at the New Lawn. Vince has attracted widespread attention in the national media for what the club serves on its plates – or, rather, what it doesn't serve. 'We stopped red meat, then stopped white meat, then went vegetarian and this season went vegan. When I first came here, we were feeding the players minced beef lasagne. I had no idea why. From a sports performance point of view, red meat is not a good thing. That was my starting point. But, secondarily, as a vegan I can't be involved in the meat trade in any way. We couldn't feed our fans and staff this stuff.

'Look at what that man's got on his plate there.' He gestures to the Forest Green fan at the next table, who thankfully doesn't spot that we're both studying him eating his lunch. 'That's a pie on a bed of mashed potato with fine shredded beets on top, plus peas and gravy. It's fantastic. What you have to focus on is not what's *in* the food, but that it's *great* food. We avoid labelling, so vegetarian lasagne is just lasagne. You're just setting yourself up to fail otherwise. "A-ha! There's something missing!"'

The eco message is carried through right across the club. The under-pitch drains collect and reuse rainwater, there are solar panels on the roofs of the stands, charging points for electric cars can be found in the car park and the whole stadium wears the colours of organic, chemical-free paint. All the beers and wines are vegan, too. 'Some fans now come up to me and say "I've gone vegetarian. It's changed my life." Others want to talk about electric cars or solar panels. It's actually working.' He beams and takes a proud sip of his pint of Venom, a vegan version of an existing Northamptonshire ale, brewed specially for the Forest Green bars.

With notable initial disquiet about the red meat ban, the changes Vince was ringing on the footballing side as well meant that the club's saviour was increasingly being viewed with suspicion. Replacing the club's colours and badge can be seen as heretical measures in football's more conservative quarters, yet the new owner didn't hesitate to do just that. 'We changed the badge because it was a rip-off of Barcelona's – and a bad one at that. Then we created a new strip because the old one, with vertical black and white stripes, was nondescript. The club needed an identity, so we now have a first-team strip that's unique to us.' They certainly do. The lime-green and black combination is the most striking on the non-league scene, at least other than Dulwich Hamlet's shocking-pink and blue kit.

'The black and white stripes had only been around for thirty-four years or something,' defends Vince. 'The club had played in a variety of strips in its history. And I don't set too much stall by tradition anyway. It's important to move with the times.' Besides, the economics vindicated the change. 'This new shirt sold more in its first season than all the other shirts put together.'

The kit change confirmed Vince's skills as a savvy marketeer. Forest Green's new colours – along with the chunky font used for the names and numbers on the back of the shirts – mirror the energy company's corporate identity. 'I wouldn't say the club is part of Ecotricity's marketing as such,' he defends when challenged, 'but it's part of the promotion of our message.'

While the fans would have been relieved and grateful that Vince's pockets both saved the day and underwrote their club's immediate future, it's a brave new owner who chooses to be so radical so quickly. His actions might have got up the noses of the faithful, but opposition has softened in the passing years.

'It was actually the thing we didn't do in the first couple of years that upset people the most – and that was sack the manager! When we first got here, the team were not only part-time but only ten players were signed up for the season. They never trained or played on a full-size pitch, except for matches. There were all these fundamental

79

problems and I felt the manager didn't have the tools for the job. I wanted to give him a chance to see what he could do. So we went full-time, brought in new players and changed the way we trained.' It wasn't until three years after the new owner's arrival that the manager was finally let go.

Because Vince clearly possesses an attribute missing from the DNA of most football chairmen – that of patience – Forest Green became an attractive club to manage, despite the results of recent seasons. 'We had some very serious people apply for the job because they knew they would get a fair shout, that they weren't going to be here for just six weeks or six months. That attracted quality applicants who wouldn't have otherwise come to the club. It pays you back in the long term. And it's no different for players. We're now able to attract players who we would never have been able to attract. We've built this reputation for the way we do things.'

'Doing the right thing' is a recurring conversational motif – and these methods and principles are borne out by the club's league position. They're currently looking down on the rest of the Conference table, having begun the season with nine straight wins. Tranmere are today's visitors, a chance to measure Forest Green's achievements against another of the division's big boys.

And with each game, with each win, they're looking closer to fulfilling at least the first part of Vince's on-pitch dreams. 'Our aim is to ultimately be a Championship football club. When we started this, we said we'd achieve that within ten years. That was four years ago, so we've got six left! It's possible, but I wouldn't mind if we were sat in League One in six years' time. That wouldn't trouble me. I'm much more interested in doing it the right way, in a sustainable way, so that once we get there, we can stay there.'

But, as he reaches the bottom of his pint, Dale Vince reveals his biggest dream of all – to build a stadium 'that's never been seen before, the kind of stadium that all fans will want to visit and tick off their list, like Wembley. A real experience.' To do this would mean Forest Green leaving their current location and resettling on a plot adjacent to junction thirteen of the M5, part of Vince's planned 100-acre eco-park split between sport facilities and business. It would put the club in comfortable reach of north Bristol, Gloucester, Cheltenham, Tewkesbury and the Forest of Dean, as well as making travel easy for away fans. It would also mean the first team, who currently train thirteen miles away in Cirencester, would be based in one location, along with the women's and academy teams, neither of whom train or play at the New Lawn.

These plans are on the table despite the fact that the existing stadium is only nine years old and certainly good enough for the requirements of League Two football, should the hoped-for promotion at the end of the season materialise. Vince shakes his head. 'The stadium would cope, but the location absolutely wouldn't. The roads get clogged on match days, people park in the local streets and upset the neighbours. There's one road leading in which is narrow and steep, and we've got only a hundred and fifty parking spaces for a stadium that holds five thousand. It's a good facility that's just in the wrong place.'

You can believe he'll get there too, to the promised land out near Junction Thirteen. He might be the owner of the Conference's longest-serving member, a club that has stayed in the same division for seventeen seasons, but Dale Vince himself doesn't stand still. He's an idealistic dreamer, for sure, but he's also a man of action. Status quo be damned. And while the Premier League gets plumper and plumper on its petrochem dollars, the green pounds this multi-millionaire is spending mean more and give more value. Doing the right thing, as he would invariably say.

* * *

'Ooo-ooo-ooo, Gary Taylor-Fletcher!'

Merseyside is known for its songwriters, but few were surely as quick-witted as the lyricists among the 481 members of the Tranmere faithful who've made the journey down to Forest Green. The club completed the signing of veteran striker Gary Taylor-Fletcher this very morning, a deal that pays instant dividends when the striker, carrying a little more weight than in his heyday, scores with only his third touch in a Tranmere shirt. Rovers are one-up against the league leaders after just five minutes and the away terrace's tribute, to the tune of Black Lace's 'Do The Conga', is immediate. A new cult hero, a new song to be sung.

It's far from the only example of the songwriters' art

we hear this afternoon. While the sheep on the steep green hill overlooking the New Lawn stadium might have provided them with some obvious subject matter, it's the meat-free environment that offers the richest pickings for the carnivorous choir's satirical barbs. An early offering, to the tune of 'Yellow Submarine', is 'We all dream of a ham sandwich / A ham sandwich / A ham sandwich'. 'Go West', the disco anthem taken to the upper echelons of the charts by both Village People and the Pet Shop Boys, is plundered for the factually water-tight '1-0 to the meat-eaters!'. But the most smiles are reserved for their take on 'When The Saints Go Marching In': 'Oh, Birkenhead / Is wonderful / Oh, Birkenhead is wonderful / It's full of beef, beef and more beef / Oh, Birkenhead is wonderful'.

Then, just as the food-related merriment seems to be wearing thin ('Who's the vegan in the black?' etc.) comes surely the intellectual highpoint of this afternoon's musical banter: 'You can stick your veggie burgers up your arse / You can stick your veggie burgers up your arse . . .'

The bonhomie grows even stronger when former Forest Green striker James Norwood doubles Tranmere's lead after twenty-two minutes. A fan just along from me – one certainly old enough to know better but presumably with a couple of pints of vegan beer in his belly – climbs onto one of the terrace's dividing barriers and somehow balances for at least half a minute while he unleashes a stream-of-consciousness tribute to his heroes. His pals in front offer a soft landing.

There's reason for such acrobatics. The home side's

luminous lime-green kit might be successfully penetrating the Gloucestershire gloom, but they're unable to penetrate the visitors' stout and resolute gameplay. Little evidence is offered as to why Forest Green are currently top of the league. And Tranmere's new front pairing are playing as if they've been lifelong team-mates.

Aside from two sighing Tranmere old boys next to me discussing former Everton manager Howard Kendall, whose death was announced this morning, the jollity remains high in the away end during the break. The younger fans clown about to the *Muppets* theme tune played to accompany a display by the school-age Gloucester Wildcats cheerleaders, and this excitability doesn't diminish when play resumes. Halfway through the second half – and clearly forgetting that earlier late capitulation against bottom-of-the-table Kidderminster – the faithful abandon their vegan-baiting in favour of a straightforward singsong, serenading the rest of the ground with 'Twist And Shout', 'Sweet Caroline' and Erasure's 'A Little Respect', the original lyrics all retained.

The two-goal advantage is, this time, comfortably held until the final whistle, an impressive victory that lifts them to fourth in the table. That heel-dragging reaction to the Kidderminster draw is long forgotten. There's now a skip in the stride as the fans leave the ground, picking their way through discarded chip trays and ripped-up raffle tickets. Tonight the fleet of coaches will head back to the Wirral full of song and good cheer. But not before their passengers issue a poignant farewell to their Forest Green brethren.

'Town full of vegans! You're just a town full of vegans . . .'

* * *

Such jollity is in short supply down at Bishop Sutton. Completely absent, in fact. The season so far has upheld the form of the last campaign. Save for the point gained from a single goalless draw, defeat has followed defeat has followed defeat. The margins are finer these days, though; the only real tonking of late was an 8-1 loss to Chipping Sodbury last weekend.

These performances are reflected in the small number of spectators dotted around the ground. The forty-three who witnessed the FA Cup defeat back in August has now dwindled to less than half that for tonight's league visit of Chard Town. The meagre numbers, though, don't stop the man on the gate taking a quid off my admission for arriving a little late. It seems the Bishop Sutton defence is being similarly generous. 'They're two down already,' sighs the master of the gate, a smile of resignation forming at the corners of his mouth. There's barely fifteen minutes gone.

But the inevitable walloping proves not to be inevitable at all. While still not on winning ways, they've managed to score at least once in each of their last ten games and do so again before the break. From what I've seen so far, it's the least they deserve for their improved organisation and confidence on the ball. It's all the more impressive considering three of the starting line-up are making their home debuts. Steve Laker is still being forced to shuffle his pack.

One of the debutants, the striker Raph Waugh, signals across to the bench. They can't hear the nature of his complaint, but they can see what's up. After a challenge from a Chard defender, his finger is at the most unnatural of angles. A collective 'eurgh!' comes from the supposedly battle-hardened backroom team in the dugout, who spin on their heels and look away. Taff the trainer is made of tougher stuff. He jogs onto the pitch and pops the finger back into its socket.

Although the score stays 2-1 to Chard, it's a much-improved performance that could have yielded at least a point if Bishop Sutton's finishing was sharper, more ruthless, more composed. Any neutral – certainly one arriving fifteen minutes late like me – would have been hard-pressed to identify which team started the match in sixth place and which team was rooted to the bottom. 'It'll come, it'll come,' soothes the assistant manager. With performances like this, it's a reasonable assessment. They might still only have notched up a single point this season, but they're just five points adrift of the next team. Plenty of time, surely.

While the performance is an improvement, other things don't change. George the gobby goalie's incessant yapping finally earns him a yellow card in stoppage time when he questions the referee's time-keeping. 'One minute of added time for five fucking substitutions?' The silence at the final whistle also remains the same, but so too does the manager's unshakable optimism. 'We still have close to ninety points up for grabs,' he gushes in the clubhouse afterwards. The relentless dreamer, clinging on to what's mathematically possible.

* * *

Less than a fortnight later, however, the relentless dreamer finally transforms into the brutal realist. On the same day that the catcalls pleading for José Mourinho's departure from Stamford Bridge get even louder following Chelsea's home defeat by Liverpool, Steve Laker falls on his sword.

A couple of hours after the team's FA Vase defeat at home to Cornish side Torpoint Athletic, he tenders his resignation to the 'not shocked, but surprised' committee. Circumstances meant his days had been numbered, his card punched. 'It's Mission Almost Impossible at the moment,' he later reflects. 'I have a team that's almost there. We're only two or three players short, those three players who are the spine of the team and who control each area of the pitch – including, obviously, a goalscorer who's going to score twenty, twenty-five goals a season. But those players, the type with experience and creativity, are unfortunately players who'd want some kind of wage each week. And it's not necessarily the odd ten or twenty quid. With the resources we've got, I can't bring those players in. I've exhausted all my contacts. I've gone through my little black book and I've only got those premium players left. Now's the time for a new manager who might have those extra players on his list.'

He's still referring to the team in the present tense, not in the sighing, regretful past tense of a manager who's just driven out of the club car park for the last time. That's because he's not leaving Lakeview – not just yet, anyway. 'Officially I've stepped down from the role of manager, but I'm staying on as a coach until such time that they find a new manager to see what his plans are. I'm not the kind of guy to wash my hands of it – unless I'm told to leave.'

The club's retention of Laker as a coach for the foreseeable has created a strange situation. With him picking the team until the vacancy gets filled, he is effectively the caretaker manager, the man charged with replacing himself. 'It's a strange one,' he agrees. 'I've said to the players that it's just a change of job title until the new manager comes in. But I am kind of the caretaker, yeah.'

That he's not embarrassed about the situation, that he's happy to continue offering up his spare time two or three times a week, emphasises his passion and commitment. Whenever reflecting on the unfair hand dealt to him in his first management job, he's never once looked for excuses or for scapegoats, never deflected the blame beyond his own shoulders. 'They're a great group of lads. They work hard. They're honest lads. But they're all inexperienced at season-on-season in the Western League. They're county-level players who've stepped up to Western League. A lot of them are under the age of twenty. We went to Devizes the other week and, through unavailability and whatnot, my back four consisted of three seventeen-year-olds and a twenty-one-year-old. They still played exceptionally well, but . . .

'I could have left it another five or six games to see how it all turns out, but without being able to find those other players, we could be another five or six games further behind points-wise.' In a sport not known for its abundance of humility, Steve Laker stands down with honour, displaying a grasp of reality and self-awareness that a certain someone at Stamford Bridge would do well to study.

4

NOVEMBER

Swansongs and encores

It had been an unprecedented few days for non-league football. The spotlight had never shone so bright before, its beam illuminating the nooks and crannies, the folds and creases, of a semi-pro scene that would otherwise have remained invisible to Joe or Josephine Public.

A week or two ago, barely anyone outside Sheffield had heard of Stocksbridge Park Steels. Football fans up and down the country now know it to be the club that launched Jamie Vardy's unstoppable rise from lower-tier anonymity to Premier League ubiquity. At the time, Vardy could only play the first sixty minutes of Stocksbridge's Saturday matches – and none of their midweek games – because the terms of a curfew, earned for an assault conviction, dictated that he be back home no later than 6 pm. To make sure that curfew stayed intact, legend has it that his parents would sit in their car at matches, turning the ignition key the moment the subs board was held to the skies, telling Vardy his time was up. Cinderella had to be home before the clock struck six.

This weekend, the whippet-thin, whippet-fast striker's penalty against Watford brought him just one match short of Ruud van Nistelrooy's record of scoring in ten consecutive Premier League games. Three days later, Vardy's reward was having an entire ninety minutes of Five Live airtime devoted to his unlikely route to glory, a programme rejoicing in the neat name of *Straight Outta Conference*. Host and guests forensically dissected the giant steps Vardy had made through the semi-pro ranks – that hop-skip-and-jump to the Premier League, via short stopovers in Halifax and Fleetwood – before becoming non-league football's first million-pound man.

With his rise taking everyone bar non-league watchers by surprise, the BBC weren't going to miss out again. Throughout the programme, presenter George Riley posed anyone near an open microphone or on the other end of a phone line the same question: could lightning strike again? Was Vardy Mk II lurking in the same depths from whence the prototype came – and, of course, from where other non-league alumni, like Chris Smalling and Charlie Austin and Dwight Gayle, emerged? The responses were open but non-committal. 'Yeah, maybe.' 'Might be.' 'Could be.' 'Why not?'

But it wasn't just the Vardy back-story that had heads craning in the direction of the pyramid's lower reaches. This overnight fascination with matters non-league came with another link to the top flight of the English game – namely the five holders of innumerable Premier League medals who, in their financially well-padded retirements, fancied a little sport. They had all chucked in some loose change to buy a club from the Northern Premier League Division One North.

Two nights before Vardy drew within one goal-scoring game of their former team-mate's record, the Salford City-owning ex-Man Utd quintet had their plans, not to mention their acumen as owners, scrutinised by the nation on prime-time TV. The two-part, fly-on-the-wall documentary *The Class Of '92: Out Of Their League* revealed the warts-and-all workings of a semi-pro football club to more than three million gripped viewers.

As well as tracing the fortunes of the promotion-chasing side, the documentary's second episode also shifted its editorial focus away from the millionaires and towards the real heroes of the club. All human life was here. People like Jim, the recovering alcoholic who revealed himself to be a one-man construction whirl-wind. Or people like Babs, the formidable guardian of the tea-bar who gamely went head-to-head with Gary Neville over his plans to resettle her in an isolated burger van behind one of the goals. With twenty-six years of voluntary service under her pinny, she was resolute in her opposition. 'I could walk way, don't worry,' she cautioned. 'Very easily.' Very few people have chosen to butt horns with one of the spikiest footballers of his generation. She became an instant folk hero for doing so. And she got her way, too.

But the documentary wasn't enough for the BBC. The very next night, Salford's home tie against Notts County, in the First Round of the FA Cup, also sat proud in the corporation's prime-time schedule, thanks to a Friday-night live screening on BBC2. The Beeb's radio-heads were also present. 'The FA Cup begins here!' trumpeted

Five Live. No one told them that it was actually the club's seventh match in the competition to date.

The last time I was here at Moor Lane, in one of Salford's leafier quarters, an abandoned TV had been dumped face-down on the pavement outside, while the main gate was adorned with a poster for a lost ferret. Things are a bit more together now. The BBC's outside broadcast trucks are neatly parked behind one goal, additional Portaloos have been hired and Babs has drafted in extra personnel to help cope with the demand for meaty pies and hot sweet tea. There's no news on the ferret's whereabouts, though.

Overnight, Salford have – admittedly through artificial means – become the country's favourite non-league team. Even without the documentary, a nation of armchair viewers would still be tuning in. The First Round of the FA Cup is the point at which the mainstream sits up and takes notice of non-league, the stage when the neutrals align themselves with the underdogs, backing teams whose locations they couldn't place on a map. This is the weekend when the part-timers – the butchers, the bakers, the candlestick-makers and, in the case of Salford skipper Chris Lynch, the night-shift gas-fitters – get the love. The fascination with Premier League shenanigans and tittle-tattle is put on hold while a nation reconnects with – cliché alert – real football.

Tonight, Salford find little resistance from Notts County. Not even the presence of a pair of ex-Man Utd players in the visitors' ranks (Alan Smith and Roy Carroll) can prevent a 2-0 reverse. The win is crowned by an extraordinary solo goal by Salford midfielder Richie Allen, twisting and turning and tormenting the opposing defenders with all the control and poise of Ricky Villa in the '81 final. It was an individual goal – and a team display – that will keep eyes on the non-league scene for a little longer. That spotlight needn't be switched off just yet.

* * *

Salford weren't the only seventh-tier team dishing out knock-out blows to Football League opposition that weekend. Chesham United, of the Evo-Stik Southern League Premier, travelled to Bristol Rovers and calmly disposed of their three-divisions-higher hosts. The victory was a bittersweet affair for Chesham's player-coach. On his way to Premier League fame with Fulham, Barry Hayles spent a season and a half at the Memorial Ground, his thirty-two goals in sixty-two league appearances granting him eternal cult status in Bristol's northern suburbs. A fortnight after that emotional return, he's back in the West Country, this time for a distinctly prosaic league fixture against Paulton Rovers.

Hayles is forty-three now, the age by which most former pros have got their feet under the carpet in cushy broadcasting roles or have reinvented themselves as loyal, dues-paying coaches or are renewing their annual membership at the local golf course. Hayles, though, can't stop playing – and is unembarrassed by seeing out his days at this comparatively low level. His roots can be found deep in this particular patch; he was already in his mid-twenties when, as a free-scoring striker at Stevenage Borough, Bristol Rovers dangled a professional contract before his eyes. Back in non-league for five seasons now, his ongoing career is a tribute, a salute, to the world from whence he sprang.

Grounds like this would have been familiar territory for Hayles in his younger days. It's just a couple of degrees above freezing here in Paulton, a wind rattling the ground to its bones. You can almost *see* the dankness on the air. And the game matches it. The romance of the FA Cup – to be rekindled in a couple of weeks' time when Chesham travel to Bradford City – is on hold for now. Today is romance-free; it's a sour game on a sour day. 'You fucking nobhead!' bawls one unnecessarily angry home fan to a Chesham player just for taking a throw-in, not knowingly nobhead-like behaviour on a football pitch. 'There's one at every ground you go,' sighs one of the photographers.

A chant goes up at the away end: 'Everywhere we go / Everywhere we go / We are the Chesham boys / Making all the noise.' This is surely ironic. They're not making much noise; only half a dozen are bothering to raise their voices. Mouths are kept shut to keep the cold out. During a lull in play, the stewards can be heard comparing the respective thickness of their thermal socks, but surely no one is colder than the gloveless physio cradling a chunky bag of ice as she scurries across to the pale shelter of the dugouts. The players' limbs seem to be protesting too and are refusing to work as they should. A sliced clearance smashes on the metal grille of the tea bar, recalling one of Richie Benaud's most memorable lines about an Ian Botham slog that went straight into the confectionery stall and out again.

Today, Hayles, aside from being part of the Chesham coaching team, is one of the substitutes. That's been his position in the squad since missing a few games through injury. A fixture of the starting XI before he picked up the knock, he's itching to regain his place in the playing hierarchy. That's obvious from his body language. Most players would gratefully accept a seat on the bench this afternoon, out of that biting wind, but Hayles is a bag of energy, a coiled spring that can't rest. His seat remains vacant. Instead – wearing a woolly hat, gloves and a pink bib over his blue training top – he's constantly dancing on his toes on the touchline.

His advice from the sidelines is a mixture of gentle persuasion and more rapid-fire instruction, all informed by a quarter-century of experience that saw him climb from the lowlands of Willesden Hawkeye to the peak that is the Premier League. He's now coming down the other side of the mountain, albeit in no particular rush. The younger players nod their acceptance of what he's got to say. Respect is unquestioningly granted to this wise elder, the man who escaped non-league when he was around their age, the man whose career they would dearly love to replicate.

Two-thirds of the way through a niggly first half of hoofs, shunts and nudges, Paulton take the lead, a scrappy bundle of a goal that's greeted enthusiastically by one orange-bibbed steward in particular. Sporting a scruffy folk-musician beard and missing a front tooth, he leaps up onto the nearest railing with an unexpected show of athleticism – and a probable contravention of the stewarding code. You can forgive his outburst. Goals are in short supply round here. His team are bottom of the league.

After the break (an interval marked by greasy tea and some insipid Justin Bieber being played over the PA to the appreciation of precisely no one), Chesham are reduced to ten men after one of their strikers is dismissed for backchat. Their boss vents his anger towards the referee, the linesman and anyone else who'll lend an ear. He invokes the spirit of Graham Taylor when sarcastically thanking the officials for the game-changing decision; that's when he's not involved in an extended slanging match with the Paulton number six. Meanwhile, Hayles quietly gets on with his task, instructing players to fill the gaps that the early departure has created. He's a pragmatic man. Inwardly frustrated for sure, but someone who gets on with dealing with irreversible decisions.

When Paulton double their lead, though, his frustration goes public – frustration at an imminent defeat to the bottom side and, presumably, frustration that today he'll be an unused sub. The fact that the nearside linesman seems able only to raise his flag after the referee has made every decision just exacerbates matters. The dying breaths of these ugly ninety minutes are notable only for the way they keep the ball-retrieving volunteers busy. During stoppage time, at least half a dozen balls are hoofed into the car park or onto the roofs of the adjacent bungalows. One ball in particular appears to be on its way to the neighbouring village. Finesse, in short supply this afternoon as it is, loses out to frustration.

After the match, the faithful dive inside to feel the warm, welcoming blast of the clubhouse's heaters. One of its rooms is festooned with the balloons and streamers of a child's birthday party. On the TV, the Liverpool/Man City game has been chosen over *El Clásico*, a decision vindicated when Jürgen Klopp's men race into an early 3-0 lead.

The showered players emerge and Hayles and I retire to the peace and quiet of the snooker room – although the young daughter of one of the players is insisting on performing forward rolls at our feet. Over a Guinness and a polystyrene bowl of home-cooked stew, the frustrations of the afternoon subside with every warming forkful Hayles takes. All big smiles and easy laughter, he reflects on the extended autumn of his playing career.

'It still feels the same. I'm not pretending to be a youngster out there, but – and I know this is a cliché – age is nothing but a number. Of course, I'm not going to have the pace that I had when I was in the Premier League, but if I can read the game a bit quicker than others and get myself in certain places where I think the ball is going to drop, that gives me an advantage. And the body's holding up. I wish I could have played today to show you what it still means. I keep playing because the passion's still there. Once that's gone, then I can settle on the sidelines. For now, though, I'm still amongst it, still hungry.'

One moment this afternoon was particularly revealing.

Chasing the game during the second half, Chesham launched a swift counter-attack. Hayles was off, hurtling down the touchline in his subs' bib, parallel to his counter-attacking team-mates and visibly struggling to stay on the right side of the white line. The instinct was still there, still kicking in. A trigger response, hound after hare.

Hayles never devised a plan that carved out a second, post-pro career and, well into his forties, his playing days have been extended on an ad-hoc basis. Never knowing whether each season might be his last, it's been swansong after swansong after swansong. 'If the phone stopped ringing, that would be it. The boots would get put away. But the phone has kept ringing. Andy the manager's already asked me if I'm going to stick around for next season. We'll see.' His plastic fork scoops up carrots, peas and chunks of indeterminate meat. 'Never say never.'

And Hayles certainly doesn't make it easy for himself. Since his professional years, he's had three spells down at Truro City. That's not his local team. Far from it. There are probably 100 decent non-league sides within an hour's drive of his home in the South East. Instead, signing for an ex-team-mate at Truro meant a 550-mile round trip every week – and, at journey's end, there was no well-appointed hotel in which to relax, refresh and recuperate. During his third spell in Cornwall, home on Friday nights was a static caravan on the mobile-home site owned by Truro's chairman.

Signing for Chesham last summer means a comparatively short hop to Buckinghamshire. It's a mutually beneficial arrangement. Not only does the Chesham boss get the benefit of Hayles's goals (ten days ago he scored a hat-trick in the Berks & Bucks Senior Cup), he also gets the accumulated wisdom of someone with right-through-the-leagues experience. 'The manager hasn't limited my input. He's given me free rein. I say what I want, when I want. He gives me a lot of freedom to express my opinion.'

The circle complete, Hayles is living and breathing (and goalscoring) proof that the big time can still beckon those who've started out at low altitude, down in the regional divisions. 'It means a lot for me to come back and share this with them,' he notes with a satisfaction that's anything but forced. 'I keep trying to emphasise this to the younger boys who've got the ability to get to the next level. A few of them take it on board, a few of them think "If it happens, it happens". But you've got to try to make it happen.' And his tale continues. He's not just going through the motions, seeing his time out in the dusk of his career. The latest FA Cup run is a very real thing in itself, another chapter in an ever-extending biography.

He's the last to climb aboard the coach on which both team and fans will travel back to Buckinghamshire. A two-hour journey home after a defeat is worse than a five-hour journey home after a victory, especially if the stench of a gross injustice – that hastily issued red card – lingers in the air. Because of their exploits in various cup competitions, today was the fifth of seven successive away games for Chesham. The players are getting used to riding on that coach, but none have clocked as many miles as Barry Hayles.

* * *

'Hoo-lee-o! Hoo-lee-o!'

They love a South American here in the North East. From the Robledo brothers wearing the stripes of Newcastle in the 1950s, via Claudio Marangoni, Mirandinha, Faustino Asprilla and Juninho – not to mention *The Fast Show*'s Julio Geordio – Spanish and Portuguese have been familiar sounds around the region's grounds for decades. Newcastle, Sunderland and Middlesbrough have all been more than partial to a little South American flair, the latter two having had their first teams illuminated by the skills of one particular Argentinian – Julio Arca.

It's Arca for whom the 'Hoo-lee-o!' chants toll here at Mariners Park, a modest ground squeezed among industrial units in the hinterlands between South Shields and Jarrow. For the midfielder – who's only thirty-four, still a perfectly respectable age for a pro – now plays for South Shields. Having almost exclusively spent his playing days in the Premier League, Arca now patrols more humdrum territory. This is the EBAC Northern League Division Two, three levels below Barry Hayles and Chesham United. It's an unlikely place to find Arca just two seasons after he left Middlesbrough.

'It wasn't a straightforward retirement,' he explains. 'I finished my contract with Middlesbrough and was trying to recover from an operation on my foot. I was in recovery for up to a year trying to get back to professional football.' Such a long recovery meant the call never came, so Arca embarked on his coaching badges instead, resigned to waving the white flag on his professional days. After around eighteen months, his foot was feeling much stronger. The itch to play might just stand up to being properly scratched.

His return to action, though, was for an even more unlikely team: Willow Pond, a pub side from the Sunderland Sunday League, for whom he'd have to pay to play – £3.50 a match. 'One of my friends, who'd been playing for Willow Pond for a long, long time, asked me if I fancied playing again. So I played a few matches – it was an adventure! You'll know what the Sunday leagues are like. I'd prepare myself on Saturday night by eating right and I'd get there on time. But they'd have been out on a Saturday night, all night, but no matter what, they'd still turn up on a Sunday. I respected them. They love football. They love to play, they love to run around, they love to compete.

'It was good for me. I became one of them. There was no difference between us. And I never felt I was targeted by the opposition. I only got a bad tackle once. I was just another player. I didn't get any special treatment and I didn't want that either. An ex-professional footballer might come along with some arrogance, but it was nothing like that.

'In the majority of Sunday games, it's long balls, throw-ins, corners, everyone fighting. My idea was to make the team play more football. I was centre midfield and we were trying to play it on the floor as much as we could. Obviously the condition of the pitches wasn't great. But it was good. I'd be running around like a chicken without a head some days. And we won promotion, so it was a good season.'

By now Sunderland had offered their former midfielder a position working with their academy. Sunday mornings were taken up with his new job, meaning Willow Pond's pub team lost their midfield fulcrum. Saturday afternoons, though, remained free – a situation that the South Shields manager quickly exploited. Fit and injury-free, moving back to playing on Saturdays was the right challenge for Arca. 'They probably thought I might not be fit, that I might be fat. But they saw me play with their lads and everything was fine. I felt I could compete at a higher level.'

From his showing in today's match against Tow Law Town (a club most famous for being the footballing incubator of a certain Chris Waddle), Arca can comfortably compete at this level. South Shields are favourites for the league title, evidence for which comes in spades this afternoon. Tow Law take an early lead, but that's all they'll get. Shields are 4-1 up by half-time.

All grace and poise on this gluey playing surface, Arca still has the full bag of tricks at his disposal. Wearing number six but playing in left midfield, he makes the nearside touchline his own. During one particular attack, he dances around his marker, leaving him dizzy and discombobulated. He's a dominant force, the player that most of his team-mates want to find with a pass. At corners, he hovers and prowls on the edge of the box, looking to outfox the keeper with an elegant side-foot or to launch a speculative thirty-yarder towards the top corner. Even when one of these efforts lands in the car park of the warehouse next door, the chorus still rings out: 'Hoo-lee-o! Hoo-lee-o!' Arca's only been with the club for a couple of months, but from the off he's been afforded instant cult status.

As dusk descends, the local kids continue to kick a ball around on an adjacent field that's being engulfed in steadily deepening shades of blue. They're curiously oblivious to the goal-fest happening just yards away under the floodlights, despite the hearty cheers of the 1,400-strong crowd, an enormous gathering for level-ten football, attracted by the presence of a North East legend. Shields are dominant throughout the second half and, in the ninetieth minute, Arca finally gets the goal he's been sniffing after all afternoon, curling one into the bottom corner from the edge of the area. It's the claret and blues' eighth of the game, but there's still time for one more before the end. A 9-1 win to keep the title chase firmly on track. For the crowd lining the perimeter fence, that's ten goals for their £5 entry. A fine return on any investment.

Despite the ease of the victory, Arca and the rest of the Shields players never dropped down a gear or two. 'I play the way I've always played. Yes, it's different playing in front of forty to fifty thousand than playing in front of five hundred, but if I make a bad pass I still get grumpy with myself like I used to when I was a professional. If I'm doing something, I want to do it right. I want to win every game, I want to win every challenge. When I find I don't have the legs to run any more or I feel like everyone's just going past me, then I'll probably stop playing. For now, I can chase people, I can tackle, I can score. That's why I still play.'

There's certainly no sense of embarrassment at a rapid descent down the slopes of the pyramid. 'The Northern League is very competitive. It's not an easy-peasy league where you can do whatever you want. There are some very good players who could make it as a professional. One of our youngest players last year signed for Hull City. I'd definitely recommend ex-pros, if they're still fit enough to run around, to have a go in the Northern League. Why not?'

Arca is not the only player with Premier League pedigree currently playing down at level ten. He might have lost his pencil moustache and nature now forces him to shave his head but, at forty-one, Julian Joachim remains a relatively quicksilver presence on a football pitch, having swapped his top-flight days with Leicester and Aston Villa for the more prosaic East Midlands Counties League, where he now wears the yellow and green of Holwell Sports. Unlike Arca, though, Joachim's journey from English football's top table down to the tenth tier took a distinctly serpentine route. His passage through the non-league system has included spells at (deep breath) King's Lynn, Thurmaston Town, Quorn, Hinkley United, Holbeach United, Boston United, Coalville Town, Oadby Town and Shepshed Dynamo. The quintessential journeyman.

Former pros can even be found further down the pyramid. Last season, one in particular could be spied on the blustery cliffs above the Pembrokeshire village of Solva, cliffs clung to by gulls and guillemots. Here, Simon Davies – the former Spurs, Everton, Fulham and Wales winger – pulled on the emerald-green jersey of the local team to take on the likes of Fishguard Sports and Prendergast Villa. Solva's home matches are held on the very playing fields where Davies honed his skills as a football-mad kid. He'd gone full circle, the homecoming king.

Arca's self-described 'adventure' on Sunday mornings isn't without precedent for an ex-pro, either. On the frost-scorched pitches that line the A10 corridor north of the M25, Fitz Hall – an alumnus of several Premier League clubs, including Southampton, Crystal Palace, Wigan and QPR – now turns out for Hertfordshire-based Percival in the Waltham Sunday Football League. Having converted from the centre-back role of his professional days to a Sunday morning striker, often in the company of his former QPR team-mate Patrick Agyemang, he's clearly enjoying his new position – and the comparative ease of this level. On his very first match upfront for Percival, he helped himself to a hat-trick against Enfield Rangers.

Colin Hendry, the former captain of Scotland, is another defender who takes up a more advanced position on Sunday mornings. He now plays upfront for Clifton Casuals, a Lancashire side for whom Hendry's old Blackpool colleague Gavin McCann also turns out. Meanwhile, over in East Anglia, that former terror of

Premier League defences, Darren Huckerby, is now terrorising the defences of the Norfolk Veterans League as the star turn for Cringleford's village team.

And on the touchlines of the Blades Super Draw Sunday Sports League in Sheffield, the fifty-four-year-old player-coach of Hallam FC's Sunday morning side has, very occasionally, been seen to strip off his tracksuit and slip onto the field of play, especially if the result is safe and his job is done. His name? One Christopher Roland Waddle.

But the most inspiring story of a former pro gracing Sunday morning pitches, though, surely belongs to Stiliyan Petrov. In 2012, the Aston Villa captain was diagnosed with acute leukemia. After extensive treatment and retirement from the professional game, Petrov decided to dust off his boots once reassured he was in remission. Wearing the number ten shirt of Sunday leaguers Wychall Wanderers, Petrov inspired the Solihull side to a league and cup double in his first season. 'It will go next to my UEFA Cup medal,' he said, clutching his Central Warwickshire Over 35s Premier Division One Cup winner's medal. The worth he put on it was unspeakably symbolic. 'It is more valuable than everything else. It is priceless.'

* * *

Down at Bishop Sutton, Steve Laker only has one match as caretaker manager. There's a new face in the home dugout – or, rather, prowling up and down outside it. Around twenty years Laker's senior, on first impressions the new boss is both avuncular and explosive. His name is Colin Merrick.

Merrick's presence has already made itself known. Tonight's match – against Ashton & Backwell United – is his second in charge. His first was a creditable draw. After just ninety minutes in his care, the first team had doubled their points tally for the season. Definitely a man for making his presence known, he was previously in charge of Wellington AFC before he was relieved of his duties. 'I got sacked for non-footballing matters,' he confesses, with a shrug. 'For getting physical with the linesman. It happens.'

That first draw might have hinted at a brighter tomorrow under the new regime, but tonight the first team are reverting to type, a 4-1 home defeat that suggests Saturday's draw was a deceptive anomaly. The task is making itself abundantly clear to the new boss: resuscitating a season that flatlined months ago.

Steve Laker, in his new coaching role, remains the most vocal force on the bench, but he's notably much more relaxed than at any point this season – or last, for that matter. The strain has left his face. There's even the occasional smile. Instead, Merrick now shoulders the burden. With each defensive mistake, with each Ashton & Backwell near-miss, he pulls his dark-grey woolly hat further down over his ears. It's a subconscious reaction to what he's seeing, a defence mechanism against the unavoidable truth. The publicly acceptable equivalent of a grown man assuming the foetal position.

He silently scans those supporters behind him,

checking which locals are saying what, which should be listened to, which should be ignored. Meanwhile, Laker is at his shoulder, offering similar appraisals of the players – under-the-breath pen portraits that advise who's largely self-reliant, who needs encouragement, whose head will drop when a third goal goes in.

This might only be his second match in charge but, like a diligent, newly appointed teacher, Merrick has already learned all his charges' names. And their preferred nicknames, too. While he's undeniably stern – capable of issuing a narrow-eyed fixed stare that fillets its target, stripping it to the bone – he's tactile too. An arm goes round the shoulder of every player he takes off. A ruffle of the hair, too. Whether the ruffle translates as 'Thanks for your efforts tonight' or 'Thanks for your efforts this season but I'll be bringing in someone new in your position', no one yet knows. The two-match audition could go either way.

The mild optimism that lightened the mood after Saturday's draw is dispensed with tonight. Dissatisfaction abounds – both with the commitment of the players and the performances of the officials. As the game deepens, the disgruntled home bench increasingly rise to their feet en masse to howl at the referee, like a pack of baying hounds left out in the rain. There's a lot of howling tonight. The only light relief is offered by an exchange between the visiting goalkeeper and one of the Bishop Sutton subs. When the latter loudly guffaws at a sliced goal kick, the keeper's come-back, delivered from forty yards away, is instant: 'You can only make the bench for Sutton and you're laughing at *me*?' The rest of the home dugout nod their acknowledgement of his 'quality response'.

Three-quarters of an hour after the final whistle, Steve Laker is holding a tactics surgery at the bar with Bishop Sutton's young left-back, illustrating his points using some time-honoured props. The back four consists of ketchup bottle, vinegar dispenser, salt cellar and pint glass. Across the room, the new manager is off duty, preferring to chew the fat at the players' table rather than swap pleasantries with the opposing club officials. The players are Merrick's people. He is the leader of this particular tribe.

'People think I'm bonkers for coming up from Taunton to take over at Bishop Sutton. But it's a challenge. It's a massive, massive challenge. I'm a man-manager and this was a job to get my teeth into.' You get the sense that he's more of a motivational boss than a technical one – a Neil Warnock or a Barry Fry. Beautifully sculpted patterns of ball retention probably aren't his forte. Under his stewardship, it's clearly going to be by whatever means necessary. He grumbles under his breath. The words 'coaching' and 'bullshit' are audible.

Merrick's role, as with all the other roles at Lakeview, is unpaid. He did receive a small wage during his time at Wellington ('peanuts really'), but chose to use the money to sign a couple more players instead. He's not in it for the extra income, the pocket money. He's in it for the pride and the passion – and, ideally, the glory that comes with avoiding relegation. 'Looking around, this club is a nice club. The people are nice people. The pitch is a nice pitch. But it's going to be hard work. We knew that. It's going to be two steps forward and one step back. It's going to be like a yo-yo.

'Obviously I want to do it for myself, too. Someone told me I'm a better person when I'm in football than when I'm out of it. When I was out of football, I found myself continually working Saturdays and Sundays. I've got my own building business. When I was doing that, I didn't really miss football. But over the months it's like a dripping tap. You'd see certain managers getting jobs. "How's that twat got that job?"'

There is something slightly Churchillian in Merrick's no-nonsense defiance and resolve. He often uses the imagery of warfare; the team are 'warriors' or 'troops', the pitch becomes 'the trenches'. Accordingly, he needs to plan the rest of the campaign like a military strategist. And the result of the battles is paramount, rather than the style of any victories. 'We're not going to set the world alight, but as long as we get enough points to get out of the bottom two, we'll be all right. But it's going to take a month to have a look and get players in.'

Coming up from Taunton, forty miles south by south-west, means a different supply of players can be tapped into – and Merrick can save them their petrol money by giving them a lift to training and matches. New recruits, though, mean inevitable departures. 'A few of the current players will be released because they're not good enough. Results don't lie. And tonight was disappointing because we just threw three goals away. We were absolutely shite. We were ragged at the back, the midfield didn't function. I'll always have time for players who give their all, but I look at some of them and they didn't do a shift.

'We've got to change it and we've got to change it quickly. It's not easy with no budget. But I might take a gamble on this striker I know. The lad's trouble but he does know where the back of the net is. He'll give centre-halves a torrid time. And referees, too. He's a nightmare. Yellow card after yellow card. But when he gets the ball, he smashes it in the net.'

A smile softens his face. 'Yeah, I think I'll give him a ring on the way home . . .'

5

DECEMBER

Hopeless devotion, unconditional love

There's a great sign outside the Dripping Pan, the curiously named home of Lewes FC, ten miles east of Brighton. It's not meant to raise a chuckle, but it must do to anyone who spots it. 'No ball games are to be played whilst the match is in progress.' It appears that this season the players have been taking the sign too literally. The club is currently bottom of the Ryman Premier.

But Lewes's league position doesn't seem to be too strenuously concerning the regulars here. There's plenty of festive spirit around, particularly from a bunch of early-arriving fans in the car park. They're watching one shopper's attempts to squeeze a decent-sized Christmas tree into the less-than-decent-sized boot of a Ford Ka. Each time the driver gets into his seat, thinking he's been successful, the boot springs open again. He goes through the routine three or four times. The good-natured laughs get louder with each attempt.

The Dripping Pan – so named as it occupies former marshland where the local monks used to pan for salt – is one of the most attractive grounds in non-league. The pitch sits in an amphitheatre, bordered on two sides by steep grass banks, with the ancient city walls running high along one length of the playing surface. They've been playing football here for exactly 130 years, a lifespan that's seen many other clubs at their level come and go. Lewes owes its continuing survival to the hopeless devotion of a fine and upstanding brigade of volunteers.

Upstairs in the office, one of those volunteers, Roger, who looks after the match-day music, is searching YouTube for Christmas songs that no one is yet sick of. Across the desk, Issi – a chartered accountant who splits her time here between a part-time salaried position and unpaid hours as a volunteer – is checking the PayPal account for recent deposits into the club's coffers. The office printer spits into action. The club secretary and his four-year-old son (both unpaid) are running out the team sheets to pin up around the ground.

Next door, the home team is noisily gathering in the only first-floor dressing room I've ever seen. Before each game, they have to gingerly descend the damp, uneven outside steps, their studs like stilettos on drunken midnight streets. They've not lost a player down them yet, though. Zero accidents on the job.

The chairman, Stuart Fuller, carefully climbs those steps, a mysterious package under his arm. He reveals its contents to the excitement of the rest of the office. It's a new electronic substitutions board that the league has insisted every club in the division must use from now on. From today, in fact. (It's unclear, though, whether the edict has come from the league's secretary, the fabulously named Kellie Discipline.) But, as ever in the wonky world of non-league football, there's a problem. The boards can't be charged because they've got European plugs.

Fuller has had to lug this subs board halfway across town as he can't get a space in his own club's car park, due to today's Christmas shoppers using it. Unlike everyone else at the club, he's not a local; this morning, Fuller has driven the sixty miles down from his home in south-east London.

His presence here in East Sussex sprang from a sense of disillusionment with the direction of the Premier League and its teams. He's not alone. It's an emotion felt by many other comparatively recent arrivals in non-league. 'I'm West Ham born and bred. My eldest daughter, who's now fifteen, used to love coming to football from the age of four or five. We had season tickets, but it increasingly felt like you didn't matter there. So I was looking for something else and a friend of mine said "You should come down to see this team Lewes. They're abysmal, but it's a great laugh. You can have a beer, the food's brilliant. And they don't take themselves too seriously."

'I came down and really got into it. This was when they were playing in the Conference. I knew the club were in trouble but I didn't really know how much trouble. The shit hit the fan the following January or February when they were within a couple of hours of going out of business. So six local guys took over the club that summer and made it a community model. One of them approached me. "Do you think you can help us out? We're trying to change some things – the website, the programme – to bring new supporters in." My day job means I spend a lot of time travelling around the world trying to spread a message. So, in November 2010, I was elected to the board and have become more and more involved ever since. It becomes like a drug.'

The decision to proceed down a fan-owned direction wasn't, unlike at FC United, born out of protest and a sense of injustice. Lewes's rebirth was all to do with financial expediency, with survival. The club now has more than a thousand owners, meaning it's on a much sounder footing off the pitch. On the pitch, though, their footing is less sure. 'At the moment, our results are in the toilet,' agrees Fuller. 'Perhaps we're playing at a level that we can't sustain. Time will tell. And that's a frustration for some of the fans. The club was really successful a decade ago, but was funded by one or two people. They were in the construction industry, so when the bottom fell out of that, they essentially withdrew their money. And that's when the club started going downhill. But we have owners all around the world now. We're not reliant on one person or two people. That's the beauty of the community model.'

As with all other non-league clubs not underwritten by benevolent sugar daddies, Lewes are reliant on the goodwill and free labour of its volunteers. This is a club of modest means, after all. Fuller explains how their wage bill is £2,000 a week for a squad of seventeen or eighteen, while estimating that local neighbours Whitehawk – just one division higher in the Conference South – probably spend around five times that on their players' wages. Such tight budgets mean that recruiting and retaining a strong team of volunteers is crucial to keeping noses above choppy financial waters.

'If we didn't have those volunteers, we'd be dead,' says Fuller bluntly. 'So I hope they feel valued. We had the volunteers' Christmas party last night and at half-time at every match we give a shout-out to all of that game's volunteers. I love the engagement, the fact that anybody can turn up at a non-league club and say "Hello, I'd like to help". And I'd say 95 per cent of non-league clubs would say "Absolutely fantastic. We'd love you to do this, we'd love you to do that." All of the board here will stand with the fans to watch the game. No one will sit in the stand. I was a fan before I got involved with the club, after all. And the players are fans, the players are owners.'

This all-in-it-together, democratised environment (some of the directors are manning the turnstiles this afternoon) is in sharp contrast to the boardrooms of so many professional clubs, an environment motivated by spin, disinformation and hidden agendas. Should the Lewes fans become disgruntled about the club's progress or ambition, it's not a case of hurling abuse, or raising a banner, towards the distant directors' box. It can be a quiet, reasoned word in the ear of a board member in the bar after the game. And, of course, the massed ranks of the club's owners are the ultimate custodians of its traditions and its future, both of which are fundamentally important here. In existence as a football pitch since 1885, the Dripping Pan is among the top ten of the longest-used grounds in the country, but so far any overtures from companies brandishing fat cheques in return for the naming rights of either stand or stadium itself have been politely declined. And quite right, too. The Bathroom Solutions Dripping Pan doesn't have a great ring about it.

As one of the club's newer fans, Stuart Fuller feels no less of a custodian than the lifers here. His commitment can be measured by the mile. 'Today I left home at eleven and will get home at seven. I'll be back down here on Monday for a board meeting. There's another game next Saturday and then another the following Wednesday.' A grin at the lunacy of such an undertaking. This is his spare time he's surrendering, after all. 'But it's worth it. Yeah, it's worth it. I think . . .'

At precisely 1.30 pm, the first click of the turnstile sends one of those precious volunteers, septuagenarian Ethel, into action. 'Golden Goal?' she calls out to the first soul in the ground, regardless of the fact that he's already making a beeline for her bright orange bucket filled with lucky-dip tickets, a couple of quid in his hand in readiness. He's eager to select the winning ticket, the one whose number tallies with the number of minutes on the clock when the first goal goes in.

It's a ritual that Ethel has presided over at hundreds, if not thousands, of matches before. 'My mum and dad used to bring me down here when I was little. I used to play on the grass bank over there while they watched the football. The club's like my family, really. When I first left school, I used to sell programmes out the front when they had the big gate there. Then I did the raffle, then they started the Golden Goal and I've been doing that ever since.'

Of all the volunteering jobs, Ethel's is something of a plum one. Aside from a quick tally of her takings once the game's kicked off, she's able to take in most of the action, which she wouldn't were she stuck behind the bar or doing the teas for the visiting officials. She watches every home game alongside her son, her brother, her sister-in-law and her nieces. 'And my granddaughter's over at the other field at the moment watching the under-21s. She'll be here in a minute.' If the club feels like her family, it might be because half of the supporters appear to be related to her.

But never mind Ethel's near-eight-decade affinity with the club. That's a trifling short period of time. She's actually intending to be connected with Lewes FC in perpetuity. It turns out her late husband – who played for the club, naturally – had his ashes scattered over the Dripping Pan pitch. 'That's where I want to go when I die,' she says defiantly, extending an arm behind her. 'Out in that centre circle.'

While I chat with Ethel, a party of around two dozen men in their twenties – distinctly middle-class, with at least two-thirds of them sporting neat, well-maintained facial hair – pass by Ethel's table. 'Students?' I venture. 'Tight, whoever they are,' she replies. Just one of the party took his chances with Ethel's lucky dip. Instead they were galloping towards the bar, the scent of beer in their nostrils.

They're a curious bunch, though, wearing pink and

navy scarves, the colours of neither Lewes (red and black) nor today's opponents Leiston (royal blue). It turns out there's no mystery. They're sporting the colours of Dulwich Hamlet, the division's in-form, on-trend club. The Londoners were supposed to be Lewes's opponents today, but their progress in the FA Trophy means they're in cup action instead.

The party knew this, but they've still ventured to East Sussex. And there's a perfectly logical reason. While they might look like an office outing of the Guild of Graphic Designers, they're actually on a stag-do. With accommodation and travel already booked before the fixture was rescheduled, they decided to head south anyway – a match in Lewes and a night out in Brighton. This is very much to Lewes FC's gain. A couple of dozen extra punters through the gates, plus plenty of cash going into the till from a thirsty party appreciative of the bar's impressive stock of craft beers.

And the club shows its appreciation in return. They've got a neat take on corporate hospitality here – four beach huts sitting on top of the bank above the nearside goal. Kevin the chief executive has given the stag-do use of three of the huts as gesture of goodwill, their windows cast wide open to take in the excellent view. The groom is easily identified (his face has been printed on the party's bespoke scarves, after all) and Kevin further rewards him with the honour of shaking hands with the players on the pitch beforehand, as well as picking today's man of the match. 'Community football in action,' the savvy chief exec whispers in my ear.

The beach huts aren't the only imaginative touch around the Dripping Pan. The takeover became a make-over for the club, which now boasts an identity unlike any other at this level. Not only are the first team's shirts sponsored by the band Squeeze (whose chief songwriter Chris Difford lives nearby), but huge imagination goes into their match-day posters, each one bespoke for the particular game in question.

The poster for today's encounter salutes Brian Clough, reproducing a youthful shot of him along with one of his finest quips: 'Rome wasn't built in a day, but I wasn't on that particular job.' For the local derby with Eastbourne Borough, the poster featured a picture of Jack Lemmon and Walter Matthau in the teams' respective kits under the headline 'The Return Of The Odd Couple'. Other designs have incorporated *Star Wars*, the opening titles to *Dad's Army* and the distinctive orange and white art-work from Billy Bragg's first mini-LP.

As the craft beer selection might suggest, Lewes are also progressive on the catering front. Here, carnivores can enjoy smoked BBQ pulled pork in a brioche bun or a pile of poutine, that hipster-approved, nutritionist-baiting Canadian dish of chips, gravy and cheese curd. As a whole package, it's a thoroughly attractive, twenty-first-century way of presenting non-league football.

It's an admirable balancing act, too – reinventing the club to appeal to new followers without alienating the existing ones who've been coming here season in and season out. PJ, the club's other Golden Goal ticket-seller, first came here to watch Lewes play Tilbury in 1967. He was six years old. 'It hasn't changed that much since. Best ground in the league by a long way.'

This is a man who's appreciated the changes in recent times. 'Everything about the club is fantastic, apart from one thing . . .' A pause for dramatic effect. ' . . . The first team. I can't put my finger on why we're so poor at the moment. It's a bit of a puzzler. We're trying to play catch-up now, which isn't easy mid-season. But no matter what league we're in, we'll still support the club. Gates will drop off if we get relegated but, having said that, if we're winning games in the league lower, they'll turn up. Probably.'

Programme-seller Gary agrees. 'If the team regroups in the Ryman South and we start winning, people will come. People support a winning team, regardless of what level they're at.' Although Gary also first came to the Dripping Pan in the mid-1960s, a devotion to Chelsea got in the way – at least, until top-flight football started to price him out. Consequently, he's been back supporting his hometown team for the best part of twenty years now. 'Here you're part of the team. In the Premier League, you're just a number.'

Gary appreciates that fans can travel to away games with the players on the coach. Such trips are fine while your team is playing in regionally segregated leagues, pitching up at grounds at most two or three hours away. That changes when you reach the national level. 'It was a step too far when we were in the Conference. Some of the away trips were horrendous. I went up all the way to Barrow in a minibus. You can imagine what that was like . . .'

To prevent slipping down a division (and it'll be a tricky escape to navigate as a full four teams get relegated from the Ryman Premier), Lewes need to start getting results – and quickly. Instead, though, it's Leiston who come flying out of the traps this afternoon. They're one up within the first five minutes. But the goal is strangely greeted by a hail of cheers from the Lewes club shop. The reason soon becomes clear. The shop's volunteers, Barry and Jon, have put their allegiances on hold because both of them have drawn the five-minute mark in the Golden Goals lucky dip, bagging them £25 apiece. Ethel comes across with their winnings. 'I reckon it's a fix!' she laughs. My tickets – for minutes twenty-six and fifty-two – go into the nearest bin.

Barry, the shop's manager, has leapt headfirst into the seasonal spirit and is sporting an elf's uniform re-imagined as a Christmas jumper. His personal commitment clearly extends to wearing deplorable knitwear for the cause of his club. Actually, his commitment goes much deeper. Not only does he man the shop at every home game and run the online shop from home, he's also responsible for organising the ordering, manufacture and printing of what is an impressively wide stock. This is no small undertaking. Aside from the customary shirts, scarves and hats, Barry's stall offers a multitude of Lewes FC-branded souvenirs. Water bottles, cufflinks, darts flights, you name it. And for thirty quid, you can even become an owner.

Barry became a regular at the Dripping Pan in the early 1990s, but only got involved in the retail side five seasons ago. 'One of the original directors was running the shop. One day I was watching the game and said if he ever needed a hand, I'd come and help. Four games later, I was made shop manager! My hours vary from week to week, depending on whether we have a match day, or two match days, or no match days. I do this on top of my normal, full-time job. One week, I managed to put in forty hours here.'

Jon also gives as much time as he can. 'I'm a teacher, so if they played during the summer, I'd have loads of time to spare, but at this time of the year I really don't. I had a couple of years where I really didn't have much time to give, but I thought "This is crazy. I can't just be devoted to teaching." So I came back and now help Barry out. When we're quiet, one of us will do the shop and the other can watch the game.'

It does beg the question as to why they devote so much of their downtime to the club. 'I played for the reserves for one season,' explains Barry, 'but soon realised I wasn't good enough. They were way out of my league. Then I had to give up football at twenty-eight because I'd got rheumatoid arthritis. I still wanted to be involved somehow so, for me, volunteering is probably a replacement to playing.

'I've worked behind the bar, I've done the PA. I've even been linesman for a couple of games.' There's a pause in the conversation as we strain to see how another Leiston attack fares in the goalmouth below us. 'Getting to see a full game is unheard of,' he laughs. 'I've had to sign up to [non-league highlights website] Football Exclusives because nine times out of ten I miss the goals. So I go back home to watch it, to see what I've missed.'

I don't want to miss any goals either, so leave Barry and Jon to prepare for the pre-Christmas half-time retail rush. The conditions are tricky, with both teams struggling to find a rhythm – and the net – in a swirling, almost unplayable wind. That early Leiston goal divides them for nigh-on ninety minutes. Then, after an inordinate and unexplained amount of stoppage time that the home fans are in no rush to question, Lewes scramble an equaliser and the ground explodes. The stag-do spills over the advertising boards and onto the pitch to mob the players. Their euphoria – admittedly beer-flavoured – is unquestionably genuine. You'd think that the club they had supported for years had just won promotion. Instead, it's just a hard-won point for their new second-favourite team.

Roger the DJ makes a swift change to the end-of-match music, swapping an anonymous, vocal-free trance track for Yazz & The Plastic Population's 'The Only Way Is Up'. The message is in the music. Appropriately, for a club nicknamed The Rooks, a pair of said birds appear to be dancing along the touchline.

The stag-do heads off to the fleshpots of Brighton, wide grins on their faces, beer in their bellies and the obligatory inflatable penis under the arm of the groom. For the Lewes faithful, and their 1,000+ owners dotted all over the map, there could just be light at the end of the tunnel. And it may not be the light of an oncoming train.

* * *

Sunday, 9 am. John Kyte carefully places his kitbag in the boot of his white Fiat Panda and glances down at a small piece of paper, running down its contents while patting various pockets. 'Watch? Yup. Keys? Yup. Phone? Yup. OK, we're all done. Let's go.'

It's a ritual that he's been faithful to for fifty-five years now, one sometimes performed up to four or five times a week. For, since the age of sixteen, Kyte has devoted every spare moment of his life to donning the referee's whistle. He's officiated at more than 4,700 matches, from youth football to FA Cup semi-finals. Most of that time has been spent in and around his native Black Country, working his way up from the Bilston Youth League to the top flight, via the Staffs County and West Midlands Regional.

Among his years taking charge of matches at semi-pro level, when he'd regularly be refereeing at places like Kidderminster, Stourbridge and Halesowen, was a fourteen-year spell running the line in the Football League, hurtling up and down the touchlines of footballing cathedrals like Anfield and Old Trafford and Villa Park. 'I'd have loved to have made the middle in the Football League,' he sighs, 'but it never came.'

However, nearly thirty years after he hung up his Football League flag, he seems to have little inclination to halt this early-morning routine just yet. Now in his early seventies, he remains in high demand on the pitches of Wolverhampton. Most Saturdays and Sundays are given over to officiating, plus the occasional week night. His full calendar is evidenced by the battered copy of the

Birmingham/West Midlands *A–Z* in the Panda's glove compartment.

Raised on a nourishing diet of watching Wolves in their 1950s pomp, those floodlit matches of misty legend against Honved and Spartak Moscow, Kyte's time as a goalkeeper was brought to a very premature end at the age of sixteen after an extremely nasty groin injury, the details of which are best left to the imagination ('The doctor said it would be too dangerous to continue'). But not content to be a mere spectator, Kyte soon took up the whistle, having been asked to take charge of a referee-less youth game which he happened to be cycling past. 'It was the next best thing to playing. The following season I took the referees' course and I've been a referee ever since.'

Checklist ticked off, we set off for the site of today's match, on the other side of Wolverhampton from Kyte's village. 'Let's take the scenic route,' he says, pointing the car towards open countryside. Going the long way round gives him plenty of time to divulge the reasons behind his enduring reputation as a referee. 'It starts when you get to the ground. Don't slope about, don't slouch. Go into the dressing room. If the law says you get two match balls, ask for two match balls. I always like to carry the ball out with me. It shows I'm in charge. And walk onto the pitch like you mean it. Show them that you are the referee and you are in control, even before they've kicked off. Put the ball down in the middle, blow the whistle and that's it. Start as you mean to go on.

'I'm laid-back, but I can be a strict disciplinarian. I get

the feel of the game to start with and then referee accordingly to that. You've got to be able to be everything. You've always got to be ready because something can always happen in a game. You've always got to be on the ball.' This approach is the backbone of his longevity. 'Looking back, there's not one game I had to run away and escape from.'

Kyte had a clear, and local, role model when it came to being the under-fire man in the middle: Jack Taylor, the Wolverhampton butcher who became the world's greatest referee. Taylor was the man charged with handling the potential powder keg that was the 1974 World Cup Final between the Netherlands and West Germany. He showed he had the *cojones* to match his appointment, awarding the Dutch a first-minute penalty before the Germans had even touched the ball.

Not that Taylor's high ranking prevented him from undertaking more menial assignments. Kyte recalls a match from the Wolverhampton Thursday League that he was due to referee. He was unaware who was down to run the line. 'Who should come and pick up the flag but Jack Taylor? If you're going to learn anything, you're going to learn off him, aren't you? If he tells you anything, you're going to listen. Every player wants to be a Cruyff or a Pelé. I wanted to be a Jack Taylor.'

Taylor was always immaculately turned out and, after more than fifty-five years of service, Kyte still insists upon wearing the referees' traditional black uniform. He gleefully recalls the time when his kit would have starched, removable collars and cuffs, and when his black boots would have had white laces that needed to be 'taken out every week, washed and put back in'. He believes smartness to be a key part of exerting authority on the pitch. 'You have to look the part. I've seen referees doing kids' matches, one sock halfway down their leg. No black, no cuffs, no badges.' He glances across from the driving seat, a hint of a grin at the corner of his mouth. 'Slovenly . . .'

He's on a roll now. The manifesto is fully formed. 'And I'll tell you another thing. Have a smile on your face. It ain't a serious thing. It's not life or death, despite what Bill Shankly said. No, you go there to enjoy it.'

It might not be life or death, but football has taken precedence in the Kyte household, as confirmed by a story from the time his son was born in 1970. 'Twelve o'clock, a phone call from the hospital. "I'm pleased to inform you that you can come and fetch your wife and son now. They're ready for collection." "OK, I'll be up there about six o'clock." "Six o'clock?!" this nurse says. "They're ready to come out now." "But I'm refereeing the Hednesford vs Worcester City cup tie this afternoon. Look, I've waited nine months. Another few hours isn't going to hurt . . ."'

What could be conceived as a mild case of chauvinism is in fact evidence of Kyte's sense of loyalty, of an innate inability to let the clubs, the league, the game down. Certainly, amassing such a number of games does demand a sense of priorities that others might not be prepared to adopt. 'To get on and get the rewards, you have to dedicate yourself. You must. The phone might go at four in the afternoon. "Can you go to Wrexham tonight? So-and-so has cried off." If you say no, you'll get no more. My answer was always "Yes, I'm on my way".'

Work has always had to bend around his sporting commitments, too. As a teenage referee, he was employed at a local steelworks. 'I had a good job. I was a shift worker, but it got in the way of football. I used to work 2–10pm or nights. Someone said I'd never get on as a referee if I wasn't available every Saturday, so I left. In them days, jobs were easy to come by. You could leave one on Friday and start a new one on Monday.'

We've arrived at our destination now, the home ground of Bilbrook Juniors in the suburb of Codsall. A couple of teams hire out the pitches here on Sundays and a gaggle of players are gathering, perching on car bonnets while chewing the fat – quite literally in the case of two less-than-athletic players currently demolishing bacon butties.

The officials are clustered at the far end of the car park. This isn't just a player/official divide. It's a generational one, too. John isn't the oldest official today. The other linesman – another local legend by the name of Harry Worrall, a man with a Black Country accent even thicker and more singsong than Kyte's – is seventy-seven. Bucking the trend, and bringing the average age of this morning's officiating trio right down, is our referee, a lad in his twenties who's currently preparing for the game by taking long, satisfying pulls on an e-cigarette.

These advanced ages aren't so unusual. At one recent match here in the Wolverhampton Sunday League, the combined ages of the three match officials clocked in at 209. 'I keep going because there's such a shortage of referees,' explains Kyte. 'If you took all the referees who are over fifty out of this league, you'd probably take three-quarters off the list. And you'd annihilate the Wolverhampton Combination League. The older referees are reliable and they turn up. With the young 'uns nowadays, there are so many other attractions. They're available up until Saturday night, then the league secretary will get a call and they've cried off. Something more interesting has come up. Maybe the Wolves are at home. We've lost a few to that.' Kyte is bemused by such a flagrant disregard of duty. 'I would never think of standing and watching a game of football when I could be running around instead.'

These seasoned sages of the local football scene confirm that these declining levels of commitment and participation are echoed on the playing side. 'There used to be ten divisions in the Wolverhampton Amateur League. There were nine divisions in the Wolverhampton Works League. Neither of those leagues exist now. There are currently seven teams in the Wolverhampton Combination League. Just seven.' Kyte turns the word around in his mouth, showing displeasure at its bad taste. 'Seven . . .'

Harry Worrall recalls a recent match he had to abandon because not enough players were left on the pitch. Not because of a mass brawl and a flurry of red cards. One side had started with ten players, the opposition with just eight. A couple of injuries rendered the match unplayable.

We appear to be tempting fate with the subject of our conversation. At the players' end of the car park, a shout goes out as a newly arrived BMW finds a space. 'We've got two now!' The call comes from the manager of one of the teams whose match Kyte, Worrall and the e-cigarette-puffing ref will be officiating. It doesn't look good. Kyte hasn't bothered getting changed, informed by his years of experience. Indeed, just five minutes shy of kick-off, the team – I'll save their blushes by not naming them – still wouldn't be quorate if they were just a five-a-side outfit. The match is called off, the opposition handed a 3-0 walkover. We're denied the opportunity to see Kyte in action and the officials have a rare couple of hours to fill on a Sunday morning. Their match fees still get paid, though, Kyte's £19 linesman fee comfortably covering his petrol costs, scenic route or not.

We fill those hours by heading back to his bungalow, where he disappears into the spare room. Here the shelves are lined with trophies and medals, the long-service spoils of officialdom. The floor is awash with cardboard boxes filled with silverware.

Kyte spills a pile of photos, press cuttings and programmes across the dining table. Each photo – almost all are era-specific Polaroids – shows a similar set-up: him and another linesman, both flag in hand, flanking a referee almost always shorter than his two assistants. Taken between the mid-1970s and the tail end of the 1980s, Kyte's wavy fringe lessens and loses its sandy colour as we flick through the photos, as we flick through the years. Similarly, the referees' sideburns shorten with each photo.

These pre-match smiles are from Kyte's time in the Football League, when he would assist some of the greatest legends of the refereeing world – the likes of Clive Thomas, Neil Midgeley and George Courtney. As any football obsessive from these times could confirm without the slightest help from Google, these particular refs hailed from Porthcawl, Salford and Spennymoor respectively. Indeed, I can hear Barry Davies in my head right now. 'And our referee today is Mr Allan Gunn from Burgess Hill . . .'

While this haul of souvenirs covers his Football League years, Kyte's entire refereeing career is compacted into a shallow cardboard box that he's now placing on the glass table. In this box is the bigger picture, the full story. It contains nearly 100 match books, soft-back notebooks no bigger than the palm of your hand, each one fifty pages in length. Every match Kyte has officiated in, no matter how lowly, has its own page, its own details documented. Date, location, score, weather conditions, that kind of thing.

Giving equal billing to each match, these books offer fascinating snapshots of a have-whistle-will-travel official. For instance, one volume reveals that, within twenty-four hours of running the line for a Notts County/ Everton encounter in the old First Division in 1983, Kyte was back in his kit, taking charge of a heavyweight clash between the Fox & Goose and Penn British Legion. Such delicious juxtaposition isn't unusual. That same year,

Kyte refereed an under-12s match one Sunday afternoon (his third game of the weekend, the records show), before flying out to Greece to run the line for a Cup Winners' Cup tie between AEK Athens and Újpesti Dózsa the following Wednesday.

Each page also has a pithy overview from Kyte. A match between Hadley Colts and Bradley Youth Club in 1960, which ended in a 24-0 defeat for the home side, is summed up by the understated comment 'Too one-sided to be called a game'. That very first match he officiated, with his bike propped up on the touchline, is immortalised by 'Good game spoilt by rain'.

Flicking through these match books, the obvious question is whether they'll reach a 100th volume. That is, whether match number 5,000 is within Kyte's reach. 'It'll be touch and go. But, as fit and as healthy as I am, I see no reason why not. However, I wouldn't do it if I was keeping a young person down. If there were twenty young referees who couldn't get a game on a Saturday or a Sunday but I had one, I'd say "No, take me off and put them on".

'I keep thinking "I'll have another season. I feel fit enough." I came off the Football League in 1988 and I've been saying that ever since. When you have that break for summer, it whets your appetite. After two and a half months off, you look forward to it. I'll be pining to get back on.'

John Kyte puts the match books back in order and returns them to their cardboard box. The energy and enthusiasm, outwardly betrayed by his heavy eyelids, remains. 'Yes, go on,' he chuckles. 'Have another season.'

* * *

Up on the Wirral, hopeless devotion takes a different form to work-for-nothing volunteers and long-serving referees. Lasse Larsen shows his love in the distances he's prepared to travel, the air miles he's willing to collect. And the object of his affections is a curious one for a young Norwegian. He's usually spotted in these parts draped in his national flag with a capital letter occupying each red quarter. The letters signify his unlikely footballing allegiance. TRFC.

If he's not Tranmere Rovers' most faraway fan – there are presumably exiled Wirralites who've retreated to sunsplashed outposts in California or on Australia's Gold Coast where they wear their vintage shirts with pride and to the bemusement of the locals – Larsen is surely the club's most frequently flying fan. A social worker from Bergen in his mid-thirties, he's become something of a cult figure at Prenton Park. He's currently in the country for his latest match this season, yesterday's 1-1 away draw to Conference strugglers Halifax. The morning, he's holding court in the lobby of the Birkenhead Premier Inn, explaining the source of his devotion.

Both his father and grandfather became big fans of English football when it was first televised in Norway during the 1960s. Larsen Jr followed suit, with one player in particular grabbing both his attention and imagination. 'It was John Aldridge all day long,' he gushes. 'He scored and he scored and he scored.'

When Aldridge pitched up at Prenton Park in 1991, the eleven-year-old Larsen began looking out for the results of a club he'd largely been unaware of until that point. When the striker became player-manager in 1996, Larsen firmly nailed his colours to the Tranmere mast. He's not looked back since, even if it took him a few years to actually make it to a match. His first experience of Rovers in the flesh was a scoreless FA Cup tie at Southampton in 2001.

'I knew I needed to go over and try a game. It was a sell-out and the away section was packed. It was a great atmosphere. I'd bought the paper every Sunday morning and read the results, but to suddenly watch them in the flesh was so special. People started to talk to me during the game. They gave me email addresses and said I was more than welcome to stay at their place next time I was over. On the plane home, it was "When can I go back? When can I mix with all these people again?"' If his enthusiasm hadn't been dented by the 0-0 at the Dell, the dramatic replay at Prenton Park – where Tranmere emerged 4-3 winners, having been 3-0 down – couldn't fail to cement long-lasting loyalty. 'That might have had something to do with it, yes!'

His presence on Merseyside often leads to people assuming he's a Liverpool or Everton fan. 'They think it's very strange and surprising that someone from Norway has heard of Tranmere and knows its history. It's not like going to a Premier League match where there'll be Scandinavians and people from the Far East. Scandinavians don't come to Prenton Park. But there's just one team for me.'

But why does a fifth-tier club in England have more appeal than a top-flight Norwegian team? 'The culture of Norwegian football is not the same,' he explains, a tinge of disappointment in his voice. 'You don't get the same experience. There isn't the social side. You go to watch the game and then go home. Here you go to the pub with your mates for three hours before the game and then again afterwards. There's something about the culture here, about pubs, good beer and friendly people. It's something I can't get at home. Plus, most of the football in Norway is played on Sunday and people have to go back to work the next day, so away games are tricky.'

Larsen has immersed himself into British culture, his frequent visits endowing his accent with a Merseyside edge. He's also fluent in the particular vernacular of the English game, dotting the conversation with phrases like 'lacking in the final third' and 'a screamer that went in off the bar'. This is a language learned through TV commentary and in the football-literate pubs of Birkenhead.

'It's my second home here. I'm so welcome. I've got so many friends. Even yesterday I made new friends on the train to Halifax. "Are you the guy from Norway? Come and sit with us. Have a beer." Everyone knows me. My wife and I got engaged in Liverpool in 2013. We've been going to Prenton Park together for the last ten years. She doesn't enjoy away games, but likes going to Prenton Park where she knows a lot of people and can chat to them in the pub before the match about things other than football. But it's the shopping and restaurants in Liverpool that she likes most. She's been with me to Scunthorpe away, but she hated it. It was such a small place. She said it was a dump. But she's fine with home games – she's made lots of friends there.'

For this trip, he was supposed to travel over with his wife and seven-month-old daughter, but they developed a flu sickness bug. His father took the plane seat instead, before falling ill with the virus himself. Rather than travel across to West Yorkshire to take in the Halifax game, Larsen Sr has spent the weekend marooned upstairs here in the Premier Inn, feverishly staring at the walls of room 116.

It's not the only bug his father has caught. Thanks to his son's evangelism, he too has become a disciple of lower-league English football. 'He's a big Man Utd fan, but he doesn't watch them. He doesn't like the Premier League. Rather than paying £60 or £70 at Old Trafford, he likes to go to Prenton Park and get an over-sixty-fives ticket.'

Now he's a father himself, Larsen is supposed to be rationing his visits, turning the heat down on his obsession. Changed circumstances, new realities. He's finding it tricky, though, especially as Tranmere's newly acquired non-league status offers new grounds to visit. 'I try to see six games every season, so my wife is not very happy that I've been over here four times before Christmas. But I know that you can't put your family aside to go to watch the football, even if you really, really love it. And I can't tell her that every time we go on holiday, it's to see another Tranmere match. That's not fair.'

Larsen may have to become more of a stranger around Prenton Park, to be content with a long-distance love affair. Not that the passion will lessen. 'Even back in Norway on a Saturday, I'm following the score and live texts and the radio. It's a big part of my life. It drags you through the working week.' It's an obsession that hasn't diminished with Tranmere's slide into non-league. 'If they're struggling, you need to support them even more. You have to hope for better times. And those better times *will* come. I just think they might take some time. When I started coming over here in 2001, we were in the Championship. We've been relegated three times since then. I've never seen us get promoted. I've never seen a play-off match. But these are things that will hopefully turn up one day to make the experience even better.'

Family commitments aside, there's the financial aspect, too. 'Of course, it costs money. I'm just a normal social worker in Bergen. I'm not a banker or anything. The flights can be expensive, the hotels can be expensive. Then there are trains and beer and food and tickets for the games. With everything, this trip has cost me about £500 or £600.' Add to this the fact that Larsen has, across the years, made more than seventy trips over to watch his heroes and it becomes a significant investment in following the fortunes of a fitful, often failing team.

Yesterday's 1-1 draw against one of the division's bottom feeders, a side reduced to ten men at that, seems scant reward for the commitment, measured in time and money, that Larsen is happy to give over. 'We're struggling against teams that are happy to get a point. They counter-attack and we can't kill games off. We prefer to play better teams like Forest Green and Cheltenham – teams that want to win themselves. I haven't been to any of those games like Braintree or Boreham Wood, but my friends tell me we look so clueless. But a play-off place – fourth or fifth – is in our own hands if we can get a good run going. I think the team is more than capable of going up.'

However, Larsen is both dreamer and realist, and has already started to plan which games he'll be flying over for if the club remain in the Conference next season. 'I'd really like to go to Grimsby. That's a ground I'd really love to go to.' He's also earmarked a few potential games in the South East. Flights to there from Bergen are cheaper, plus the area boasts more family-friendly places to visit and things to do. The growing brood have to be factored in now, after all.

Not that he'll be abandoning his beloved Prenton Park. 'I've got a plan,' he concludes conspiratorially before heading upstairs to check on his poorly dad. 'If, when my daughter's older, she says she doesn't want to go to the football, I'll tell her I'll take her to the Disney store in Liverpool first. She'll be happy then. Maybe . . .'

* * *

Lasse Larsen might have a plan, but the Tranmere faithful are wondering whether Gary Brabin does. The draw against Halifax continues a run of just two wins in eleven league games, leaving them twelfth in the table. It's hard to see how this form will haul them up into the play-off places.

It's rare that a football club stays in one gear, the highest gear, throughout the season. The imperious Liverpool side during the closing years of the 1980s managed it, so too Arsenal's defeat-free Invincibles during 2003–04. For mere mortals, there's a natural ebb and flow to a ten-month campaign. After a bright start, there might be a lull around the time the clocks go back, before a New Year revival restores the faith and reboots the dreams. There will be the odd peak and trough, but seasons tend to trace a gently undulating parabola. Tranmere's season, though, is less of an arc and much more of a jagged, stuttering line. The smooth tarmac of a comfortable win one weekend, swiftly followed by a sharp detour onto a bumpy verge the next. Then smooth tarmac again. Repeat to fade.

Brabin shrugs his way through the post-match press conference, reaching for the comfort blanket offered by concentrating on the positives. Tranmere certainly played a tighter game than they have done of late; they also hit the woodwork more than once, while Halifax scored with their solitary strike on target. These positives do give hope and, yes, the margins are fine, but dropped points are still dropped points. The manner of the performance is what's clung onto by Brabin, the shield between himself and the press pack, the sharks who might just be able to detect the scent of blood in the water.

Shrugs alone can't fix the widening gap between Tranmere and those above them, the teams that can't stop winning. For those unable to develop that habit, the short days and long nights of December test the resolve and devotion of fans, players and managers alike. And, most markedly, of chairmen with itchy trigger fingers.

6

JANUARY

The greasy pole

Matt Hanlan holds two unique claims to distinction. He scored the winning goal the last time a bunch of part-time non-leaguers dumped a top-flight team out of the FA Cup. And, two days later, he became the only person to have ever appeared on *Wogan* having been building a new branch of Asda that morning.

Such were the crazy events, and the crazy aftermath, of Saturday 7 January 1989, a date cherished by Hanlan almost as much as his wedding day or the births of his children. 'I've been dining out on that ever since,' he beams, conversely declining the offer of lunch and sticking with a cappuccino in this Borough Market café. It's twenty-seven years and a day since, as a twenty-two-year-old Sutton United winger, his close-range volley dispatched Coventry City from the competition. Since then, Hanlan and his team-mates have been embroidered into the rich tapestry of FA Cup folklore, an act of giant-killing second only to Hereford United's mud-coated vanquishing of Newcastle United seventeen years earlier. Coventry had, after all, won the cup less than twenty months previously and were sitting in fifth spot in the

143

old First Division. Sutton United – a motley crew of builders and insurance salesmen presided over by a pipe-sucking, poetry-quoting manager – were drifting in mid-table obscurity in the GM Vauxhall Conference.

With that wide smile and infectious willingness to offer up chapter and verse about that January afternoon at Sutton's Gander Green Lane ground more than a quarter of a century ago, Hanlan has clearly never tired of revisiting his greatest footballing triumph.

'When Coventry came out of the hat, I remember being a little bit disappointed. We could have had Man U or Liverpool or Arsenal. It wasn't until the following day that it sunk in. When you ran through their players, you realised it was a proper game. They'd be bringing their first team. And Keith Houchen, who scored in the final two seasons earlier, ended up only being on the bench.

'We trained on the Tuesday as normal. On the Thursday night, the local BBC cameras came down and then another film crew on the Friday, so I nicked a day off work and, with a couple of the other lads, filmed some set pieces, including me smashing a volley in!

'I can't imagine what Coventry thought when they saw the pitch. The groundsmen had worked hard and you were able to play football on it. But there was a lot of sand up the middle. Whether it was youthful exuberance or arrogance I don't know, but I don't remember being fazed by the occasion at all. I just went in on the day, did some training, had beans on toast and scrambled eggs, and soaked my feet because they were cold. That's all it was. It wasn't until afterwards that it was "Hold on. What's happened here?"'

Hanlan recalls his sixty-first-minute magic moment in admirably forensic detail. The lead-up to the corner. The short ball played to Sutton's right-midfielder approaching the apex of the penalty area. The players that his cross evaded. The point at which Hanlan made his run to coincide exactly with the arrival of the ball in the box. Who knows how many thousands of times he's replayed it in his mind, doubtless always accompanied by John Motson's commentary. 'Oh, and driven in! And number eleven Matthew Hanlan followed that in! And Sutton have done it again from a corner kick, bringing this little ground to life once more. The Coventry defence were standing still . . .'

Hanlan's celebration – which included an angry, arm-swinging rant at an unspecified target – shares an equal standing in FA Cup history with the goal itself. 'I don't know where that came from. There was a time when I wasn't particularly well-liked by a certain section of the crowd at Sutton. Maybe that had something to do with it. But it wasn't premeditated, it wasn't thought out. It just happened.'

On the final whistle – after Coventry had besieged the Sutton goal in search of an equaliser and a face-saving replay at Highfield Road – Hanlan the bricklayer was consumed by a whirlwind of media attention. 'I was whisked off to be interviewed by Trevor Brooking for Radio 2, then straight on to the Final Score part of *Grandstand*. Barry the manager went off to do *Match of the Day*. We had press around us until the small hours – and it didn't stop. I went to work on the Monday. We were building a new Asda. The site manager rushed over. "Your dad's been on the phone. You've got to go home." "What's happened? What's wrong?" This was before the days of mobile phones. I rushed home. "The BBC have been on the phone. You've got to go on *Wogan* tonight . . ."'

The café is now busy with office workers looking for somewhere to perch while they eat. But we need the table space. Hanlan reaches below the table to pull out a bag full of mementoes that he spreads out, the centrepiece of which is a scrapbook put together by his parents and crammed with press cuttings and other ephemera. Even included is the remittance advice from the BBC, detailing the fees paid for various interviews. Back then, it appears you could pocket £50 for a couple of breathless minutes of euphoric post-match words on *Final Score* and £150 for a more considered but still fleeting spell on the *Wogan* sofa. Hanlan reaches deeper into the bag and the real prize emerges – the number eleven shirt he wore on the big day, a gold polyester relic from times past. It's not seen the inside of a washing machine during the intervening years. The Gander Green Lane mud, vintage 1989, is still visible.

'The whole thing was a little taste of what it must be like to play for Man U or Real Madrid up in the top echelons of the football hierarchy,' he wistfully concludes, folding the shirt back up. The taste didn't linger long on the lips. In the next round, Sutton were hammered 8-0 by Norwich.

Now a director of a building firm, he's no longer involved in the game, save for his Crystal Palace season ticket and those annual requests to relive *that* day. He still speaks fondly of his own little crazy gang who upset football's apple cart that January afternoon – Micky and Lenny and Tony and the others. They reconvene occasionally, perhaps for a charity game, perhaps merely to reminisce. And their forensic powers of recall, like Hanlan's, remain tack-sharp. Every touch, every nuance.

He's surely part of a dying breed – the part-timer who did battle with household names and emerged victorious. These days, even if a semi-pro non-league outfit scooped a plum Third Round draw against Premier League foes, it would inevitably be a below-strength side they'd be facing, the superstars rested in readiness for matches against more elite, more testing opposition. Giant-killing tales of beating a Premier League team's anonymous reserves wouldn't hold the value and the improving vintage of tales like Hanlan's. Unknown names, unrecognised faces. These would not be Speedie or Kilcline, Regis or Ogrizovic.

Matt Hanlan's story is future-proof, bathed in aspic. He can tell it until he dies and people will still listen.

* * *

Who's going to be Matt Hanlan today?

You can't hear the tip-tip-tap of the rain above the ceaseless growl of the adjacent motorway, but you can see it, making the small but growing puddles blink and shimmer. Puddles have been a fixture here at the appropriately named Silverlake Stadium in Eastleigh for weeks, not just in the car park but at regular intervals along the touchline and across the pitch.

This might be the Third Round of the FA Cup, the point at which non-leaguers traditionally get a tilt at toppling a side from the country's top two divisions, but this weekend Conference side Eastleigh are the only minnows left in the competition, carrying the weight of the entire non-league pyramid on their shoulders. It's the first time in forty-seven years that the semi-pro game has had such poor representation in the competition at this stage. The cup that kicked off back in the summer heat all those months ago has slammed its door shut on all but one last bunch of hopeless romantics.

Today, Bolton Wanderers of the Championship are the giants facing potential ignominy. But the drama isn't reserved for the 3 pm kick-off. It appears we've got a whole day of it.

10.15 am

'Breakfast!' The shout goes out across the Silverlake pitch, echoing around the empty stands. It's a call for the volunteers out in the centre circle to refuel, those hardy souls who've been busy with forks, rollers and brooms for the last three hours. Even some early-arriving Bolton fans, who flew down from Manchester this morning, are lending a hand, having packed wellies and waterproof trousers in their carry-on luggage.

'You should have seen it on Wednesday when we put the covers on,' says one of the volunteers, whose wide broom is ushering waves of standing water down a drain hole. 'It's so much better now. More than playable.' 'They're still not going to like this, though,' says his mate, referring to the relative footballing sophisticates of Bolton. 'They're not going to like this one bit.'

The gallant, round-the-clock efforts of the voluntary crew may well have saved the day, the biggest match in the club's history. The pitch will invariably cut up later, but they've removed hundreds of gallons of water from the pitch over the last few days. Huge white tarpaulins cocoon and shelter both penalty areas from the showers that are forecast, while a TV technician places a stepladder in one of the goalmouths in order to fix a camera to the top corner of the net. The stepladder sinks lower into the turf with each rung he steps on.

Mark Chapman, anchorman of this afternoon's coverage on Five Live, is here already, clutching a polystyrene cup of stamina-sharpening instant coffee. He's broadcast from elite stadia right across Europe, but it's grounds like this – the Silverlake is penned in by a motorway, a railway line and an airport runway – that really get his juices flowing. 'I was just chatting to one of the guys from Eastleigh and I said "This is brilliant, isn't it?" He said, "Do you really think that?" "Yeah, I absolutely love it. This is what going to football's all about." I know it sounds a cliché, but it's a cliché because it's true. First and foremost, I'm a football fan. I just happen to do it as a job as well. A hot cup of coffee and feeling cold and it's raining – that's what it's all about. It's not about sitting in a Chelsea press room with a bloody seven-course buffet before you go and report.

'Here you bump into people around the club and you have normal conversations. You go into a lot of professional clubs – and not just in the Premier League, you can go quite far down – and your arrival is met with an element of suspicion. I just asked someone here where I should park my hire car as all the spaces are numbered. "Just park anywhere. It'll be fine. Don't worry about it." You wouldn't believe the hoops and the rigmarole you have to go through when you're doing a top-flight game or a Championship game. This is the attraction of these kind of places. People are normal and proper and how you would want everyone to be.'

Chapman is steeped in non-league football, a regular face, when work allows, in the crowd at another Conference side – Altrincham. Bearing in mind the fact that Eastleigh are the sole remaining non-leaguers in the competition, is it not annoying that this tie wasn't selected to be one of the BBC's live games? 'It's annoying in the sense that those of us on-screen seem to be held accountable for what our bosses decide. I have no input at all into which games are chosen. But I firmly believe that there's a responsibility when you are picking live games in the early rounds – and therefore money is going to those involved – to make sure that money goes to the clubs that need it. If you pick an all-Premier League tie as the live game, which you're perfectly entitled to do, the money that you pay for that game shouldn't go to the two clubs involved. It should be dropped down to the non-league side who are still in the cup. That's me talking as a fan.'

11.00 am

The referee, well aware that the pitch requires deep scrutiny, arrives earlier than expected. Dan Walker, the *Football Focus* presenter who'll be going live to the nation in little more than an hour, grabs him to get a sense of, literally, how the land lies.

Kenny Amor, Eastleigh's young general manager and uncanny Peter Kay lookalike, keeps his distance. Nervous is what he is. Nervous about the logistics of the day, nervous about the game not going ahead, nervous that the week's long hours getting the pitch into what he hoped would be a playable condition may all have been in vain.

Twenty minutes later, the referee and his assistants have changed out of their suits and into their match attire. The giant tarpaulins are carefully peeled back to reveal what lies beneath. The inspection starts. And it doesn't start well. The referee tosses a ball into the air and it slops down onto a patch of mud. No bounce. Glued to the pitch. A collective wince from those watching from the touchline.

The referee is certainly thorough in his assessment. Escorted by the Eastleigh groundsman, he particularly spends time in the far corners, where the ball not only fails to run true, it fails to run at all. The skies are darkening again and the rain resumes. There are universally anxious looks along the touchline on the faces of club officials and broadcasters alike. Eastleigh's thirtysomething boss, Chris Todd, arrives from his home in Devon. He's in his Saturday best – sharp blue suit, tan winklepickers and a handkerchief immaculately folded into the chest pocket of his jacket. Despite his woefully inappropriate footwear, he gingerly ventures onto the pitch to placate the referee with smiles and jokes. The tense mood needs lightening.

The rest of Five Live's on-air team – commentator Ian Dennis and summariser Steve Claridge – are here now. I take shelter in the away dugout next to a head-shaking Claridge who explains that, in his 828 league appearances, he took to plenty of pitches in far worse nick than this one. The referee's coming back to the touchline now and a crowd gathers. He announces that there are four areas he needs the groundsman to work on ('potential leg-breakers', he calls them) and that he'll re-inspect at 12.30. As he speaks, the ground staff are already shovelling sand along the touchline. Chris Todd makes the point that, during this particularly sodden winter, the ball has had trouble bouncing on plenty of Conference pitches. 'It's the norm.'

12.30 pm

Prayers are offered up to the weather gods, who respond in kind. The forecast was for heavy rain from noon until beyond sundown, but instead the battleship-grey clouds have parted to allow some much-needed sunshine to be cast onto proceedings. Both Mark Chapman and Dan Walker have gone live on their respective networks. While we wait for the referee to re-emerge, the cabaret that is *Football Focus* unfolds before us. Walker and his guests – Dion Dublin, Graeme Le Saux and Oxford United manager Michael Appleton – are a blur, racing from location to location for the next set-up. They take their chances with the slippery touchline to assume position in the home dugout, all the while chastened by the impatient instructions of the director. 'Live in twenty seconds!'

Meanwhile, the referee's back out in the middle. The general consensus is that, had the forecast heavy rain come down, his decision would have been much easier. The sunshine has further muddied the already muddy waters. 'He's walking across it as if it's shark-infested!' laughs Chapman who, if the game is called off, will have to speed over to the St Marys Stadium four miles away to present the rest of the show from the Southampton/Crystal Palace tie. Alongside him, Bolton manager Neil Lennon, a man who once masterminded a Celtic victory over the mighty Barcelona in the Champions League, doesn't like the conditions one bit. Chris Todd isn't so concerned. A couple of yards away, he's happily explaining Eastleigh's intended formation to the diligent Ian Dennis.

More activity. The groundsman speeds across to the far side of the pitch in his John Deere. He's heard the referee's verdict already. The verdict is a non-verdict. Another inspection at quarter past one.

1.15 pm

With his broadcasting duties done for now, Dan Walker joins the referee on that third inspection. The presenter returns to the touchline and the signs don't look good.

153

Everything might seem fine from a distance of eighty yards away, but Walker reveals that while he was over in the far corner, he actually sank an inch into the ground when just standing still. The concern shows in his eyes; like Mark Chapman, for him this is one of the season's red-letter days.

'I grew up watching non-league football,' he reveals. 'Crawley Town in the Dr Martens Premier. I love it. It feels earthy, it feels real. It's the noise, it's the Bovril, it's the smell of a pie that's been there a week and a half. I feel that people who support Arsenal or Manchester City or Manchester United – not that there's anything wrong with that – miss out on the passion and that real feeling that you're involved with something that is hugely import-ant to a small community. To people who moan about football, shut up and go to watch a local non-league side. Even if it's a 0-0, I guarantee you'll enjoy yourself.'

Walker is also a fierce advocate of the importance of the FA Cup to the non-league game – and of the televising of these delightfully mismatched David vs Goliath clashes. 'There's a huge appetite for them. When we did the First Round – Salford City against Notts County – three and a half million people watched that game. That's a million more than watched Manchester United against Liverpool on Sky. So don't tell me that no one cares about the FA Cup. They do. The Third Round has been something so intrinsically linked to football for generations and hope-fully will be in the future.'

The rain has relented for more than an hour but, at 1.27 pm, three minutes before the gates are scheduled to open, the referee is still in conference with his assistants in the troublesome far corner. Then, just as the deadline approaches, the three of them stride across towards the touchline where 100 or so players, officials, broadcasters and journalists have gathered. He's made his decision. A single thumb raised. A collective sigh of relief. Game on.

2.15 pm

The pitch continues to be a flurry of activity – as it's been all week – right up until kick-off. The line-marker marches his machine around the perimeter, while one of the ground staff uses a leaf-blower to remove any surface water. From the arcs of spray being produced, there still looks to be plenty around, especially as light rain is now falling again.

Neil Lennon is back on the touchline, watching his goalkeeper being put through his paces. With hands thrust deep into the pockets of his puffa jacket, those flinty blue eyes cast a critical look over what his side will soon be facing. He's got little to win and much to lose this afternoon. Bolton are currently anchored to the bottom of the Championship, as well as being mired in a potentially grave financial situation. Facing debts totalling £172.9 million, the club have warned their staff that wages might not be paid at the end of the month. Lennon anxiously needs a slice of good news, however small. The mud flats before him may well not readily yield that.

The rest of the ground is in better spirits, though – relieved the match is going ahead and, in the Eastleigh ranks at least, excited about the very real prospect of an upset. Despite only making the transition from player to manager less than three months ago, Chris Todd has got his side riding high in the Conference and the fifty-two league places between the two teams will largely be rendered meaningless this afternoon.

The turnstiles clack with rhythmic regularity, while the tea bar queues lengthen. The obligatory replica FA Cups, fashioned from cereal-packet cardboard and tin foil, are being held aloft by kids for whom this may well be their first-ever football match, let alone their first-ever Eastleigh game. They're ready for history. So too are the Eastleigh old-timers, like the nonagenarian Derik Brooks, the man who founded the club the year after the Second World War ended; the club's first dressing room was an air-raid shelter. As well as being interviewed by the local TV news last night, Derik is commemorated by a flag behind one of the goals in the Shed End. 'Forever Thankful' says the banner.

3.00 pm

The floodlights have snapped into action and a 5,000-strong crowd has packed, cheek-by-jowl, into the Silverlake. The lucky ones have a roof over their heads; those less fortunate are exposed to the elements for the best part of the next couple of hours. The Shed End will be the noisiest quarter. It's home to not only a drummer, but also someone who, rather annoyingly, has liberated a police siren for the afternoon.

As the rain continues to fall, Eastleigh start brightly, refusing to be intimated by their troubled opponents. If you were looking for signs of who might be the hero of the day – the Ronnie Radford, the Matt Hanlan – Eastleigh's sprightly right-winger, Yemi Odubade, looks the most likely candidate. He's tying the Bolton left-back in knots early on. But his hamstring goes after twenty minutes, cruelly removing him from proceedings, from the biggest game of his career.

The longer Bolton don't steady themselves by scoring the opening goal, the more intense the pressure, the tighter the screw. Everyone in the ground knows this and so the goalless first forty-five minutes is greeted with good cheer at the half-time whistle by the Eastleigh crowd, by the faithful and the first-timers alike.

But that good cheer is nothing compared to the explosion of joy that's unleashed in the fifty-first minute when Bolton's centre-back slides the ball neatly into the bottom corner of his own net. The giant-killing that the town, the neutrals and the entire non-league world are longing for is on. No matter that, if the score remains so, there'll be no equivalent of Radford or Hanlan. A 1-0 win with only an own goal to separate the teams? They'd take that. No problem at all.

But the score doesn't remain so. With just three minutes of normal time left, Bolton scramble a scrappy equaliser at the Shed End. The drums fall silent, as does the police siren. At the other end of the ground, the Bolton fans are sent into delirium, delighted that their collective 470-mile round trip has not been in vain.

A rare reason to be cheerful in an otherwise dismal season.

For Eastleigh, what has been achieved – parity with a team three divisions higher – gets slightly lost in the contemplation of what was so nearly achieved. Just three minutes away from immortality, there's a palpable sense of deflation. The giant was allowed to stagger back to his feet. The knockout blow wasn't quite powerful enough.

5.00 pm

There might be deflation on the final whistle, but the dominant emotion is one of relief – relief that the game did go ahead, relief that it *was* one of those classic, blood-and-guts FA Cup ties. Neil Lennon is clearly satisfied to be taking the tie back to the smooth turf of the Macron Stadium, while the referee is almost certainly breathing easy in his dressing room. Not only did his diligence ensure we had a match to savour, but also there were none of his feared 'leg-breakers'. Even the pitch invader who joined Eastleigh's attack at one point in the second half before sidestepping the advances of the stuck-in-the-mud stewards came away unscathed.

Kenny Amor is beyond relieved. He is finally smiling (it turns out he even has the same smile as Peter Kay). Like a music promoter too busy to see the live show, Kenny didn't get to watch the match but will catch the drama on *Match of the Day* tonight, safe in the knowledge that there's no unhappy ending. Not only does the team live to fight another day, but the replay will also provide some of the revenue that the BBC's curious decision not to televise the game denied them.

Chris Todd is smiling, too, engulfed in a blur of microphones and dictaphones. Everyone wants a piece of him. The position in which he finds himself is a remarkable one – not just because he was simply a member of the Eastleigh playing staff at the start of the season, but because seven years ago he was diagnosed with leukaemia. After battling the illness through the use of the chemotherapy drugs he continues to take today, Todd resurrected his football life, playing on for another six seasons before moving into management. He is the true hero of the hour.

Once the herd of reporters have their quotes and disperse, I grab Todd for some quieter reflections on the day – although not before we're rudely interrupted by a crew from ITN. 'We go live in six minutes!' They only need to record something short for the early evening news, so Todd, still looking immaculate despite the conditions and all the excitement, is soon back with me.

'Everything today has been unbelievable,' he gushes in his Swansea accent. 'It's been like a little storybook. It was on and it was off and it was on. All credit to the referee. He could easily have called it off. Let's be honest, it ain't good out there. I was worried that the linesman wasn't going to last the full game. He did a fair few runs up and down that line beforehand.

'I'll tell you what, wherever Chris Todd goes, there's always a frigging story. I turn up and I'm doing an interview with Dion Dublin and Graeme Le Saux. Then I walk out here and all of a sudden I'm talking to Five Live as I'm walking around. And look at all this lot standing here talking to me. It's bonkers. I'm a Conference manager and I'm standing here with twenty people sticking their bloody microphones in my face. But I love it. All I can say is that I feel alive at the minute, I really do. And after what I've been through in the past, I'm so lucky.'

Ten days later, luck is in short supply as Bolton edge the replay 3-2. Eastleigh's cardboard replica trophies have another outing but, by the time the supporters' coaches start the long journey back south, they're wilting with disappointment. The FA Cup fantasy is over. Not just for them, but for all of the non-league world, put into storage until summertime and the Extra Preliminary Round of next season's competition.

* * *

Up at Salford City, the FA Cup dream dissolved before Christmas. After the Notts County game in the First Round, they welcomed another league side to Moor Lane – Hartlepool. Again under the scrutiny of a live BBC audience, they held the League Two side to a draw but, like Eastleigh, were unable to conjure up the magic again in the replay.

A month after the cup exit and two months after the BBC documentary was transmitted, I venture back up to Greater Manchester on a chilly Tuesday night with a crystal-clear angle to take, a single overriding question on my lips. What's life been like with the spotlight switched off, after the cameras departed?

Within minutes of arriving, that question proves itself redundant. I'm chatting to striker Gareth Seddon, one of the 'stars' of the documentary and the first Salford player to arrive tonight. But I can sense a presence at my shoulder. I turn and find a lens just a couple of feet away from my face. It turns out that the cameras never left. Normality was never invited back. The documentary was such a success that a second series was quickly commissioned and this season is being documented in the same forensic detail as the last – including, it appears, my shambling interview technique.

'At first it was really strange,' says Seddon of the cameras' ongoing intrusion. 'You were always guarding what you said. "Am I allowed to say this? Am I allowed to jump on someone naked in the dressing room and wave my bits at him, which I normally do?" After a month, they were like "Gaz, you do what you want". Everyone says it, but you do forget the cameras are there. Sometimes that gets me into trouble – "Gaffer's a right dick". But it's real life. What you saw is what you'd see at six hundred other football clubs. It's just how it is.'

The programme-makers couldn't have wished for a more dramatic arc to document last season, with Salford overcoming a double-digit points deficit to snatch the Northern Premier League Division One North title from arch rivals Darlington 1883. 'It was unbelievable. We were so far behind in the league, the manager got sacked, the new managers came in and we won the league. Everything just fell into place, a real Roy of the Rovers story. Even the guy from the TV said "Jesus Christ, we couldn't even have written that".'

The documentary's stranger-than-fiction narrative ensured it made fascinating viewing – as well as making minor celebrities of Seddon and seemingly peripheral characters like Jim the handyman and Babs in her tea-bar. Seddon has instantly become the most recognisable non-league player in the country. A natural attention-seeker, he's been in hog heaven. 'It's been brilliant. It's as though I'm actually a decent player and I'm famous. When I went out in Manchester before Christmas, just after the programme finished, it was crazy. I'd got out of the car and within two minutes I'd had fifteen people ask for pictures. Workmen would come down from their scaffolding. "Seddon! Over here, lad. Let me get a picture with you." And not one person has come up to me and said "You're a nob, you". Everyone's been really good.'

This recognition, this modest fame, doesn't come with riches, though. Despite, at £400 a week, being Salford's highest paid player, Seddon's wage – like those of his team-mates – runs dry after the last game of the season. Pilloried in the TV documentary for missing a match to take a modelling job in Germany that would provide enough income to see him through the summer, Seddon still needs to make ends meet. At one point while we chat, he spots something shiny in the mud under the pitch's perimeter fence. He's disappointed to find it's just a bottle top.

They say that every dressing room has its joker. Seddon is Salford's, his lengthy playing career at various clubs giving him an excess of confidence around these younger players (he's actually older than both joint managers). Plus, his work as a model means he has no shortage of showing-off genes. 'I'm thirty-five going on twelve,' he grins toothily, chugging on a pre-match can of Red Bull.

As well as the camera lenses, last season found five pairs of owners' expert eyes, belonging to a quintet of heavily decorated international footballers, scrutinising every touch, every tackle, every turn. Seddon and his team-mates had it from all angles. 'Those guys, especially round these parts, are living legends. When you've got someone like Scholesy watching you, if you make a ten-yard pass and miss the man, you think he must be laughing and wondering how this lad has made a living out of football. On the other hand, knowing they're all watching you inspired us to do well in every game. We couldn't just turn up, rest on our laurels and expect to win the game. Every time we played, we wanted to impress those guys. That translated into us winning the league because we kept up our high standards. It wasn't just because of the attitude of our managers willing us to win. We also had those other eyes on us.'

Those joint managers – aka Anthony 'Jonno' Johnson and Bernard Morley – are next to arrive at the ground, fresh from an honest day's work as truck driver and builder respectively. Jonno grabs himself a restorative hot drink (he's been up since 5.30 am) before offering his take on the most remarkable twelve months in his and Morley's managerial career. It's almost a year to the day that the pair took over, their appointment coming just a month after they brought their Ramsbottom United side to Moor Lane – an occasion marked by a red card for Jonno after he hurled a Salford player to the floor.

'I don't think there'll ever be a season at this club where it's just relaxing and sitting back. If you get comfortable in a job like this, you're out the door. We're under no illusions. We're at a club that matches our ambitions and backs us. And our stock will keep rising with them. Me and Bern have been managing seven years now. He's thirty-one, I'm thirty-three. But we don't settle, we don't get our feet under the table. We're out every night, watching players, watching as many games as we can.'

The pair's modus operandi – bad cop, bad cop – may seem brutal, but it gets respect from the players. While we talk, several of the first team arrive, a series of handshakes and fist bumps with Jonno before they plonk themselves down in front of a TV in the clubhouse. The ruthless management technique clearly works; the pair have won four promotions in six seasons. 'We won't pretend. We won't tell them any lies. If players want to conform to the way we do things, they'll enjoy it. We have fun. We have some mad times. That's why they keep coming back. But there's also a side to us that, if you're not conforming to what we are, there are consequences.'

With another promotion push very much on track, the double-hard double act have kept the squad grounded, despite all the recent distractions. 'I don't like to blow our own trumpet because we're not like that, but I do think one of my and Bernie's strengths is keeping the lads' feet on the ground. So they've been on TV, they've beaten Notts County, but we'll get them in on the Sunday and we'll graft them. We'll absolutely blitz them. We train like we're underdogs, we act like we're underdogs. And we try to keep some perspective. The lads clean the changing rooms at every away game.'

Despite the recognition that the documentary has pushed his and Morley's way, Jonno also remains grounded himself. That's an easy thing to do when the alarm clock goes off at 5.30 am and you're going to be behind the wheel of a truck until six in the evening. 'People say "You're famous now". Well, the fact that I drive a wagon during the day tells you I'm not . . .'

The hard graft, both in the day job and in his football-ing second life, continues. 'Clubs get a bit of money and think people will open doors for them, that they'll just walk through the leagues. Well, no. We understand that sides want to beat us even more because we've been on TV, because there are cameras at every game. Listen, if sides want to use that as their team talk, more fool them.'

He then offers a line that cuts to the heart of his and Morley's management ethos. 'Everything's got to be set up knowing that everybody's coming for you.' He leans in, his nose just two or three inches from mine. 'Everybody.'

Behind us, Karen Baird is being introduced to a new player who was signed today – Chorley's Josh Hine, the leading scorer in the division above, his capture a meas-ure of Salford's pulling power. But she's forced to do so with, of course, a camera poking its nose into the conver-sation. It's the perfect introduction for the new lad to the goldfish bowl that is Salford City FC.

Baird has been Salford's chairman (she swiftly corrects me when I use 'chairwoman') for two and a half years, a key figure in brokering the Class of '92's takeover deal. She's the conduit between the owners, the committee and the fans – a tricky task, especially when the new regime starts making fundamental changes, such as switching the club's colours from orange to red. It doesn't seem to faze Baird, who, by day, runs five accountancy practices with a staff of 130. 'I'm used to dealing with different people.'

While not a fan of being in front of the cameras ('They tried to get me on BBC *Breakfast* the morning after the FA Cup win. No thanks'), she is appreciative of how the coverage has affected turnstile numbers. 'Crowds have gone up massively. More than the documentary, I think, it was the FA Cup run that put them up. People hadn't realised how good the football is at this level. On the Tuesday night after the Notts County game, we had a Doodson Cup tie. Normally you'd get a hundred men and a dog, but a thousand people turned up. We ran out of everything and they were still coming through the turnstiles. It was just so unexpected.' They've made new fans all over the map, with visitors from as far north as the Scottish Highlands and as far south as Jersey having made the pilgrimage to Moor Lane.

As well as keeping the joint managers in check ('They're scared of me, them two,' she chuckles. 'The hardest men in football . . .'), Baird also has to shoulder the demands of the more opinionated members of the ownership team. Well, one owner in particular. Gary Neville. How easy is it to stand your ground? 'I'm the same, to be honest. Me and Gary have a few arguments, but we get on well. He's the most amazing person I've ever met. He's so passionate about everything he does. He's demanding, but it's good. He brings out the best in everyone.'

Being products of the Man United youth programme, none of the Class of '92 had much experience of the non-league game. 'They absolutely love this level – the fact that you can stand at the side of the pitch, have a drink and watch the game, and that the players come into the bar afterwards. I think they like being here more than at United.' A wry smile. 'The football's better, too.'

While the owners were a strong presence on the sidelines last season, other commitments – most conspicuously, the Neville brothers' respective appointments to the management structure at Valencia – have seen them take less visible roles. 'Obviously they're not here as much since Gary went, but he's on the phone constantly, or texting or on WhatsApp at five o'clock in the morning. They're still very much involved.' The direct, face-to-face meetings in sleek city-centre offices that were a feature of the documentary have been replaced with conference calls. 'We've all just got bigger phone bills now . . .'

The players are coming out now to the strains of The Pogues' reading of 'Dirty Old Town', Ewan MacColl's paean to his Salford birthplace. It's a crisp, dry night. It snowed a couple of days ago and the remains of a snowman are visible behind one of the goals. Two lads having a kickabout are using him to form a defensive wall they're bending free-kicks around.

Psychologists would have a field day studying the respective demeanours of the joint managers. Bernard Morley is quieter, impassively observing the game while standing motionless. The more enigmatic of the pair, he was described by Gareth Seddon in the documentary as looking 'like he could kill someone'. Jonno is the opposite, a live wire who singularly fails to respect the restrictions of the technical area. He trespasses onto the touchline time and time again, nipping in the ear of the linesman ('You're just making stuff up!') and trading barbs with the Stourbridge officials in the visitors' dugout. His interaction with his players is no less intimidating. After a defensive lapse that almost gifts Stourbridge the opening goal, he warns: 'Stephen, that doesn't happen again.' Stephen doesn't do it again.

But his full fury is reserved for the moment, shortly before the half-hour mark, when Salford striker Jordan Hulme is sent off for a late challenge on the opposing goalkeeper. His heavy-set assistants either side of him, the diminutive, bespectacled Stourbridge manager offers his appreciation of the referee's decision. The Salford fans aren't impressed. 'Get back in your box, Penfold!' is the shout from the terraces which, while amusing, doesn't diffuse the situation. The two dugouts explode with anger at each other. There are no fisticuffs, but plenty of jostling. The simmering pot has come to the boil.

Jonno sits in the stand in the second half, silently, moodily watching from the top row. He's not been sent off, though. Karen Baird has suggested, for his own protection and to avoid the kind of touchline ban he's got prior experience of, that he take himself away from the heat of the dugout. It would take a braver person than me to suggest he's been put on the naughty step.

The well-organised Stourbridge side take the lead with twenty minutes left and successfully protect it from ten-man Salford until the final whistle. A definite dent in the promotion challenge. The Salford players disappear into the Portakabin that's the home dressing room, readying themselves for what will be presumably be a noisy post-mortem conducted by Jonno and a now-vocal Morley. To be a fly on that Portakabin wall.

But we can be. Before the door slams shut, one of the cameramen slips inside, the post-mortem to be preserved and presented to a television nation at a later date. Probably best broadcast after the watershed, though.

* * *

It's the twenty-third day of January and, somewhat remarkably, Bishop Sutton are unbeaten since Boxing Day. That's twenty-eight days without defeat. Not so remarkable, if truth be told. They've not lost because they've not played. After an extended deluge lasting at least forty days and forty nights, the club's former cow field resembled a paddy-field. The Western League's pitches haven't had a hope of coping with the biblical weather, so the table remains the same, frozen in time. Bishop Sutton bottom, deux points.

For today's visit of Calne Town, the grass has been left much longer, partly to protect the pitch and partly, you suspect, to hoodwink the referee that conditions are perfectly acceptable. If so, it's worked. He doesn't need the three extended inspections that Eastleigh's pitch warranted. The game is on; the season can resume.

There's a renewed sense of optimism around Lakeview, the players eager to get back into action after an enforced, month-long winter break. The pain of endless defeat seems to have been forgotten during their time away. There are some new faces in the side, too; Colin Merrick has been busy drafting in some experienced heads to shore up Bishop Sutton's season.

That optimism lasts precisely fifty-three seconds. A Calne free-kick into the area, an uncontested header and the first goal. A new year, but no new leaf. The same old story, the same moans from bench and fans alike. Emotions that had gone into hibernation have been rudely reawakened.

Soon after, Bishop Sutton lose their new sweeper to an ankle injury after a heavy tackle. You could hear the bones crunch from eighty yards away. But, unlike in months previous, heads don't go down, spirits don't deflate. This is partly due to the new Bishop Sutton captain, Brendan Abood, a fortifying presence in midfield. A second Calne goal on the stroke of half-time, a scrambled effort from another free-kick, doubles the visitors' advantage and is a cruel blow that doesn't reflect the play. The home team should be level at the break, if not ahead. Chances created but not taken. While the conditions aren't ideal – a stiff, swirling wind; grass up above the boots – it's nonetheless the most together performance from them yet seen this season.

The second half is goalless and that win – any win, an ugly win, a really pug-ugly win – remains out of reach. Towards the end, frustration begins to etch itself on Merrick's face as he increasingly appeals to the supporters behind the dugout to validate his interpretation of the match. And with George the gobby goalie having left the club, it's the boss who now provides the potty-mouthed cabaret. His best line of the afternoon? "Ere, Brendan. Nail that twat there.'

The silence that, until now, has greeted every final whistle is replaced by applause from the thin crowd, rewarding the effort and endeavour that kept the defeat to two goals. Sutton created enough clear-cut chances to win the match, but the ongoing absence of an out-and-out goalscorer remains their Achilles heel.

In the clubhouse, George Williams the chairman – the man who marks the pitch, who cleans the dressing rooms, who washes the kit and so much more besides – has every reason to be exasperated with the ongoing winless streak. Not that he shows it. Tall, slightly stooping and with a baseball cap permanently perched on top of his head, he's riding out the turbulence of recent seasons with good humour and admirable resolve. This is the man, after all, who is most responsible for building the club up from nothing over the last forty years, from being occupants of that cow field to champions of the Western League Premier. Nearly forty seasons' worth of results are in his head, most of them in Bishop Sutton's favour. He is the club.

Once he's finished detailing the long trail of trophies

and medals, Williams moves on to that swift, dramatic decline. Having so gloriously won the Western League Premier two and a half seasons back, the club became a victim of its own success. For promotion to the Southern League to happen, certain ground improvements had to be made. 'It was going to cost about a hundred grand. We'd get an FA grant of fifty grand, but we still had to find the rest. We just couldn't afford that.'

And then came the episode that caused the club's recent dislocation and slide down the divisions. 'We won the league and had to go to Torquay for the trophy presentation. We got there and people were saying "Congratulations, but it's a shame about your manager". "Why, what's he done?" "He's leaving." I didn't say anything that night, but got hold of him on the Monday. "Yeah, I'm going and I'm taking the players. We've had a big offer from Bristol Manor Farm. They've got the facilities and we can go up to the Southern League." All seventeen players went with him, the coaching staff, everybody. He took the entire lot. It absolutely crucified the club.'

Chairman George had paid the players' modest wages the season they won the league. They repaid him with betrayal. 'The world's changing,' he sighs. 'Players are changing. Their attitudes are not what they used to be. They can take it or leave it. But if you've got money – if you're offering fifty or sixty quid, that's what it's all about. It's all about money.'

It wasn't just the sudden exit of manager and squad that made Chairman George's lot tough. He also feels let down by the local community, believing that the club could punch harder and higher with improved support. 'It's a village of over two and a half thousand people, but we get half a dozen locals if we're lucky. People in the village are bank managers, they're police inspectors, they work in insurance. They go to work every morning, come home at night, close the door and that's it. They've no interest in the village at all. We used to have a coach that would be filled up with players and supporters for away games. Not now. Village life as we knew it has totally gone.'

These setbacks, not to mention the first team's current form, have definitely left him bruised. But bruised doesn't necessarily mean beaten. 'How much longer I can go on, I don't know. But I'll make sure we get our team back together. I can't watch this club go down the pan after all we've done, after all the work we've put in. How could I walk away? I couldn't. I couldn't live with that.'

Five days later, Longford AFC – a team with an even worse record than Bishop Sutton this season (eighteen defeats from eighteen games, one goal scored) – make national headlines when they announce that their shambolic statistics have enticed fiftysomething Stuart Pearce to dust off his boots and add ballast to their chronically leaky defence. In all the excitement, most people seem to ignore the fact that Pearce's signing appears to be a one-afternoon-only arrangement – not to mention that the deal seems less romantic than at first glance, that it's been brokered by a publicity-hungry insurance company. But it does set me thinking.

I've interviewed a number of former internationals in my time. What if I were also able to persuade one of them to dust off their boots, just for ninety minutes, and turn out for Bishop Sutton? Their appearance would attract a fair few hundred punters paying their six pounds at the gate, with the proceeds spent on what the club has been unable to get close to affording: the modest wages of a proven-at-this-level, twenty-five-goals-a-season striker whose prolific ways could inspire one of the greatest of football's great escapes.

While avoiding relegation remains mathematically possible, the dream still has a faint pulse. The season can be revived. It just needs a superstar signing to make it happen.

I reach for my contacts book.

7

FEBRUARY

Sunday worship

'I'm over the Marshes every Sunday unless World War III breaks out or her indoors ties me to the bedpost.'

At eighty-two, Johnnie Walker has seen plenty in a long life dominated and defined by amateur football. He's not travelled far, though; this weekend warrior has spent almost his entire sporting life in one place. Homerton Road, London E9. The large green patch of London otherwise known as Hackney Marshes.

Walker first trod this turf as a teenage player in 1948. Nearly seventy years later, he remains the venerable chairman of the Hackney & Leyton Football League, the man charged with upholding and protecting the traditions and legacy of this totemic 340-acre site, the seventy-five-pitch symbolic home of Sunday morning football.

The Marshes couldn't wish for a more determined, more defiant protector. While his mobility might be a little compromised now, Walker's mind remains as agile as that of someone half his age, a sharp thorn poking itself into the side of the authorities. 'I'm quite outspoken,' he admits, almost apologetically. 'I've got a bad reputation up at the FA.'

Talking to Walker here in the lobby of the Hackney Marshes Centre is an easy task for an interviewer. No probing required. You'll get the full story from Walker regardless. Just switch on the dictaphone and he's away, pinballing from rosy memory to heinous grievance and back again.

'I started playing football when I was evacuated up to Lancashire in the war. We played on cobbles with a tennis ball. That teaches you ball control.' Back in London in peacetime, he started playing on the Marshes as 'a little winger, because I had quite a lot of pace. Then, after that, I fancied myself as Puskás. He was a marvellous player. So I took the number ten shirt. I even had a spell at centre-forward for two seasons when I was about thirty-two. I really enjoyed that. I don't think I ever ran back beyond the halfway line. What a lovely experience! When I was about thirty-five, I dropped back to play sweeper. It was an absolute doddle. You just had to read the game. I could have played there for years if I hadn't had a heart attack when I was forty.

'I had to give up playing then. But after about six months, I started playing five-a-side. It filled a gap for a while. But you can't go on forever, as much as you'd like to. Once you get an injury, it takes longer to heal. I remember getting a hamstring. I didn't know what it was. I'd never had a hamstring in my life. It took about eight weeks to heal, so I thought I'd better turn it in. So then I took up managing. I ran a very successful side when I was a manager. We won the Premier five years running.' He pauses, his smile straightening. 'It's not as good as playing, though.'

Walker is fascinating company, his words painting a vivid portrait of times past, when players would wash their boots and faces in the same freezing water of a cattle trough. 'You'd go home caked in mud. And most of us didn't have bleeding bathrooms in them days.' That would only be after they'd dragged those mud-caked bodies into a favourite pub, having scraped together enough loose change for a couple of post-match light ales.

There are at least two volumes of memoirs in Walker's head, the accumulation of nearly seven decades of adventures across these acres. He rattles off stories and anecdotes like a comedian pumps out one-liners. One of his best involves a twenty-two-man melee where the corner flags were used as spears and batons. Not that, while recounting these colourful episodes, he's keen to uphold the popular perception of Sunday mornings on the Marshes being a tad shambolic when it comes to the quality of play and the application of players, all beer breath and bed hair.

'People think it's Mickey Mouse football down here, but our Premier League is really good. We get some class players. It's not all rubbish, lurching around drunk from Saturday night. Anyway, it's more like this now . . .' He raises thumb and forefinger to his mouth and takes a drag from an imaginary joint. The sweet smell of marijuana is certainly detectable on the touchlines later on this morning.

The quality in the league's upper echelons possibly has, very slightly, something to do with higher-level Saturday players making illicit appearances on Sundays. 'I still think there are some contract players slipping through, but I'm not a bleeding policeman. There are always going to be ringers. We had the whole Enfield team playing in this league years ago. Their manager phoned up. "You got any of my players playing in your league? They're apparently playing for such-and-such a team." I looked them up and, of course, none of the real names were there. "No, not to my knowledge . . ."'

The quality may be decent, but the quantity has dropped off since the league's salad days. At one time, such was the popularity of Sunday morning football that more than 120 pitches had to be squeezed onto the Marshes to keep up with demand. 'They were so closely knitted together. You'd take throw-ins while standing on the next pitch.'

Now, certainly compared to those crowded days, participation is lessening. The Hackney & Leyton Football League started this season with fifty-five teams over its four divisions, four teams fewer than last year. Not the most humungous of declines, but a decline nonetheless – and part of an undeniable downward trend. Walker's eyes show regret and sadness. 'If I'm speaking honestly, grassroots football is in a right state. I've no idea what it's like nationwide because it's very hard to get hold of those figures, but in London we're about 200 clubs down from last season. That's a considerable number.

'And not only that – the leagues themselves are

disappearing too. We've not done enough to keep people interested in playing. There's less football in schools and that breaks my heart. As kids, we'd play two or three games a week, whether for your school or for the place you lived. And you don't get many people organising. I mean, look at me. I'm eighty-two now. I'm still running the bloody league. My treasurer is eighty-two and all. The secretary is seventy-eight. Jermaine, the referees' secretary, is the youngest. He's about fifty, I should imagine.'

You get the sense that Walker likes a good gripe, but he's put in the years to gain this perspective. He's more than qualified – and entitled – to speak out. 'I'm continually having a moan at the FA. I've written to the last four chairmen there and, with all due respect, they've written back. But what they write is a load of cobblers. "Believe you me, we've got grassroots football uppermost in our minds." They don't know what it is! Grassroots football is park football. They think it's the Conference!'

Then there's the prickly subject of the Olympics. Due south of the Marshes are the pristine lines and geometrical perfection of the Olympic Park; the cool curves of the velodrome are the closest, just across the A12. Further south, the cranes of Docklands continue to reshape the skyline. The Marshes are the permanent fixture of this particular corner of the capital, one greatly unrecognisable from how it looked in 2005 when London got the nod from the International Olympic Committee. Nearly four years after the last medallist left town, the wound left by the Games continues to seep for Walker.

'They took the East Marsh for Olympic parking. They concreted over that whole area of twelve pitches and it was hardly used. Sometimes there were only half a dozen vehicles over there. It was so unnecessary. Our facilities were locked down a year earlier than they were supposed to, so our players were changing out in the open or in their cars. No washing facilities, no toilets. People are born to expect more these days. They don't grow up in a society without bathrooms. They don't put up with what we put up with.

'And where's the legacy? The Olympics has had no effect on the take-up of sport. Over the last thirty or forty years, half the nation's playing fields have been sold off. And that's criminal.'

The fields of Hackney Marshes, though, remain held in a strange, ephemeral affection – from a plummy-voiced 1953 Pathé newsreel celebrating its Corinthian values ('All equipment is provided by the men themselves and they generally manage a smart turnout') to Lionel Messi's helicopter landing on the fields sixty years later, via the Eric Cantona-starring Nike ad of the 1990s. Several ex-England internationals – among them David Beckham and Trevor Brooking – claim to have cut their footballing teeth on the Marshes.

Maybe there are future internationals among the players now arriving for their mid-morning date with destinies either glorious or dispiriting. I let the chairman get back to his duties. He's largely based here in the lobby on Sunday mornings, chewing the cud with players and his fellow league officials, physically unable to get himself out across the fields to the distant matches. 'That aspect has been stripped away from me,' he sighs. 'But you see the same people every week and it's a sort of community.'

He can't, though, resist a final pop at the authorities. 'It's undervalued. I think the council undervalue it. We never get a mention. It's always someone with bleeding sandals on putting some trees in somewhere. Football never gets a look-in.'

* * *

The corridors of the Hackney Marshes Centre are busy and bustling now, home to a seemingly infinite number of dressing rooms. The keener players, the ones who arrived early and changed early, impatiently knock balls back and forth across the concrete floor. Latecomers are chided good-naturedly.

Pep talks are being given at an unnecessary loud volume. Two middle-aged players, clad in immaculate scarlet kit, are engaged in a full and frank exchange of views with a third. 'Are you prepared to give yourself to this team? Are you committed? Listen. Listen to me . . .' The line of questioning is answered by the body language of the subject of their interrogation. Eyes roll, shoulders slump.

As hundreds of players funnel out towards the faraway pitches, last week's glories are keenly remembered. So too are last week's thumping tackles, still sore, still felt. 'He cleaned me right out. Went right through me. Couldn't put any weight on it until Thursday.' But the victims have returned to the scene. Never in doubt.

Battered, bruised and possibly disguising a limp in order to make sure they're in today's starting XI, they can't bear just one week off from this giant field of dreams.

Outside, crows keep high sentry this morning in the tall, leafless trees, while coots bob on the meandering River Lea that cuts the Marshes in two. The shadow of a low-flying airliner moves across the grass as the plane arcs westwards, straightening up for its approach to Heathrow on the other side of the city. An ambulance parks up on the far side, ice packs and suture kits at the ready.

Across the pitches, the same scene is being replicated: the lightest member of a team sitting precariously on the broad shoulders of his most solid team-mate to fix nets to crossbar. Winger riding centre-half. The frame of every goal wears the marks of matches and seasons past, each one covered in little strips of silver or black gaffer tape, the net fixings of last week, last month, last year.

A late-arriving player rides his bike right across several pitches, leaving a narrow, diagonal scar across the playing surfaces as he takes the shortest route to make kick-off. One team's manager tries to call a recalcitrant squad member into the pre-match team talk, but he's more interested in the packet of ten Silk Cut cradled in his hands. On pitch N17, though, all have arrived on time and all are focused on their manager's words. Bow Badgers – appropriately clad in shirts of black and white stripes – are ready to resume their weekly mission: to escape the depths of the fourth division of the Hackney & Leyton.

As they line up to face today's orange-clad foe – the curiously named Dynamo Gobbler – a stiff wind blows a Tesco bag-for-life across the pitch, its progress only halted when it gets tangled in a player's studs. Across the way, another team is playing in orange. Their opponents are in pale blue and white stripes, instantly recalling the 1978 World Cup Final between the Netherlands and Argentina. But there's no repeat of that match's glorious ticker-tape reception. Just a crisp packet tumbling across the turf, soon overtaken by a fast-rolling empty Lucozade bottle.

A distant siren is a reminder of real life beyond the fields, but for the next couple of hours it's pure escapism, the Marshes a green fantasy island among the sprawl and the regeneration projects. That Bow Badgers are less than immaculately turned out isn't important. Like a schoolboy team forced to wear whatever they can salvage from the lost-property box, very few wear matching shorts. And they only have eleven shirts today; later on, this causes the substitute to hurriedly put on the jersey of the player he's replacing. But sartorial uniformity is low priority. A decent performance, one of heart and soul, is all.

While Dynamo Gobbler isn't the most amusing name for a less-than-serious amateur team (see here Arthritic Bilbao or Borussia Munchingflapjack), they do have comedy credentials, having previously included the comic actor Tom Rosenthal in their ranks. Rosenthal – star of *Friday Night Dinners* and *Plebs*, son of TV anchorman Jim – was 'a bit tasty' as a player, too, according to the Badgers. Gobbler appear to be missing him today. Their mannerisms and gesticulations are straight out of the Premier League, but their technique is not. It's not even kick and rush. It's kick and jog. They fall one behind to the bottom team within five minutes.

It's the only score of the first half, a lumpy forty-five minutes that nonetheless prompts one Badgers player to excitedly question the last time they were ahead at the break. They double their lead early in the second period, despite playing into that buffeting wind. A much-welcomed win is in the offing. Minds are focused, eyes on the prize. 'Own it, bro'. Own it.'

The handful of spectators are a little less loyal. They might be girlfriends or wives, mothers or brothers, but they can't resist stealing a glance whenever a neighbouring match sounds more exciting than the one they're contractually obliged to watch. Celebrations ring out on the pitch to the left; tempers are raised to the right. Cheers in one ear, expletives in the other. It's a truly stereophonic experience. One striker on an adjacent pitch is getting particularly exorcised by being, in these linesman-free games, continually ruled offside by a referee thirty yards off the pace. The Sunday morning verbal barrage would make a vicar blush.

Bow Badgers see out a comfortable 3-0 victory, one that their collective ranks clearly weren't expecting. 'We might not win again,' one of them points out. 'We should soak this up.' There's no spraying of champagne, though, just a shower of mud clods as Jay the captain smashes the studs of his boots together. But even the euphoria of a rare win can't get in the way of the housekeeping that's familiar to anyone who's ever undertaken the thankless task of organising a football team. 'Who's paid? Has Elliott paid? Richy, have you paid? Alex, no?'

Bikes are retrieved from where they were thrown down on the touchline, as the Badgers join a couple of dozen other teams making the long walk back to the Centre. The excitement of victorious players ('Did you see that lob? Did you see that lob?!') mixes with the blame-game being played out among the ranks of defeated teams. Fresh memories, fresh recriminations.

Back in the lobby, team sheets are handed in to the league secretary. Anchored to his station, he studiously collects and collates the details of matches he never gets to see. The scores are coming in thick and fast. A flurry of paperwork. Two half-eaten sandwiches lie neglected on a plate next to him.

The Bow Badgers result seems to be that morning's headline news. 'You won?' laughs Jermaine, the incredulous referee's secretary. 'I should have gone down the bookies!' He's joined by an equally disbelieving Johnnie Walker, a man still eager to hear the match reports after all these decades on the Marshes, after this life of Sundays. He shakes his head. 'They mucked my bleeding pools up!'

Half the Badgers team decamps to the nearby Adam & Eve pub where, restorative pints to hand, they ruminate over today's game, while also dissecting the reasons why they exchange a warm Sunday morning bed for ice-cold municipal playing fields. Jay, the team's Bow-born-and-bred captain, started the team five years ago 'after getting into both drinking and putting on weight'. He filled the side with old school friends and those who answered ads placed online. 'We ended up with eleven players to begin with but before we knew it, people were getting in touch. I still get contacted every week by someone who wants to play for us.' Accordingly, they resemble a patchwork of different backgrounds and back-stories.

James (centre-back, originally from Newcastle, works in marketing): 'Since I moved down about three years ago, I've been in and out of five-a-side and six-a-side, but no one's really committed to a team. It's start and stop. No one can really be bothered. The reason I started looking for a proper eleven-a-side was for that commitment – the discipline that says "Maybe I shouldn't have twelve pints on Saturday because I've got football tomorrow morning". And I can get away with more in an eleven-a-side. If I hoof the ball in five-a-side, I get told off. But here it's all right.'

Jay: 'Playing Sunday morning means I'm not drinking as much on Saturday night. Not that it's ever really beer cans on the sidelines with us. Everyone gets passionately into it. It's still taken seriously enough. You need to be of a certain fitness, otherwise you just get found out.'

Robin (centre-back, originally from Manchester, works in engineering): 'I moved down a year and a bit ago. I didn't know anyone in London and hadn't played for a team for years. I just found them on the internet and they seemed like nice guys. I live in Bow, so they're my local team. People like me and James are young professionals moving into east London where it's getting more gentrified. But at least we're playing footy on the Marshes. We're part of something that's been here before. There's some connection to the community.'

James: 'I'd heard of the Marshes, but didn't know much about the place. I knew it was an old institution, but that was about it. Since starting playing here, I've done more research. It's a fascinating place. And we feel part of its history, even though we're the bottom team.'

Robin: 'We're not as angry as we should be when we get beat, though. We're making excuses when we've lost by a ton.'

Dom (left-back, originally from Essex, works in banking): 'One of our players, Bobby, is nineteen. Every week the rumours are flying around about him having trials for West Ham, for Palace, for Fulham. But every Sunday he turns up and plays for us. We are bottom of the bottom division of the Hackney & Leyton League – very close to the bottom, if not the actual bottom, of the entire football pyramid. But he turns up every week. He loves it.'

James: 'There's something romantic about joining the bottom team in the bottom division on Hackney Marshes, but still having that commitment from everyone.'

Dom: 'For me, it kicks in on Saturday night, watching *Match of the Day*. It comes on and I start thinking about Sunday morning. Am I going to be left-back? Am I going to be right-back? Or will I finally be allowed to play in midfield? Are we going to play like Leicester today or are we going to be a shambles like Newcastle? We're a good team that's underachieved. Maybe we're like West Brom.

Yeah, we're the West Brom of the Hackney & Leyton League.'

James: 'Today could be a turning point, though. We've never played like we did today. We could be talking about this one for a good long time.'

Robin: 'In my opinion, we've got the best squad in the division. I don't think that's exaggerating. We've got quality players. We're just less than the sum of our parts. If we decide to play as a team – like we did today, we played solid – maybe promotion next season and reaching the final of one of the cups.'

Jay, the team's founder, has set his sights somewhat higher. 'Personally, I want the Bow Badgers brand to be big. I want to be able to go on holiday to China and see our replica kits on sale there . . .'

* * *

Monday. The morning after the morning before. The Hackney Marshes car park is empty now, save for a handful of vans belonging to the various dog-walking companies serving this end of London. The changing-room corridors have fallen silent, too. Sunday's footballers have become Monday's workers, cursing at alarm clocks, late trains and pointless meetings about meetings.

Aaron Bobb has no meetings to worry about, no office politics to navigate his way around. As the Marshes' head groundsman, he has a very relaxed start to the week. 'I never come to work with a plan,' he says, striding out across the plain in hobnailed boots, green overalls, sunglasses and flat cap. This is the first job of every week for him. Walk the land, assess the damage, get a measure of the next few days' work. This is clearly a favourite part of his week, especially if he likes what he finds. The wind in his sails, fresh air in his lungs.

There's been quite a downpour overnight and miniature silver lakes now exist where twenty-four hours earlier they didn't. The winds of the incoming Storm Imogen are beginning to gather, too. An academy team is beginning its training session, their luminous yellow defensive dummies bowing and rocking in the stiff breeze. Dogs splash and crash into faraway puddles, their balls thrown wind-assisted record distances. But the conditions – in particular the surface water – hold no concern for Bobb. Built on the rubble that much of London was reduced to by the Luftwaffe, the Marshes boast universally excellent drainage. If the rain holds off today, those puddles will disappear by late afternoon.

Bobb's predecessor was steeped in the game. A former YTS goalkeeper at Fulham who succumbed to a couple of anterior cruciate ligament tears, he worked in coaching and scouting alongside his duties on the Marshes. Indeed, he only left damp Hackney because he was offered a position in desert-dry Qatar to be their turf specialist ahead of the 2022 World Cup. By contrast, Bobb doesn't have that football pedigree, that connection with the game. For him, it's all about the groundwork. 'I'm not a big football fan,' he concedes. 'It's unusual, I know. I was a golf-course green-keeper for about ten years and I didn't play golf either.' He is not here because of sporting dreams that failed or went unfulfilled. It's his love of the soil that motivates him.

Despite his lack of sporting genes, Bobb still understands how important Sunday mornings are to the footballing wannabes of east London. 'For a lot of people, it's their life. They don't really do anything else on weekends. It's a very, very big thing to them. On the rare occasion we cancel football, for them it's "What am I going to do instead?"'

Even during a winter that will be remembered for its near-constant downpours, postponements at the Marshes have been rare. Unlike almost all the semi-pro leagues above them, this season the Hackney & Leyton Football League has once again prided itself on the absence of fixture pile-ups.

'I've only cancelled football on one weekend this season,' Bobb announces with a beaming smile, 'and that was the weekend it was pretty much cancelled everywhere. There was heavy rain on Wednesday, Thursday, Friday and Saturday, so we had to call it off. I wasn't the most popular person, but when I showed everyone I wasn't the only idiot calling off football, it was fine. It's not daunting to make that kind of decision. It's just that people don't understand. They think you're closing football just because you've got the power to. I'm not. It's that I want them to play next week and the week after.

'But I've found out over the years that you can't tell a sportsman anything. A sportsman will tell *you*. That's always the way. Whether it's bowling greens or golf courses or cricket pitches or football pitches, they know best. You've just got to pretend that you're going to do everything that they say. It's "Yes, yes, yes, yes, yes". But they have no clue really.'

We've reached the North Marsh now and Bobb is more than content with what he's seeing. Depending on how hard Storm Imogen fancies shaking the capital, it looks like a straightforward week for his team of fifteen. Yesterday's battering, by the massed battalions of amateur footballers, was far from severe. One or two pitches might get rested next weekend, but there's more than enough capacity to cope.

With no teams populating them this morning, the empty Marshes seem to stretch even further into the distance than yesterday. At regular intervals, the undressed goalposts stand motionless and lonely. Ghostly, even, like a series of Anthony Gormley sculptures replicated towards the horizon. The local crows, on their daytime roosts atop the crossbars, give the scene an extra gothic edge.

We make a 180-degree turn and start the long walk back to the Centre. Bobb's pace noticeably slows. This is a man in no hurry to conclude his survey of the pitches. 'I love just walking around out here. It's a dream job for me. I had an office job once. I was an area manager, managing grounds maintenance. Similar to my boss's job now. But it wasn't me. You can't manage green spaces from an office, but try explaining that to people who think you can. "Oh, it'll just run itself." It won't. It's the same as a factory, it's the same as anywhere else. The job was unpleasant – very stressful and very uncomfortable.

So I got out and came here. I took a £6,000-a-year pay cut, but I was quite happy with that.

'I'm very active. I can't be sat looking at a screen, tapping away all day. I just can't. Even if it was £50,000 a year, I probably still couldn't. I have to be out there in the fresh air, involved in what's going on. On the field, in the soil, in the grass . . .'

There's a whiff of gasoline in the air as the line-marker's John Deere buggy zips past. Further away, a pair of litter-pickers are filling their black refuse sacks with yesterday's detritus – shin guard tapes, crisp packets, partially drunk bottles of water and, one to warm the cockles of the traditionalists, the discarded peel of half-time oranges. Bobb explains how larger items are often dumped. 'Anything they bring with them that they don't need to take back home stays out here. For instance, they might have bought a brand-new pair of boots and they now don't need the old ones, so they leave them. They know someone will come and pick them up.'

Bobb and his extended team of grass-cutters, line-markers, tractor-drivers, gardeners and litter-pickers are the true heroes of Hackney Marshes. But they're the unappreciated heroes, too, invisible when the hordes descend on Sunday mornings. Not that Bobb would expect it to be any other way. 'The players don't care who's done what. They don't care how that grass got there. They just want to get on that field and pretend to be Lionel Messi or whoever for an hour and thirty minutes. But it's their little freedom moment. That's when they get to express themselves, to pretend to be whoever they dream of being, to believe they're playing in the Premiership.

'And there's nothing wrong with that.'

* * *

It's the last day of February and, this being a leap year, Gary Brabin has an extra day to contemplate the season so far, to mull over the misfortunes and dissect the disappointments. He's at home in Aintree on the far side of Liverpool, a whole city and a significant body of water between him and his office at Tranmere. This gives him sufficient distance to make a measured, unhurried assessment, away from the pressure pot of Prenton Park.

It's twenty-four hours since a 1-0 victory over local rivals Chester moved Tranmere up three places in the Conference and into the top four. They've now only lost two in the last eleven. This is better news. The pressure that was gathering before Christmas after that draw to Halifax has noticeably dissipated.

It's been a difficult few months as players and fans have adjusted to life in an alien division. But, as a manager with Conference experience at Cambridge United, Luton and Southport, Brabin predicted the season wouldn't be the stroll in the park that a certain swathe of Rovers supporters expected. 'I've been in this position before and I understand the ups and downs of the job. But I've always been level-headed. I don't get too carried away when we're winning games or too despondent when we're losing games.' Tranmere's yo-yoing form is well-suited to him, then. His equilibrium is maintained, despite the club's broadly 'win one, draw one, lose one' form this season.

'Being Tranmere Rovers, it's easy to expect to win games. The club has great history, but history alone won't get you back in the league. There's a lot of ex-league clubs who've not only not been able to get out of this league, but who have actually been relegated into the league below this one. Look at the likes of Stockport and Chester. Over the last three or four years, it's definitely become stronger at the bottom. It's more competitive down there. There are no gimmes any more.'

Gary Brabin didn't have to put himself through this. He chose to be here, scrapping it out for whatever the team can get, while absorbing criticism from all angles. Nine months ago, he held a position that made him far less susceptible to the verbal slings and arrows of an impatient fanbase. He was part of the under-21s coaching team at his beloved Everton, arguably one of the most secure positions to hold in the managerial ranks, one that quite often survives regime change at the very top. So why leave a dream role at your boyhood club in order to return to the firing line, where the rifle sights of 5,000 devout fans are trained on you, waiting for the slightest wrong move?

'I had no intentions of leaving Everton. I was really happy with the role and had turned down managerial jobs when I was at Goodison Park. I flatly refused them. I had no intention of going back into management. Or back into the Conference. But then it came about with Tranmere. When I first came into management, they represented a realistic level at which to aim. After meeting the chairman, he inspired me. I could see the scope to improve the club and hopefully bring it back to where it belongs. It was a tough decision, but Everton understood and were genuinely excited for me to take over one of their neighbours. It's as tough as I thought it would be, but as enjoyable, too.'

His reputation as a combative midfielder for the likes of Doncaster, Blackpool and Hull lessened as he shaped a gentler managerial personality. In conversation, there's very little of the bullish bravado favoured by other, less emotionally secure managers. He's controlled and calm, the slightest hint of a lisp softening that Liverpudlian accent. In post-match press conferences, any anger stays under wraps. Mild frustration is as much as the press corps are going to get. Perhaps he saves it all for the dressing room.

Maybe the fans, quick to turn when the team snatches defeat from the jaws of victory, want Brabin to more readily show the fire in his belly. But it's probably the steadiness that made him appeal to Mark Palios. Care and consideration are very much Palios-esque attributes. There's definitely steely ambition; it's just not shouted from the rooftops. After all, the downward turn at Prenton Park in recent years has certainly meant it's not a natural home for hyperbole and big talk.

Even with his words tempered by the reality of Conference life, he can't resist thoughts of an immediate return to the Football League. 'It would be nice to look back at this season with fond memories.' His eyes glisten.

'It would be marvellous if we had just the one non-league season in the history books.'

On the other side of town, in a cloud-scraping apartment block that looks out across the lead-grey Irish Sea, James Norwood admits to giving in to an unlikely temptation. Like his boss, Tranmere's top scorer said one thing and did the other. Halfway through last season, Norwood served notice that he was leaving Forest Green Rovers in the summer. His justification for not signing a new contract was an all-consuming desire to have a proper tilt at the Football League. But he never got there. Instead, he too renounced his words having been shown the set-up at Prenton Park. After four seasons in the Conference and despite, at the age of twenty-four, being at a pivotal junction in his career, he plumped for another season – maybe even two – in the fifth tier.

'Things had got a bit stale at Forest Green and I was playing in a position I didn't enjoy. Leaving seemed the right thing to do. I had interest from league clubs. About twelve or thirteen of them rang me up in that first week. But then I got a call from a man called Steve Beck, who was Gary Brabin's agent, saying that Brabs would like me to come up and have a look. So, about ten days into the summer, I came up here. I didn't expect the enormous stadium. I didn't expect the standard of everything. It was all at Championship or League One standard. I was overwhelmed. I met the chairman and he seemed brilliant. And the first thing the manager said was that he wanted to play me upfront. Everything just clicked within two or three days. I knew it was the right club for me. Even when the stadium was empty, it just had this aura about it.

'It was another level. At Forest Green, players wouldn't do a lot of extras, in terms of weights and finishing. I remember walking into the Tranmere gym a couple of weeks into pre-season and there were about eight people in there, doing weights and stretching and rehab. They were staying for an extra hour, an extra hour and a half. They were making sure their bodies were right, that they were stronger and quicker. I just thought, "This is the mentality of winners."'

Norwood, like Brabin, had had his doubts extinguished, and his appetite sharpened, by the pretty persuasion of an owner-chairman whose precise plan of action, set out on a giant whiteboard in his office, was watertight in its logic. Both had taken the bait of restoring a sleeping giant's glory years. 'There's a lot of talk in football. But this wasn't just talk. I looked at him and believed every word he said. It sounded realistic in terms of timescales. I didn't hear "Oooh, we're going to do this in three months". He said "It's going to take time, but we'll get it right. And this is what I want to have done by the end of it, however long it takes."'

Norwood is more than your average footballer. Yes, there's the armful of tattoos and, yes, there's an inexplicable collection of day-glo boots in his cupboard. But his insight reaches a little deeper. He seems more able to place things in a wider context, not just game by game, season by season. This is a player doing his utmost to shape and steer his own career trajectory. The goal is a clear one – he has scores to settle. After just four appearances for Exeter City as a teenager, he's anxious to prove himself in a second spell in the Football League.

Whether Norwood took the best option – joining the most professionally organised non-league club rather than signing for a league club of more modest means – will be clear by the time the final scheduled match of the season rolls around, a home match against play-off rivals Grimsby on the last day of April.

All the indications of this undulating season point to the Grimsby match being decisive. 'Down to the wire' is a phrase ceaselessly echoing around the corridors of Prenton Park. Having spent all of his twenties in the Conference, Norwood is able to offer a convincing analysis of Tranmere's fortunes, insight seasoned by his time at Forest Green. 'I think it's to do with the start of the season. There were three or four of us who were fully experienced in the Conference and everyone else had come from League One or League Two. It took them a little longer to adjust to playing the right way to win this league, to go up. It's a lot tougher down here – in terms of refereeing, in terms of time on the ball. It's frantic. Control the ball and four people are round you.

'We drew at Braintree and I said "That's a good point. Not a lot of teams will come here and win." Everyone else was saying "No, it's Braintree away. We should be beating teams like this 5-0." But any team can beat any other team in this league on their day. Teams are picking up results everywhere.' The proof is in the league standings. Yesterday morning, before the lunchtime win at Chester, much-derided Braintree were above Tranmere in the table. Today, Rovers are only ahead of them because they've played three games more.

As well as correcting opinions in the dressing room, those Tranmere players with Conference experience have had to appease the fans with explanations of the challenges this league presents. It's a very different kettle of fish between Gloucestershire and the Wirral in terms of expectations on the terraces; Norwood's former club are in their rudest-ever health, while his present club are at the very lowest ebb in their history.

'The fan base at Forest Green isn't massive, but it is very loyal. The expectations here, though, are huge. If we draw or lose a game, Twitter blows up. You're a terrible player, we're the worst team in the world. If we win, everything changes. At the start of the season, everyone thought we could win every game 5-0. We had League One players and we had money in the bank, so the feeling was that we should be winning this with a hundred and thirty points. It's taken a while, but people have come to realise it's a tough league. They appreciate that we're pulling results out of the bag. And the fans know they can play a vital part. They can get behind us, they can intimidate other teams.

'The players who are part-time or at mid-table teams come to the likes of Cheltenham or Tranmere or Forest Green or Grimsby and raise their levels an extra 20 per cent because they want to move to these kind of clubs. Our striker coach said that I'd probably have had another ten goals, but the keepers have been motivated to come out and make saves they'd never normally make because they want to sign for the clubs at or near the top. Every player is trying to get out of this league.'

Norwood is, too. He's hoping his goals, like the needles of his favourite tattooist, are going to ink in the career path he's already sketched out for himself. 'I've got a point to prove,' he says, a restlessness in his voice. 'I don't want to be that guy with six hundred Conference appearances. I don't want to be in the pub when I'm sixty talking to lads and going "You know what? I used to be quite a good player . . ."'

8

MARCH

Collecting the intangible

'Rule One of groundhopping is that there are no rules.'

Chris Freer is a man on a mission. Not for him the trifling matter of visiting all ninety-two Football League stadiums. Too easy. Child's play. A cinch. Instead, Freer – for reasons he alone can understand and explain – has set himself the target of travelling to, and watching a match at, each and every ground in the top ten tiers of the football pyramid. Today we're en route from his home in the Derbyshire town of Long Eaton to the space age-sounding Euronics Stadium in Barton-upon-Humber, home to Barton Town Old Boys of the Toolstation Northern Counties East League Premier Division.

The name of the ground isn't too important for Freer. It's more of a numbers game for him. Today's destination will be better known as ground number 689.

Those who surrender their spare time and social life to visit as many football grounds as humanly possible are happy to be called groundhoppers. It's an epithet that's worn with pride, a badge of honour that describes what they get up to on Saturday afternoons and midweek evenings. And any other time of the week that twenty-two men are chasing a ball around a football field.

Groundhoppers can come in all shapes and sizes. They tend not to, though. They're mainly middle-aged and male. Freer points out that they're easy to spot at games; the carrier bag tends to give them away. But while they share a common demographic and an ultimate end goal, groundhoppers also celebrate the individual, each operating to a variety of self-prescribed criteria. As we turn east onto the M18, Freer provides the in-car entertainment as he runs through the most bizarre quirks of his brethren, behaviour that really ought to encourage their nearest and dearest to arrange some kind of intervention.

Freer runs through his own foibles first. 'My philosophy is that a game's got to start, even if something happens and it's abandoned after a minute. Some say it has to be the whole ninety minutes. For me, if the game starts, there's been a game, so it counts. And it has to be an enclosed ground where you have to pay to get in. So no park pitches – nothing that's been roped off. And I only count grounds if there's a competitive fixture involving the home club's first team. Some count friendlies and some will happily see reserves or juniors.'

These might sound like arbitrarily drawn lines in the sand, but it's soon apparent that Freer occupies the more moderate end of the groundhopping spectrum. After all, he's not disturbed by a goalless draw. Others are. For them, a 0-0 doesn't earn a tick in their book. They have to make a return visit – which might, of course, be anything up to 600-mile round trip – and see a goal scored there before the ground can be added to the tally.

One groundhopper only visits non-league grounds, but if a Football League side drops into the Conference, he has to be at their very first home game of the following season for it to count. No other game on their fixture list will do. Others feel they have to revisit a particular ground if a new stand has opened since the last time they were there. One curious soul has to touch the match ball at some point during the game. These are his own rules, let's remind ourselves. No one's making him do that. It conjures up an image of a carrier bag-wielding, middle-aged man hurling himself into a gorse bush to retrieve a stray ball before emerging, bloodied but smiling, to enter a satisfying tick in his notebook.

One particular groundhopping tale has the South Yorkshire landscape resonating with our roaring laughter. 'There's a guy who has to touch both crossbars,' Freer reveals. 'At one game, he couldn't reach one of them and complained to an official. It transpired that the bar was at an incorrect height and the game was called off. Of course, he didn't get the tick. Justice!'

Others have been known to undertake long journeys but to leave before kick-off if no programme is available. Freer looks a little ashen-faced at this point. 'I must confess that I've been to a couple of grounds where there's been no programme and thought "Sod it" and gone somewhere else. I think I've mellowed a bit on that now. The lower and lower you go down the scale, the less chance there is of them doing a programme. The word that's used is "issuing". If the club "issues", it means it produces a programme. Most clubs are obliged by their leagues to issue. Some don't and take the hit. Sometimes it's easier to take the fine than produce a hundred programmes and sell about ten copies.'

Unsurprisingly, groundhopping can't really be described as a unisex pastime. There are very few women within this mysterious society; the ones that are tend to be in the company of groundhopping partners and husbands. 'Long-suffering' probably gets close to the mark. This is a pursuit that speaks to a particularly male sense of achievement, one that's measured in list form. It is, after all, a short, duffel-coated shuffle from standing on freezing railway platforms with a tick-list in hand to standing on freezing touchlines with a tick-list in hand. Freer holds his hands up. 'Ninety-nine per cent of us are blokes – blokes who are forty-five onwards. We're all trainspotters or ex-trainspotters. Most of the guys fit the stereotype.'

His phone signals the arrival of a text. It's from a groundhopping pal who's currently paying a visit to the football leagues of Serbia and is reporting the half-time score between Radnički Niš and Novi Pazar. He's presuming that his mate back in England is on tenterhooks, impatiently waiting for the update. It's 0-0. Barely worth the price of a text from Eastern Europe. This particular pal is even more committed than Freer. He goes to matches six days a week. On the seventh day, the traditionally football-free Thursday (free of football until the

Europa League came along, that is), he sees his girlfriend.
More long sufferance.

A psychoanalyst would have a field day dissecting the
workings of a groundhopper's brain. The source of Freer's own obsession was 'probably passing my driving test
and having a car. When Forest weren't playing at home,
I'd get in the car and go somewhere else. Maybe Lincoln.
Maybe Mansfield. I had a little chart of grounds that I'd
been to and grounds I wanted to go to. This would have
been the 1976–77 season.' I am in the presence of a pio-
neer. Freer was a groundhopper before the notion of
groundhopping had been conceived.

He's been doing it on and off ever since. After splitting
up with his girlfriend at the end of the 1980s, zigzagging
across the motorway network from modest stadium to
modest stadium seemed the best way to mend a broken
heart. An extended spell as a pub landlord in the 1990s
wasn't conducive to weekend awaydays and, when he
emerged from the licensed trade, he only had eyes for
one team in particular. A return to groundhopping
remained on hold while he developed a particular affection for a team a couple of hours from his East Midlands
homelands.

'I spent two years watching Darlington home and
away. There was a little gaggle of us going up from the
Midlands. There'd be a car going from Hinckley that
would pick us up at Leicester Forest East services on the
M1. We just liked their ground. And obviously they were
no-hopers. There were like an anti-team.' This explains
why today Freer is wearing a Darlington shirt under a

double layer of coats. Not that the neutral groundhopper ever shows such unilateral partisanship. The Darlington top is offset by a royal-blue Dorking FC woolly hat.

'I followed Darlington for a while, then we had kids, which slowed me down a bit. Then, on New Year's Day in 2004, I decided to pick up the cudgels again. I went to see Burton Albion play at Tamworth. And on every weekend since then, aside from the odd Forest and Darlington match, I've been to a different ground.' His pursuit is aided by the fact that his twins are a few months shy of adulthood and so can fend for themselves, and that his wife spends a large part of her weekend tending to her horses. Freer's taking full advantage. 'In twelve years, I've gone from about a hundred grounds to nearly seven hundred,' he beams. The name of his blog is in woeful need of updating; it's called '300 grounds and counting'. As well as humorously documenting his adventures, the blog also rates each ground according to certain criteria; things like toilet provision, quantity of floodlights, presence of local birdlife . . .

With the Humber Estuary – and its plentiful supply of wading birds – in sight, we're getting nearer to ground number 689. We take the last exit off the A-road before it launches itself across the Humber Bridge and head into town, Freer issuing instructions from an unfolded piece of paper in his hands. It's not the only paperwork he's brought with him. In the unlikely event of the Barton Town Old Boys game being called off, we also have a list of several alternative matches being played nearby this afternoon, at other grounds over whose threshold he has yet to pass.

There are plenty of such grounds in his sights. This season, Freer is focusing hard on both divisions of the Northern Counties East League. Scattered either side of the M1 and points further north, and covering from Nottinghamshire up to North Yorkshire, many of the league's teams bear testament to the region's coalmining past – the likes of Nostell Miners' Welfare, Rossington Main, Pontefract Collieries and Armthorpe Welfare. With pit heads sealed up, head gear dismantled and slagheaps grassed over, football and brass bands remain the only visible memorials to an industry that has otherwise been smudged off the landscape, destined to become ancient history within a couple of generations. Sometimes these two pastimes go hand in hand. For instance, Tuesday nights at Maltby Main FC near Rotherham are usually double-booked. There'll almost certainly be a match on, accompanied by the sounds of band practice in the clubhouse. The band members, carrying their precious cargo of cornets and euphoniums, are forced to pick a path back to their cars through the piles of kitbags and discarded boots slung on the ground.

Freer and I arrive at the Euronics Stadium, located down a narrow, dead-end lane and butting up against a single-track railway line. Freer's phone is straight out of his pocket, snapping a picture of the ground's entrance for posterity. Now in his early sixties, he asks the old guy on the turnstile about the club's concessionary rates, laying the flattery on thick. 'I'm sixty-two, like you,' he tells him. 'I wish to fuck I were,' is the gruff reply. 'I'm eighty-three.' The tactic works, though. Freer saves a couple of quid on the price of admission.

Taking an admiring glance around the place, he has a set routine to uphold. Before anything else, he takes a look across the pitch, ascertaining which corner flag is showing least signs of life and therefore which will offer most shelter from the biting wind coming off the river. Over on the far side to the left is where we'll stand today, even if the centrally heated upper floors of the semis that look out across the turf might be a preferred vantage point on this double-coat afternoon. We make a slow circuit of the pitch, stopping every few yards for Freer to take photos from different perspectives. We're the only ones paying such close attention to the fabric of the ground, suggesting we're the sole representatives of the groundhopping fraternity to have made the long schlep up to Barton-upon-Humber today.

Notes made and photos taken, we head for the warmth of the clubhouse. Freer, the former publican who now publishes magazines for the licensed trade, is disappointed but not surprised by the lack of ale on tap. He plumps for a bottle of Lucozade instead, before retiring to a table on the far side of the room. It's here that he'll peruse the programme to see if anyone of note will be playing this afternoon. We're in luck. Today's visitors, Worksop Town, have Chris Waddle's son Jack in their starting XI.

At the next table, a Heston Blumenthal lookalike is noisily appreciating an outsized sausage roll. Beyond him, a pair of away fans recount how they missed the turn for Barton and enjoyed an unscheduled return trip across the Humber Bridge. Eyes are rolled in the direction of the navigator. There was no danger of such a diversion for us. Thanks to his endless jaunts travelling from coast to coast, Freer seems to know the correct lane to be in at every motorway junction in the land. You suspect that he also knows the time of the last train back home to Long Eaton from every nook and cranny of this isle. Or at least every nook and cranny that boasts a football team in the top ten tiers of the English game.

A groundhopper needs to be organised, after all. A pescatarian groundhopper even more so. For pre-match sustenance after what might be a long trip, Freer will have an insurance policy against the exclusively meaty menus of many grounds. He'll either have researched, the day before, a nearby hostelry offering suitable fare or will have packed a couple of Holland & Barrett porkless pies to keep hunger at bay. We took the former option en route, the local pub where they serve cheese baguettes as chunky as a stevedore's forearm.

The match itself is of secondary importance to the groundhopper – as long, of course, as it adheres to the criteria he himself has set. For the record, today's match isn't half bad. Barton (sky blue) and Worksop (fluorescent tangerine) share four goals, all of which are scored at our end; Freer's choice of vantage point serves us well. Jack Waddle, the Worksop number eleven, is instantly identifiable. He's not only facially the spit of the old man, but he also shares his dad's on-pitch body language – the same bowed head, the same droopy-shouldered slouch.

And when there is a lull in the fiercely competitive play (on one occasion, the break is to retrieve the ball from the railway line), an overly friendly cat entertains the hardy souls here on the far touchline, performing light-as-a-feather gymnastics on the perimeter wall with all the poise of Olga Korbut on the balance beam. The occasional single-carriage train sliding past is another distraction, its passengers getting a fleeting glance of football at NCEL Premier level. They don't look too impressed.

After the game, a small crowd gathers outside the dressing rooms. An open window is allowing them to hear every vitriolic syllable of a Worksop manager apoplectic at his team squandering a 2-0 half-time lead and conceding a late equaliser. Not everyone in the visiting party is getting quite so worked up, though, especially the Worksop fan with the enviable task of making room in his car's boot for the forty-two-inch telly he's just won in the raffle.

Ungraciously seething that our tickets weren't the winning ones, Freer and I pull out of the car park and head south. The day is done, the task complete. Football attracts the collector who chooses to amass autographs, ticket stubs, programmes, kits – the kind of items that can be admired in a display cabinet in a museum. Freer, though, is accumulating an ever-lengthening series of experiences. These are only of value to him; the value is knowing he was there, that he made the effort, that he earned the tick in the book.

'I'm a guy who's quite happy collecting the intangible,' he concludes, gazing out of the window over the flat fields of eastern England. 'I've got stuff, but you can't touch it. It's in my head. There's nothing there to pass on.'

* * *

Like thousands of others across the country, Al Crane has spent the morning of Easter Monday doing a spot of DIY. But while others might be mending a wobbly dining-room chair or assembling some flat-pack Scandinavian furniture, for the last few hours Crane has been stuck inside the tight confines of a shipping container. More specifically, he's been sawing sheets of MDF to precise specifications, ready to turn them into shelves and a shop counter. His productivity is impressive, especially as he's been working alone, albeit fuelled by a packet of Cadburys Mini Eggs left over from the day before.

For today is a momentous day for Dulwich Hamlet Football Club. This afternoon, the one-person garden shed that houses the club shop looks likely to be shutting its hatch for the last time. Crane is confident that this much larger shipping container – a retail space that will offer the revolutionary concept of allowing customers inside to actually peruse the stock – will be fit for purpose in time for next Saturday's game. This is an estimate based on expertise. He's an architect by trade, one whose exacting professional standards are being tested by the floor-to-ceiling uPVC window that's been installed during the week. 'There's as much frame as there is glass,' he tuts, adopting the haughty voice of an art critic, his tongue not a million miles from his cheek.

There's a reason why Dulwich Hamlet need a bigger shop. This is the best-supported club in the Ryman Premier League, one whose home gates regularly clock in around the 1,400 mark, making them far and away the biggest draw in level-seven football across the country.

But the crowd-pulling success of Dulwich Hamlet isn't welcomed by all. They're no strangers to attempted character assassinations. If you swallow the popular perception of the club – one conceived by those outside SE22, at least – you'd expect the terraces here at Champion Hill to be dominated by both the chattering classes and ukulele-strumming hipsters. Believe what you read and the air must surely be awash with idle talk about Tuscan villas and artisan cheeses, or with noisy comparisons of the length and fullness of various spectators' Victorian-style beards. Here's a clue: it isn't.

Like any cliché, though, it didn't come from nowhere. It's based on at least a scintilla of truth; there's no coincidence that the rise in support for the football club has climbed in parallel with the growing gentrification of the immediate area. Indeed, evidence of the club's middle-class appreciation is conspicuous. The match-day kit is sponsored by a local craft brewery, while their training tops bear the super-stylish logo of a local free-range butcher. These are atypical sponsors for a non-league football team. Usually they're more prosaic benefactors, such as Stan Robinson Pallet Network (Stafford Rangers), Paul Robinson Solicitors (Billericay Town) or, in Tranmere's case, pound-stretching superstore Home Bargains.

However, this outsider's perception of Dulwich infuriates Duncan Hart, the chair of the club's very active supporters' trust. 'The hipster thing is just utterly lazy,' he sighs. 'It obviously annoys a lot of fans as a whole part of the story gets missed – the much broader appeal of the club. Young and old, families – a whole gamut of different people. And what is a hipster, anyway? Is it somebody who likes to come to non-league football, support their local team, have a beer by the side of the pitch and have fun? If so, they're very welcome!'

Hart puts the sneers of others down to plain old jealousy – jealousy at the size of Dulwich's gates, at the club's pulling power, at the buoyant, unrestrained atmosphere on match days. We get an instant illustration of others' attitudes courtesy of an early-arriving fan of today's opponents, Tonbridge Angels. 'They're only famous because they were on *The Apprentice*,' he sniffs to his friend as they shuffle by, referring to the episode where the latest deluded bunch of 'Britain's brightest business brains' found themselves jet-washing hardened chewing gum off the Champion Hill terraces – all in the name of sharpening their commercial acumen, apparently.

Speak to any long-time home fans around the ground and they'll name two clear reasons for the inflated crowds that have risen fivefold in the last six or seven seasons. There are the performances on the pitch that have seen Dulwich – led by the long-serving Gavin Rose, one of very few black managers in the semi-pro ranks – find success on the pitch of late, including being Ryman Division One South champions a couple of seasons back, as well as reaching the Premier play-offs last May. A winning team is always a magnet, after all, whatever the level. And then there's the imaginative community initiatives the club and the trust undertake, as Hart explains.

'We've put a lot of work in to make this club a better place where everyone feels welcome. Non-league has traditionally attracted more senior people, but we get a more mixed crowd in terms of age. Also, our anti-discrimination work makes the club stand out. We don't just put a banner up saying "Kick out racism" or "Kick out homophobia". We actually get out there and, for example, play Stonewall FC. And that's the right thing to do.'

There's also a sharp grasp of marketing at work here at Champion Hill. 'We have a ground that can hold three thousand,' reasons Hart, 'so all the while you haven't got three thousand in, you might as well give out free tickets. People will come and they'll spend money on food, on drink, on merchandise. And next time they'll be paying on the gate. Maybe a third of those will come again occasionally. Maybe ten per cent will come back regularly. And maybe five per cent will become season ticket-holders. The proof's in the pudding. We've gone from crowds of three hundred a few years ago to averaging just over a thousand last season.' It's the same logic that, through the placement of enticing, loss-leading products at the store entrance, wouldn't be unfamiliar to the marketeers from the branch of Sainsbury's directly behind the main stand.

Another member of the supporters' trust board, Mishi Morath, is in full agreement about the effectiveness of such initiatives. 'We don't lose money on it. Not a penny. When those people come through that gate, they're filling empty space. A hundred per cent of nothing is nothing. They wouldn't be here otherwise. Also, we have a very deliberate policy here of having really cheap concessions. It's only £4 for over-sixties, twelve- to eighteen-year-olds, students, unwaged, local NHS workers, blue-light services, armed forces . . .'

Such community-facing innovations seem strikingly obvious and logical, ideas that any other team could adopt. But others don't seem to be as sharp-witted as Dulwich, whose level of progressivism stands out at a non-league level defined by caution and tradition. Like Hart, Morath despairs of the external perceptions of the club. 'You do one thing that's outside the box and it's all "Look at them. They're all left-wing."' He shakes his head at the miscasting. 'It's not left-wing. It's doing what's right for your community.'

A self-diagnosed 'natural-born pessimist', Morath is the polar opposite of the Johnny-come-recently brigade, a Dulwich Hamlet veteran of more than four decades. Highs, lows and all points in between. As such, he's the perfect person to assess the impact of the arrivistes on the club's more established fanbase.

'I've been coming down here since I was a seven-year-old. I grew up on the council estate over the back, so they were my local team. We're getting so many more people here now for so many different reasons. The football, the atmosphere, the disillusionment with the professional game . . . Some people coming down here have never been to football before. Other clubs have a pop at us, the old-school fans with a bit of a chip on their shoulder. "Look at them. They're not proper fans." I say "Yeah, but look at the crowds we're getting." In the old days – and I'm talking seven or eight years ago – I went to away games not because I wanted to, but because I was *expected* to. It was a chore that I'd never look forward to. Now I get a buzz. I've been coming down here for more than forty years and I'm having the best time I've ever had. How can you criticise that?'

And the crowds that help provide that buzz are a reflection of the changing make-up of Morath's East Dulwich backyard. 'The crowds were only a hundred and fifty midweek, two hundred and fifty on a Saturday. When a few new people started coming in, it wasn't so much distrust as curiosity – "Who are they?" You start talking to one or two of them and they start going to away games. Then it snowballs.

'Like it or not, it is a much more middle-class area these days. We have an influx of people into the area who want to come along to the football but can't afford Football League prices. On our terraces we have Shrewsbury fans, Northampton fans, Portsmouth fans, Southampton fans, Man City fans . . . That's the beauty of non-league. It's OK to have two sides. But they're all passionate Dulwich fans to me.

'Don't get me wrong,' he concludes, with a big smile. 'We don't all like each other, but it's like that in all walks of life. But we all get on. There's a common cause.'

The crowds keep growing, the fanbase keeps widening. Al Crane, who's downed tools for the day now that kick-off is approaching and he's needed to run affairs in the old garden shed for the last time, knows the tills in that new shop will continue to do tidy business. 'We get new fans every single week. We sell dozens and dozens of scarves at every game. Surely everyone's got a scarf by now, haven't they? It just keeps going on and on, with new people coming to every game.' It's more usual than not for Crane and his colleagues to sell 100 scarves at a home game. Indeed, throughout the week, the navy and pink scarves seem to be de rigueur in the cafés and on the school runs of East Dulwich.

Run by the supporters' trust, the shop hands over 50 per cent of profits into the club's coffers, albeit with the proviso that they have to approve what the revenue is earmarked for. Duncan Hart explains that the trust's two key objectives are for Dulwich to have a permanent home and to be under fan ownership. The club is currently owned by a property development company, a situation that, in normal circumstances, would ring loud and piercing alarm bells in the ears of the diehards. After all, in such an increasingly gentrified area, the Champion Hill site is a prime location for development. Indeed, the owners do want to build flats here, but only once the football ground has been shifted towards the far side of the site. Then the developers, the ones who rescued Dulwich from administration back in 2014, would place the club into fan ownership. The best of both worlds for all concerned.

That's a goal that's somewhere in the middle distance. For the time being, all efforts are focused on Dulwich climbing out of the Ryman Premier and into the Conference South. After topping the table as recently as the first week of last month, their form has dipped of late – or, as Mishi Morath poetically puts it, 'we've been shit for weeks'. There's the chance of a play-off six-pointer today, though, with the visit of Tonbridge. The fixtures computer has come up trumps, scheduling an Easter Monday encounter that pits fifth place against third, the best-supported team in the division against the next-best-supported team.

Champion Hill is filling up nicely. Behind the goal, Dulwich's famed noisy section – the Rabble – are finding their voices. This afternoon, there appear to be no drums being beaten nor trumpets blown (nor, indeed, ukuleles strummed), so they'll be singing a cappella – that is, when they're not accompanied by the percussive whirring of the air ambulance buzzing back and forth from nearby King's College Hospital.

The Tonbridge fans have brought a bass drum, but it stays largely silent for the duration. Dulwich are two-up within ten minutes, giving the visiting fans very little to celebrate for the rest of the afternoon. By contrast, the home fans are relentlessly noisy; the terraces fall silent for no more than four or five seconds at a time. Much of their output is directed at the Tonbridge keeper, who has tied some of his hair into a pigtail on top of his head – a popular option in La Liga, but not so much in the Ryman Prem. To the tune of 'He's Got the Whole World in His

Hands', the Rabble burst into song: 'He's got a rat's tail on his head . . .' The lyrics are swiftly altered to offer an update on the scoreline ('He's got two goals in his net . . .'), before another variant references the keeper's thermal undergarments ('He's got his mum's tights on his legs . . .'). To his credit, when he collects his bag and drink from the back of the net at half-time, the Tonbridge shot-stopper joins in the song.

The sense of bonhomie stretches right around the ground. There's a distinct absence of alpha-male strutting. Indeed, outside of a Women's Super League fixture, there's probably no ground where such a high proportion of the crowd is female. Similarly, there's a much stronger racial mix on the sidelines. And, as expected, the tribes aren't quite how Dulwich's detractors would have it. For every hipster who looks like he's come straight from central casting's Shoreditch offices, there's a rocker or a dread. The beard quotient is no higher than at South Shields or Eastleigh or Didcot Town or anywhere else for that matter. Champion Hill proves a draw for dogs and pushchairs, too.

This diverse, motley crew is certainly a departure from the typical non-league demographic of older men grumbling about how the modern game is a pale reflection of what it used to be. And those here this afternoon who might well fit that particular profile seem to have no quarrel with the club's new ways – certainly if the pair of pensionable-age Dulwich traditionalists tucking into their non-traditional bratwurst are anything to measure against.

The Rabble changes ends at half-time, during which time I chat with two of its newer members. Sophie and her partner Neil are in their late twenties (teacher and retail analyst, respectively) and started coming to Champion Hill halfway through last season after they moved to the area. Neil was well-versed in matters non-league, having spent a fair proportion of his teens following his hometown team, Needham Market. Sophie was at first reluctant to come; her modest experience of football spectatorship was limited to the one time her dad took her, at the age of thirteen, to see his beloved Birmingham City. It was a testosterone-fuelled experience that scared her off ever since ('I learned some new swear words that day'). The first Dulwich match that she and Neil came to, a 4-1 victory over Leatherhead on New Year's Day last season, was a revelation for her.

'I never knew going to the football could be like that. And I'm sure it isn't like that in too many places. Everyone was just so happy – and not just because of the scoreline. There was no sense of menace or danger. I felt at ease straight away. We didn't know anyone in the area at the time, but the people here were so welcoming. When my dad came to stay with us, we obviously brought him down here and he loved it, too. I bought him a Dulwich scarf for Christmas and they're his second team now. And he's just bought my stepmum one for her birthday. We're all converts.' So, that's two of Al Crane's impressive scarf sales accounted for.

When the choir strikes up again to usher in the second half, Sophie throws herself into the chants with admirable gusto. What's even more commendable is that, despite a comparatively short amount of time as a Dulwich fan, she seems to be word-perfect on all the songs. Just as some of the Bow Badgers on Hackney Marshes, these newcomers are flushed with a sense of belonging that might otherwise be absent in a strange part of the city.

The song that's sung with most feeling, most pride, salutes Edgar Kail, popularly considered to be Dulwich's greatest-ever player. This is no small accolade, bearing in mind the future professionals who learned their trade on the Champion Hill turf; these include not only Peter Crouch but also a fair few who went on to play for Crystal Palace, among them Alan Pardew, Andy Gray, George Ndah and – albeit after just a single appearance for the Hamlet in a pre-season friendly – Ian Wright.

It's partly the fact that Kail never turned professional, never turned his back on Dulwich, that accounts for his near-sainted reputation. Plus all those goals. Despite scoring 400+ times for the club between 1915 and 1933 – and despite three full caps as the last-ever non-league player to represent England – Kail elected to keep football as his unpaid pastime, a respite from a busy job as a drinks salesman. That loyalty is rewarded nearly a century later by the voices of a few hundred Dulwich fans ringing out the tribute. 'And could he play!' is the massed refrain. They're taking history's word for it that he could.

As stirring as the singing is, it's not conducive to getting babies off to a post-feed sleep. One mother, a newborn strapped to her chest, jiggles from one foot to the other to provide suitably undulating movements, while on the opposite touchline a young father is adopting a different tactic, marching around the perimeter of the pitch while pushing a pram at some speed. It takes three laps for junior to drop off.

Those kids will surely be the Dulwich diehards of future decades, the next generation to sing the praises of Edgar Kail's excellence and exploits. Certainly the passionate partisans who define this club – the polar opposite of those objective, unaffiliated groundhoppers – won't be abandoning their posts any time soon. The locals, whether old-timers or arrivistes, have no need to go anywhere else. Similarities with Chris Freer and his ilk can be found, though. These fans are collecting the intangible, too – amassing a collection of shared memories shot through with a sense of community and neighbourhood identity rarely found in the capital.

On the final whistle, the passion doesn't relent. Big gobs of rain, shortly to become tough beads of hail, fail to silence the chorus. This is the soundtrack to a home win, to a play-off campaign getting back on the rails.

It's a soundtrack that continues out of the ground, past Sainsbury's and down Edgar Kail Way towards the station. It's also a soundtrack that drowns out Al Crane's garden shed shutting its creaking hatch for the last time.

* * *

With the deftest of flicks, the Syrian winger steps inside the approaching Eritrean left-back and fires the firmest of crosses towards the small Glaswegian striker. His header does justice to the inch-perfect delivery, looping over the boots-in-glue keeper and into the top corner.

This is just a normal Thursday night on the synthetic pitch of Whitehill Secondary School in Glasgow's East End – the alma mater of the singer Lulu, actor Bill Paterson and, most appropriately, Scotland international midfielder James McArthur. Tonight, it's occupied by United Glasgow, a club set up to offer the opportunity for the disenfranchised living in Scotland's biggest city to play football, especially refugees and asylum seekers. Although there are no formal ties between them, the club's anti-discrimination work would mark them out as kindred spirits with our friends in Dulwich.

To describe United Glasgow as an international outfit would be a gross understatement. Since forming five years ago, no fewer than fifty-seven different nationalities have worn the club's colours. At present, the men's Saturday side includes players from Somalia, Ghana, Sudan, Syria and Spain, as well as a couple of Kurdish players. The Sunday team has particularly strong African representation, among them regulars from Congo, Zambia and Guinea-Bissau.

'I think it's a real testament to our coaches that they can put together coherent football teams out of so many players from so many different backgrounds and with so many different languages.' Alan White is on the touch-line here at Whitehill tonight. He's the club's founder and chairman, and a strong advocate for the healing power of football. As he explains, the lives of some of its players away from the football field can be rather grim, existences well worth escaping – for ninety minutes, at least.

'One of our players hadn't been to training for a few weeks. I just thought he'd joined another team. Then he turned up again about a month and a bit later. "I'm really, really sorry I've missed training. I've been at Dungavel detention centre. They didn't believe my asylum case and they detained me for six weeks until my lawyer could get me out." I was like, "Well, you know what? Missing training isn't the worst thing in the world. I can't really drop you for that."'

United Glasgow are committed to providing very low-cost – or even zero-cost – organised football. With those in the asylum system unable to work while their case is under consideration, the club helps out by providing boots, shin guards and the like. Social-security provision is insufficient while they wait to hear their fate. 'The government expects them to only make one trip on a bus per week,' explains White, 'which is ironic because just to get to and from the Home Office – to sign on to prove you've not run away – is two journeys.

'In 2000, the government set up a dispersal programme to, as they put it, take the brunt of immigration off London. Central government offered funding to various local authorities around the country to offer up housing and services to asylum seekers. Glasgow was the only city in Scotland to take it up. Housing that had been deemed unsuitable for human habitation was made available. And because there was no consultation with the local community, there was a lot of resentment in the early 2000s. The flats had previously been emptied, but now the council had the money to put things back in, like white goods. So there was this perception that the asylum seekers were getting something for free. It wasn't the case. It's just that these homes were being made habitable again.'

Outside perceptions are difficult to reverse. Asylum seekers are the recurrent punchbag for tabloid leader-writers – demonised and dehumanised, a faceless mass depicted with arms outstretched, palms upturned. On the take and on the make. But the club will do all it can to reverse these perceptions. Up until the start of this season, the men's Saturday side played in the Scottish Unity Football League, a broadly internationalist set-up but one not without its limitations. They now line up as part of a more mainstream organisation – the Western Scotland Amateur Football League. This is the place to truly test, and possibly challenge, opinions and stereotypes.

'We were really worried about what would happen when we took a team with significant numbers of Middle Eastern, African and Asian players into a predominantly white league. You know, amateur football in Glasgow can be pretty aggressive. And one of the things about the new league is that we don't just play in Glasgow. We go to tiny villages in Ayrshire or further north. These aren't exactly metropolises with bustling, diverse communities. We expected to have had more issues, but it's been all right so far.'

Jazz Rogers, the player-coach of United Glasgow's

women's team, is also on the touchline tonight, rolling a ball back and forth with her foot, clearly itching to join in with the training drills. She explains a simple, time-worn approach to challenge preconceptions. 'You ask someone, "What is that person wearing on their feet?" "Football boots." "What are you wearing on your feet?" "Football boots." "What do you think they're going to do?" "Play football." "What are you going to do?" "Play football." It works really well in challenging people from the off.'

Often just getting the opposition to talk to the united colours of United Glasgow does the job. 'We have a well-established connection with a team from the Western Isles,' explains White, 'a team of fishermen and the like. The first time we went out there, they sat down and spoke to some of the players from Somalia and Guinea-Bissau and places like that. They were astounded and horrified about how they were being treated. They said "Why don't you just come and live here . . . ?"'

Issues of integration and acceptance also raise their head *within* the club. 'In the Unity League, it was very much a case of there being an Afghan team, an African team, a Chinese team . . . Our whole belief was that you don't break down barriers by making these teams play *against* each other. You break down barriers by getting them to play *together*.'

Rogers nods her agreement. 'If people are in a new environment, they'll drift towards what's familiar. So when you're coaching, you have to say "You go there, you go there". But it works really well. And even if you can't communicate verbally, there is a way of communicating on a pitch playing football. You do find ways of bonding.'

'We've had some pretty beautiful friendships,' says White, 'and some pretty beautiful centre-half pairings. East End of Glasgow and Mogadishu. Shetland and Accra . . .'

The international language of football is being spoken right now on the school pitch. The last horizontal strip of late orange sun is disappearing behind the tenement block beyond the twelve-foot perimeter fence, turning the sky from powder-blue to violet. The floodlights pop into action. A few more players drift towards the session; the team's time-keeping isn't that immaculate, unlike that of the clock-watching school caretaker who will later bring the training session to an abrupt end by plunging the pitch into darkness the second it turns 9.30 pm.

Abdul, the cross-supplying Syrian winger, looks the best player on show tonight. When he arrived, a chill was beginning to descend on the evening after a glorious Glasgow day and he wanted to play in his jeans, but the coach insisted he find a pair of shorts among the various kitbags. He did, however, keep his stripy pullover on. His lithe movement and immaculate distribution prove that the wearing of comfortable knitwear is no restriction to showcasing your raw talent.

During a break in the session, Abdul explains his foot-balling back-story. 'I had a contract from Qatar, but my father told me no. He closed the doors. His brother was a good footballer in Syria but when he retired, he didn't have anything. No one paid him every week like a professional. He just played for a jersey and boots. It was hard for him after he retired. He didn't have a job. So my dad told me I shouldn't want to be like my uncle. He wanted me to study, so I did electrical engineering in my country. I was in my second year when the war started and then I came here. I've been studying English and I've applied for university. Hopefully I'm going to be doing chemical engineering. I'm getting a scholarship from the university.'

Abdul's not the only player with pedigree who's stepped over United Glasgow's threshold. White recalls one player who was with the club for a while before revealing that he used to play for Paris Saint-Germain's under-19s; another player, a Ugandan who previously plied his trade in Kenya's top flight, moved on from Glasgow to sign for non-league Tooting & Mitcham. 'We do have a few mercurial players in our Saturday team who are a joy to watch, but if you do have a very good player, you don't have him for long. If there's an opportunity to get paid for playing, who's to stop them?' The tension between collective improvement and individual ambition, between team and self, is omnipresent, no matter what level.

The club's work in unifying people through football takes on extra significance bearing in mind Glasgow's reputation for being divided in two by the sport. 'It's good to see the city celebrated,' says Barry, a Glaswegian centre-half for the Sunday team. Not that liberal means uncompetitive. United Glasgow's approach is far from softly-softly, gently-gently. 'No one's lacking passion or determination,' he explains, 'or that little bit of bite that you need to play football at any sort of level. But it's an awful lot more positive. I've played for other teams in the past and some of the attitudes and behaviour were too much. I've seen a player run after a referee with a bag of bricks. You don't get that here.'

A grounding in the politics and culture of Old Firm derbies is given to newcomers to the city. 'We do try to educate our players about what and what not to do when Celtic play Rangers,' explains White. 'Which bars not to walk past in a certain shirt. But, to be perfectly honest, the level of their interest in Scottish football is minimal. You don't get too many Sudanese Celtic supporters or Zambian Rangers fans.'

United Glasgow's players just want to play. Football is where they can regain their dignity after the harsh hand they've been dealt. 'I didn't know anybody when I arrived in Glasgow,' says Abdul, anxious to get back to firing those firm crosses into the box. 'So football was very important. It got me into the community and I've made so many friends through it.

'Football is a way of life, a language. It doesn't matter where you're from, what your origin is. You step onto the pitch and you lose everything else. You forget it all.'

* * *

In the end, there was no Stuart Pearce-style, big-name signing heading to the Chew Valley and ninety minutes of sporting ignominy in Bishop Sutton's colours. It wasn't for a lack of trying. Several household-name former pros were approached (even including an ex-captain of England), but for whatever reasons – a lack of fitness, a lack of inclination, the realisation of just how far away Somerset was – they chose not to grace Lakeview with their presence. Chairman George sadly had no reason to cordon off a parking space for a top-of-the-range supercar carrying a member of footballing royalty.

But maybe, just maybe, that one-night-only, marquee signing wasn't necessary. The seemingly impossible might just be happening before our very eyes. We're into stoppage time at Bishop Sutton's home match against Roman Glass St George and the regulars standing just along from the dugout daren't say a word, nor move a muscle. The team – crammed even more full with teenagers than ever tonight – have been defending a 1-0 lead from the fourteenth minute when a dipping long-range effort from that reliable winger Josh Dakwa put them ahead. Since then, nerves have been steadily tightening and fingernails chewed down to stumps. No one can remember the last time Bishop Sutton were in front for so long in a match. In fact, no one can remember the last time they were in front at all.

The home side have even survived a Roman Glass penalty, Sutton's seventeen-year-old keeper making the save of a hero. He's been outstanding tonight, the reason why – with seconds left – the team finds itself in such uncharted territory.

One last save, one last punt up towards the farthest corner of the pitch and there it is. Three long blasts of the referee's whistle and the unimaginable shame of going an entire season without winning a single league game has been avoided. It's been a long time coming, stretching back to November of last season. Sixteen months. 492 days. forty-eight matches. That woeful record is over, erased in ninety-odd minutes of hard-fought, bodies-on-the-line rearguard action.

In a season that's tested the resolve, spirit and possibly even the very existence of this football club, this is their cup final moment. Players sink to their knees, others high-five, most are whooping. Colin Merrick and Steve Laker, manager and ex-manager, hug each other. Collective delight, collective relief.

By the time the modest clump of fans makes its way round to the clubhouse, the songs of celebration are already playing in the bar. The volume's turned right up to make sure the victorious players can hear it in the dressing rooms out the back. Chumbawamba ('We'll be singing / When we're winning . . .') are followed by McFadden & Whitehead's 'Ain't No Stoppin' Us Now'. This is a compilation that's clearly been held back in reserve for more than a year, a layer of dust wiped off the CD case on the sound of the final whistle.

When they emerge to collect their sausages and chips to cheers from the faithful, the players look exhausted but exhilarated. They might still be seventeen points adrift, still nailed on for that bottom-of-the-table finish, but, tonight, that's of no concern. This is a win that feels like a promotion.

George Thorne, the young defender who's been so impressive all season, is the one most stoked at the victory. Despite his gangliness, he's been a rock at the centre of defence. Indeed, still a month shy of his eighteenth birthday, he was the second most experienced member of the back four tonight, a defensive line-up that also included two sixteen-year-olds. To offer a sense of their youth, this pair were born just a few months before the millennium. The veteran striker leading the line tonight is a full three decades older than them.

Thorne can't stop beaming. This season, he's had the toughest imaginable baptism into men's football, being a regular in a leaky defence that's overseen that lengthy, lengthy series of spirit-sapping reversals. Call it the blind optimism of youth, but Thorne's outlook remains strangely undented by the whole experience.

'If I'd stayed playing under-18s, I wouldn't have improved as a player. I've been learning in every single game. Now I feel so much more confident on the ball. I've got to thank Steve for initially letting me have the game time. He could have just kept me on the bench. He's put a lot of trust in me. If ever I do make it, he's definitely getting a shout-out in my autobiography!'

When your team's getting stuffed left, right and centre, when the strikers you're marking are scoring with ease, it would be the easiest thing to drop your head, to lessen your commitment, to slip away from the club. A good few players have done just that this season. But Thorne has stood tall, allowing the experience to take him from boy to man. After this season of multiple pummellings, he now knows how to cope with defeat and dejection. Character development is swiftest in times of adversity.

'We've never seen Messi lose every game, have we? It would be interesting to see how those kind of players would cope if they did.'

With this A-level student's sights set on medicine and its seven years of intense study, Thorne will need to find a balance between academia and football if he's to continue his upward trajectory through the leagues. 'I'll have to juggle my time. The dream is for football to pay my university fees. That would be incredible.' Certainly just a couple of months of the most modest Premier League wages would wipe out any student debt in one fell swoop. The future, though – both immediate and distant – remains unwritten. If Thorne ends up studying at Bristol, he'll surely reject the overtures of university football to return to Lakeview, a fixture of the Bishop Sutton defence again next season. After all, no season could be quite so harrowing as this one. 'It sucks when you lose every week. That's why tonight I'm so buzzing. I've got school in the morning but I don't care . . .'

There's an obvious irony that everyone is avoiding. All season, the talk has been about getting some experience in the team, about acquiring two or three seasoned players with the nous and worldliness to get the club back to winning ways. In the end, it was the Bishop Sutton side with the youngest average age this season that managed it. Alan Hansen was proved wrong again. You *can* win something with kids. Admittedly he wasn't talking about a bottom-of-the-table clash in the Toolstation Western League Division One, but still . . .

Chairman George places a large jug of orange squash

on the players' table. 'Is that all we get for a win?' squawks Sam Downes, one of the senior players, who doubles up as the youth team manager. 'Squash?!' Bearing in mind the tender ages of half the team, it's all that a fair few of them are legally entitled to.

It's not quite all they get. A chocolate Swiss roll emerges from the kitchen and is placed in the centre of the table. To the victors, the spoils. This is their win bonus.

Wise men say only fools rush in, though. If Chairman George has been holding back that particular treat until this long-awaited victory finally arrived, someone might just want to check the best-before date first.

9

APRIL

The stone-turning starmaker

Ken Ryder sets his phone down on the pub table, knowing that any attempt at conversation over the next hour will be punctuated by a series of pings announcing incoming texts or voicemail messages. Normally he'd be taking these calls on his car's speakerphone, but today Sheffield Wednesday's head of recruitment has been marooned. His hard-working Nissan Qashqai – a vehicle that covers in the region of 40,000 miles each year – is in the garage for some much-needed work. Its equally hard-working driver, for today at least, is forced to stay on the Lancashire side of the Pennines, the side that he calls home.

Ryder isn't just any old head of recruitment. After three and a half decades as chief scout for Middlesbrough, Oxford United, Wolves, Swindon Town and now Wednesday, he's a man with a particular affinity for non-league football. And at no time was this affinity sharper than during his five-year spell in Wiltshire. For it was then that his pickaxe hit a diamond in the Wessex League's Premier Division, nine storeys down. That diamond was future England international Charlie Austin.

'You know when you've seen The One,' he explains, his Northumbrian accent untouched by living in and around Bury for several decades. 'It doesn't come around very often. I remember wanting to shout from the rooftops about Charlie but I couldn't. That would have alerted everybody else and spoilt the deal. Of course, every chairman would love to find another Charlie Austin or another Jamie Vardy, but they don't grow on trees. You've got to go and find them. It's about putting the legwork in. It's about not being afraid to go somewhere on a Friday night instead of going home. You've got to get out and turn the stones.'

The success of strikers like Vardy, Austin and, to a lesser extent, Crystal Palace's Dwight Gayle, caused plenty of league clubs to line up the semi-pro ranks in their crosshairs during January's transfer window. The in-form players were worth a gamble in the winter hunting season. Up the M1 from Ryder's office at Hillsborough, Barnsley were the busiest, taking three non-leaguers into the Football League. These included two strikers currently among the goals: at twenty-four, Shaun Tuton's capture from Vardy's old club FC Halifax Town suggested an attempt to prompt history to repeat itself, while the teenager Bradley Ash, signed from Conference South side Weston-super-Mare, represented a more long-term investment.

While the window remained ajar, Premier League clubs were also snooping around the non-league fringes. Norwich signed a pair of young attacking midfielders from Dartford and Dulwich Hamlet respectively, but it was Spurs who made the purchase that caused eyebrows to replicate the shape of the Wembley arch. Ebbsfleet youth-team starlet Shilow Tracey moved across the Thames to White Hart Lane, despite his first-team experience being restricted to a single substitute appearance of four minutes' duration.

In this season of Vardy-mania, a low-risk punt appeared to be the best policy. No chief scout fancied a carpeting from his manager or chairman at some point in the future, an inquisition as to why a newly minted household name had slipped through the net a year or two previous.

Sheffield Wednesday resisted this winter's gold rush, instead relying on Ryder's patience and wisdom, the attributes of a man who first started scouting for Middlesbrough during the 1980–81 season. At the time, he was still otherwise employed as an envelope salesman. 'I'm always open to non-league, but the problem we have is – because of the Charlie Austins, because of the Jamie Vardys – non-league clubs now think they're going to make a lot of money. They've suddenly become very good at deals! And it's right that they think like that. I don't blame them. It's probably their one and only chance to set the club up for life.

'And I've noticed that a lot of agents have non-league players now. I've been watching a non-league player in Ireland who didn't have an agent when I started watching him. Suddenly he's got one and suddenly his wage demands are six grand a week. And the kid's part-time. How do you justify that? How's he going to get that money at seventeen years of age?'

Even if a league club, like Wednesday, has dedicated non-league scouts, it's still most likely strikers who grab their initial attention, who float to the surface. They're easier to spot from afar. Dependable, unspectacular performances by right-backs or defensive midfielders don't create even the limited headlines that non-league football makes. Goals do, though. And a rapidly accumulating goal tally does so even more. Ryder nods his agreement. 'Plus, every club is looking for a striker, everyone's looking for a goalscorer. I don't care what level you're at. If you're a defender, you've got four chances of getting a game. If you're a striker, you're a striker. You're a one-off.

'I still think there's a gem lurking somewhere. In fact, I just had a phone call yesterday about a kid at Harrogate. Somebody else has told me about a striker at Chorley and I'm also looking at someone at Tonbridge Angels. His dad phoned me up and asked whether there was a chance of his son getting watched. And I'm happy to agree to that because you just never know how good that kid is. It's best to have players checked out. You never know what level they're at, what physical attributes they've got. They might well step up. It's no good looking back and saying "Bloody hell, someone told me about him three weeks ago and I missed it". So I'll do it. I'll get someone to go there and watch.'

If it's as simple as making sure you've got a pair of reliable eyes watching a player, why didn't Charlie Austin have a gaggle of suitors forming a disorderly queue for his signature? 'Without sounding disrespectful, I think there are a lot of lazy scouts who do not want to go and pay ten quid to get in and stand on a wet touchline, getting soaked through. I call them "social grazers". They're quite happy to go and sit in Old Trafford, but they're not happy to stand next to a pitch on a Sunday morning and watch a player. I am. I'll go anywhere. I can't remember the last time I was at a Premier League game. On a Saturday, I'll watch an academy game in the morning, then pick up a lower-league or non-league game in the afternoon.'

It was certainly Ryder's willingness to put in the leg-work, to go the extra miles, that paid off where Austin was concerned. Bournemouth had been keen on the then Poole Town striker, but were hamstrung by a transfer embargo. Ryder took full advantage, driving down to the south coast to run the rule over the player.

'At Swindon, we'd just come out of administration and Andrew Fitton, who was a brilliant chairman, just let me do whatever I wanted. He trusted my judgement, he trusted my experience. I went through the non-league top goalscorers and noticed Charlie had scored numerous goals for Poole. When I went to watch him, I paid to get in. I just stood with the punters and earwigged what they said. I listened. And all I could hear was Charlie's name being mentioned. It was absolutely throwing it down, but he scored four or five and I thought "Oooooh".

'I rang Danny Wilson, who was Swindon's manager at the time, on the way home. I couldn't wait. He told me not to get too excited. "Danny, I'm telling you. He's the real deal. He's got everything." Then I did a thing that I never ever do. I sent a scout to watch Poole, but didn't tell him who he was supposed to be watching. I didn't give him a specific target. I said, "Just have a look". He rang me at half-time. "It's the number nine for Poole, isn't it . . . ?"'

Austin – at that time working as a hod-carrier for his dad – was soon paying League One Swindon a visit, thanks to the swift-moving Ryder. 'I rang the Poole vice-chairman on a Saturday morning and said, "I'd like to offer a trial to Charlie Austin, if you wouldn't mind". He said, "Would you mind if I didn't tell him until after today's game? It's an important match. We're going for promotion. I'll mention it to Charlie afterwards and, if he's interested, he'll ring you." Five past five that afternoon, I had a voice on the phone saying, "What time do you want me?"

'He came in on the Monday morning and we played Swansea under-21s. Billy Paynter was just coming back from injury and between them they scored nine goals. Danny Wilson said to me, "We'd better sign this kid". Within three days, he was a Swindon Town player.' He was an instant success at the County Ground and, after thirty-one goals over a sixteen-month spell in Wiltshire, Austin moved on up to Championship challengers Burnley. The raw talent that Ryder and Wilson had paid £10,000 for had been polished, in double-quick time, into an enviable commodity with a high yield. Swindon's coffers were now better off to the tune of around £1.6 million.

Today, the starched and pressed uniform of the club official – one usually worn to impress the parents of a prospective young player – remains on its hanger. The comfortable leisurewear favoured by the football world stays in its drawer, too. Ryder's checked shirt and jeans indicate that he's off duty this lunchtime. Partially, at least. 'It's an eight-day-a-week job. You never switch off. My phone never stops. It's on 24/7 because you never know what the next phone call's going to be.' Right on cue, there's another ping from the phone, another approach from an agent anxious for his client to be added to the hall of fame of this particular starmaker.

Ryder's easy conversation is littered with the household names he's worked with – Jack Charlton is mentioned here, Glenn Hoddle there – but never in an ostentatious, name-dropping way. He reserves as much respect for the game's lesser lights as he does the brightest shining stars. This is a man who knows everyone and everything. And, at his age and stature (Ryder was beckoned from retirement three years ago to reshape Wednesday's recruitment structure), it would be easy for him to simply command proceedings from the lofty perch of his office. The world of service-station dinners and late-night motorway closures could be left to those younger, hungrier men.

Ryder has nine such men under his control, scouts placed in strategic locations around the country, from Scotland to Hertfordshire and at several equidistant points in between. Four of these exclusively study Wednesday's upcoming opposition; the remainder follow the romantic pursuit of discovering the heroes of the future. It's the thrill of this chase – possibly chasing something that isn't even there – that warms their souls on cold, unforgiving plastic seats at the likes of Carshalton Athletic or Solihull Moors or North Ferriby United. The quest is so irresistible that Ryder, despite – or, rather, because of – having hit gold with Austin, can't give it up himself just yet.

'I was looking at individual players last night at an under-21 game. I'll be at Blackburn on Saturday, doing the same. I was at Wolves last week looking at players we might want to bring in. We've got to keep the cogs moving as we don't know what league we'll be in next season. At the minute, we've got a thirty-seven-man first-team squad, most of whom are on longish contracts, so if we stay in the Championship, we'll be set up. But if we get promoted, I don't know what we'll do. The Premier League is a different ball game. Wages go through the roof. In my first two years at Wednesday, certain agents wouldn't contact me. Now, because we've got a millionaire chairman, agents are getting in touch who would have never darkened our doorstep before.'

Not that the bottomless pockets of Wednesday's owner – the boss of the world's biggest seafood manufacturer – mean that hunting for bargains in non-league becomes a redundant activity. Two of Ryder's scouts are dedicated to scouring the semi-pro scene in search of rough-edged promise that could be polished. He knows he's blessed by their presence on his staff.

'The scout I have who lives in Luton can spot a

footballer five miles away with a blindfold on. I don't tell him where to go.' The talents of a self-reliant scout, granted the freedom to roam, come cheap. 'All he wanted from me was a coat and a book. I took him down a club coat and an old scouting book that I had. "That's me done," he said. "That's fine." He just wanted a coat to keep dry, with a club badge on it to let people know who he was working for. Happy as Larry.'

Not all scouts wear their club's logo as a conspicuous badge of honour. As Ryder did at Poole, merging into the crowd has its advantages. Sometimes a scout needs to employ the guile and deceit of a Le Carré spy to throw both the parent club and – more importantly – other clubs off the scent. 'When I was at Swindon, I was camped out at Alfreton, watching Aden Flint. They didn't know why I was going there that often. Their secretary said, "Do you want a season ticket? You're here every other week." They actually thought I was there for their centre-forward Liam Hearn, a prolific goalscorer who ended up going off to Grimsby.

'But it was Flint the centre-half who I was after – the guy at the back, not the guy at the front. He looked like a cross between a gazelle, a giraffe and Bambi. Six foot six, no coordination. I watched him and watched him and watched him. I was convinced we should buy him. So Danny Wilson said "I'll go and watch him. I'll put my hat on and go incognito." He walked through the door and bumped into John Ward and three other managers! We got him in the end, though.

'People think that Charlie Austin is the only one I've

unearthed. But he's not. I could give you a list as long as my arm. I've signed Matt Ritchie, I've signed Simon Cox, I've signed Michael Kightly, I've signed Aden Flint. But my best pound-for-pound signing was a lad called Les Robinson. Oxford paid £60,000 for him – a right full-back who played for them for ten years. He was never going to be an international footballer, but I think he was players' player of the year eight seasons in a row.

'It's not always the big signings that excite you. I look as far down as I can. There's always a chance that some-body's been released by a top club and has gone all the way down and is building back up again. And I just want to be there if this guy comes back to life.

'People will be very quick to tell you that Sheffield Wednesday released Jamie Vardy, but they're not quick to tell you he was fourteen at the time. He's now twenty-nine. It wasn't that we released him at twenty-five because he was no good! But that's part of the process. Charlie Austin got released by Reading because he wasn't big enough. He's six foot two now and has scored goals at the top level.'

If a player who found subsequent success had been let go or overlooked, critical eyes would be turned towards the recruitment team. It's a vulnerable, insecure line of work, as Ryder confirms. 'When a club's in trouble finan-cially, it's the foot soldier that gets sacked. But he's not been playing for them. He's not the one who's got them relegated. It's the highly paid, second-rate players who have.'

And, even if these easily expendable foot soldiers are

fortunate to find themselves in an ongoing arrangement, they're almost invariably beneficiaries of a raw deal. The lucky ones are on a retainer from the club they so faithfully serve, but most are doing it for mileage costs alone, somewhere between thirty and forty pence a mile. If the car of a particularly active part-time scout has clocked up 10,000 miles in a given financial year, mileage then reduces to 25 pence, a rate at which he might actually be losing money.

But the discernment of these experienced watchers is regarded as indispensable by Ryder in these times when the cold, hard science of technology is attempting to outmuscle, to *outprove*, instinct and intuition. Not that he himself is a tech-fearing Luddite, having been among the first to install the industry-standard Scout7 software into a professional football club.

'People took the mick and said I'd done away with my pen and paper, which was far from the truth. Analytics do have a place. They're probably a necessary evil. I think it's how you use them. I wouldn't want it to mean the demise of the foot-soldier scout. When you're watching on a big screen, even on Sky, you cannot see the big picture. If you're watching a centre-half and the game is on the telly, the camera will follow the play. What is that centre-half doing when the ball's in the opposition penalty area? Is he going to sleep? Is he attentive? Is he organising? You can't see that on the telly.

'Plus, if I'm an agent and you're a manager, I'm not going to send you a DVD of a goalkeeper letting the ball go through his legs. I'm going to send you clips of his best saves. Similarly, if I went to my boss and said "Have a look at that television screen because I want you to sign him", he'd think I was having a laugh. You have to go and watch. You don't get the feel of a player otherwise.

'Hours have to be put in – to do the research, to find out who they are, to check their character off the pitch. You're bringing them into a professional club that's totally different to what they've been used to. From training maybe twice a week, they're suddenly thrust into a completely different environment, so you've got to check their characters out as best you can before you bring them in.'

Even sitting here in his civvies, Ken Ryder could never be accused of not putting the hours in. The messages stacking up on his phone attest to that, as will the diagnosis of the mechanic currently tinkering with his high-mileage car. Wherever there's a match, there's always the outside possibility that one of the players could cut it in the big time. The hope of discovery is what drives the open-all-hours scout, the star-seeker who never lowers his telescope.

* * *

There's been nothing particularly remarkable about this Toolstation Northern Counties East League Division One match between Worsbrough Bridge Athletic and AFC Emley, little to set the pulse racing on a Monday night in South Yorkshire. It's a match that's been speedily rearranged after the previous week's postponement, when one of the goalmouths resembled a small bomb crater filled with rainwater. Emley, a side still trying to piece together a late surge towards a play-off place, are two-up at half-time. It's going with form. Nothing untoward about that.

Then the visitors bring on one of their subs, a short, stocky striker who immediately sets about the Worsbrough Bridge defence with hunger and gusto, notching a twenty-two-minute hat-trick as well as creating two other goals as Emley run out 7-0 winners. Reminiscent of Jermain Defoe in the way he gets the ball to his feet quickly and strikes it early, he shows both pace and neat finishing for his first and third goals. The second is a sweetly taken free-kick from twenty-five yards.

It's not as if it's particularly weak opposition he's terrorising; until recently, the two Worsbrough centre-halves were at Sheffield United. Even more remarkably, it's the striker's third game in as many days, including scoring in a cup final for his Sunday team twenty-four hours earlier. Small wonder he started on the bench this evening.

For any other player, this would be one of the games of their lives, an episode they'd hold dear for the rest of their playing days and beyond. But to Ashley Flynn, this twenty-six-year-old from Huddersfield, such a performance is comparatively run-of-the-mill, not especially noteworthy. For the three goals tonight were, respectively, his 78th, 79th and 80th goals of the season. The cliché 'he just can't stop scoring' has never been more appropriate. When Flynn is around, the ball hits the back of the net with ease and astonishing regularity, as if there was nowhere else for it to go.

Such prolific goalscoring has, of course, not failed to attract the attention of Ken Ryder's brethren. Scouts have been crowding Emley's touchlines all season, eyes and ears assessing whether Flynn could follow in the boot-prints of Vardy or Austin. Indeed, his early career shares similarities with that of the Leicester striker; he too was released by Sheffield Wednesday as a teenager. Well, not quite 'released' . . .

'It was my own error at Wednesday,' he admits after the game. 'I hated travelling and I enjoyed time with my friends. We used to train Tuesday and Thursday, and stay overnight in a hotel on Saturdays. We'd travel to the game on Sunday, I'd get back home that night and then go to school on Monday. I'd be too tired to see my friends on Monday night, and then it was back to training on Tuesday. I had no time for mates. So when it got to the end of the season, I told my mum that I didn't want to play at that level any more. "If I'm good enough, they'll pick me in a couple of years." But then I stopped playing. I lost interest altogether. I was only thirteen.'

That's another similarity with the arc of Vardy's career – an extended spell out of the game, experiencing life like any other teen, not cocooned in the cosseted, character-straightening world of the academy.

The presence of scouts in the crowd throughout the season hasn't turned Flynn's head nor has it affected his game. He seems quite matter-of-fact about the atten-tion. 'I've had quite a lot come to see me. Twenty-one clubs have wanted to sign me this year – a couple have been Conference North teams, plus a lot from the Evo-Stik Northern Premier. Some have been official approaches and some have been unofficial. I had one club offer to buy me a car.'

Flynn's goal rush demands the conclusion that he's simply way too good for this division. At times, the mismatch might resemble a teenager having a kickabout with some eight-year-olds. A player scoring thirty goals over a nine-month season suggests that a move up the non-league ranks is necessary for him to find his natural level. Flynn had reached that number by early October. On the second day of December, he'd chalked up the half-century.

The notion that Flynn is bigger and better than this division is one he would probably agree with. 'I scored four in three games against Hemsworth, who won the league, and I scored hat-tricks in both games against AFC Mansfield, who finished second. Bottesford finished third and I scored a couple against them too.' Twelve goals in seven games against the top three suggests the upward career move has to happen now.

'I'm banned from driving at the moment, so that's what's kept me at Emley more than anything. But I should get my licence back in July. I think it would be stupid not to go after I've had such a great season. It would be silly to stay.'

The driving ban may well be why attention hasn't come Flynn's way sooner. After all, who wants their main striker to be dependent on public transport or the kindness of friends and family? He's certainly proved his talent in years past; this current season is no anomaly, no one-off. A couple of seasons back, he scored forty-two for Emley – and this despite not playing between January and April due to recurrent hamstring problems. After that came a spell at Shaw Lane Aquaforce where he 'scored thirty-odd before me and the manager had a few disagreements'.

'Going professional would be my ambition now. That's why I need to try to play as high as I can. If I score goals there, I'm more likely to get a trial at a pro club. Hartlepool have been watching me all season. They were really interested. One of my friends from Huddersfield was contacted by [the then Hartlepool boss] Ronnie Moore. He told him, "He's class. If he's got better players around him, he'll score you goals." But a week and a half later, Ronnie Moore had been sacked. It's all about luck.

'There's a guy who comes to see our games quite often who brought four or five Guiseley season ticket-holders to come and watch us play Hull United. We were 2-0 down with nine men, but I managed to score twice and we drew. A couple of them told me I needed to contact the Guiseley manager to ask to train with them. They said, "You're better than our strikers". And Guiseley are in the Conference, so that was a nice little touch. If they think I can make it, then maybe I can.'

With those twenty-one interested clubs likely to be joined by a few more sniffing around at season's end, selecting which one is best for him at this stage of his career becomes a difficult task. 'I only want to go where I'm going to enjoy my football. I'd rather that than make loads of money.' He follows the equation through to its natural conclusion. 'If I'm not enjoying it, I know I won't be performing. And if I'm not performing, I'll be sat on the bench.

'I'm going on holiday in June for two weeks and pre-season will start at the beginning of July, so I guess I'm going to have to decide while I'm on holiday. If I decide at the start of the holiday, I can have a nice break and then come back and get straight into it.'

A willingness to travel to a club up to an hour and a half from his Huddersfield home – 'if it were a good club and it seemed right' – would put him in reach of the numerous sides dotted around Greater Manchester who play in the Conference North or the Northern Premier. But wherever Flynn's next move takes him, he has no intention of trimming down his day job as a legal executive.

'I'd probably stick with the hours I work, but be more flexible. I'd just save the football money and put it to one side. I've been on £10 a goal, but I end up just spending that in the club bar. I'd get a drink for my mate who'd bring me up there and I'd get one myself, a bag of crisps, a chocolate bar and it would be gone.'

It's Flynn's raw talent, rather than his dubious post-match diet, that has bagged him these eighty goals. Not that, though, it is officially eighty goals. A couple of days ago, Lincoln Moorlands Railway resigned from the league, unable to fulfil their remaining two fixtures of the season. Their record was expunged, their matches wiped from history. This means the two victories Emley chalked up against them now don't officially exist. More pointedly for Flynn, the seven goals he scored against them don't officially exist either. His tally, after tonight's game against Worsbrough Bridge, actually stands at seventy-three. Technically, at least, if not morally. 'I've put eighty balls in the net,' he pleads, as if I have the power to overturn the ruling, to nullify the league's regulations.

But whether it's seventy-three or eighty, this season Flynn has answered his critics, those who only know of him for one particular episode. Last season, he went viral on the internet – and not for a good reason.

In a match against Hemsworth Miners Welfare, Emley were awarded a penalty. Flynn stepped up to take it and elected to try a Panenka. Sadly, unlike those before him who'd successfully executed the nonchalant chip in moments of high pressure – the likes of Andrea Pirlo, Zinedine Zidane and the Czech midfielder after whom the kick was named – Flynn failed to fool the keeper. His soft-as-butter chip just offered a dolly catch into the Hemsworth keeper's grateful gloves.

That a tenth-tier player had chosen to take a penalty in this manner wouldn't normally have made any waves. It wouldn't have been headline news. But it happened before the disbelieving eyes of a sizeable contingent of groundhoppers, one of whom recorded the howler on his phone. Footage of what was quickly dubbed 'the worst penalty in the world ever' went global. He shakes his head at the icy pain of the memory. 'Everyone saw it. My friends in America were saying that their college students were even talking about it.'

After tonight, in the remaining two weeks of this season, Flynn doesn't score again. No goals in Emley's final four games marks his leanest, most barren spell of the entire campaign. But it's during their very last match where his shooting boots most significantly desert him. On the last day of April, the play-off final against Bottesford Town goes to penalties and Flynn is, naturally, among the initial five nominated to take a spot-kick.

But for a man who's been firing goals in from every conceivable angle and distance over the last ten months, he fails to hit the target from twelve yards out. It's an uncomfortable irony. Having sensibly decided not to attempt a Panenka this time, he instead skies the ball over the bar. One of his team-mates follows suit, consigning Emley to playing in the same division next season.

There, they'll surely be without their talismanic striker, the man whose overhit penalty will almost certainly be the last ball he'll kick in an Emley shirt. It's onwards and upwards for this particular hot property, the record-breaking striker with options aplenty.

* * *

Mark Palios's handshake is as firm and resolute as it was eight months ago, suggesting a sense of purpose and determination undented by a season that's felt a fair few potholes under its wheels. That same steely resolve, first observed back in August, remains.

We take the exact same seats in the main stand as we did back in those optimistic days of summer. In a couple of hours' time, Tranmere's final game of the regular season will kick off. Despite such a topsy-turvy campaign, the outside chance of scraping into the play-offs still remains. The equation is a simple one. They must win this afternoon and, down in Essex, Braintree Town must lose.

The season has been every bit as tricky as Palios was expecting. 'We knew what it was going to be like. You have to have acceptance of where you are – but purely as a basis from which to plan going forwards. I don't think that acceptance should ever be misunderstood as resignation. There's a difference between the two. I believe that you should have great expectations of life, but not great expectations of everybody else. *You* have to do it. Nothing comes for free.

'We'll review the season coldly and calmly, to look at how we've performed and what lessons we've learned. I've asked Sven-Göran Eriksson to do that in the past, so I can definitely ask Gary Brabin to do the same. If there wasn't a stand-out feature, then I'd be worried. But the season boils down to our home form. We've got a defined problem. We've just got to find an answer to it.'

More pressing is this afternoon's tea-time kick-off. The odds might be long and the optimism short, but plenty of variables ensure the destiny of that final play-off place isn't a given. While Braintree have home advantage, their relegation-haunted opponents Altrincham have to win to stand any chance of staying in the division. The fact that they won their last match 5-0 instils a little belief, however microscopic, into Tranmere hearts and minds.

The Merseysiders' own opponents are third-placed Grimsby, already safely ensconced in the play-offs. Rovers' perverse record – of getting better results against the division's stronger teams – suggests they shouldn't balk at who's lining up opposite them today. What's giving Tranmere the most wobbles is that they're playing here at Prenton Park, the 'fortress' where they've lost a full nine games this season, double the number of home defeats experienced by any of their play-off rivals. This afternoon, it could be a case of home disadvantage.

'The whole season is sullied by the fact that we play here in front of five thousand people and we haven't done well in front of those five thousand people. Yet when we've gone away, we've played in front of five hundred fans and they've seen us have a record season away from home.' Palios is right. While misfiring so chronically on home turf, perversely they're unbeaten on their travels since a scoreless draw at Boreham Wood all the way back in November.

'I'm not just being platitudinous or speaking in clichés, but all we can do this afternoon is win. Whatever happens at Braintree, happens. It'll be impossible not to know what's going on there because everybody will be clued into it. As a player, you know about it. But we'll do the best we can.

'I always look back down the season. For me, the most fantastic result was at Barrow. I've watched it several times and I still don't believe we're going to do it! In the ninetieth minute, when we were 3-1 down, my wife had her head in her hands and said that coming back to Tranmere was all my idea. In the ninety-fifth minute, when we were 4-3 up, it was all her idea again!

'When I rewatched it, I watched the players' reaction. When we scored the third to equalise, if that had been me it would have been "OK, lads. Let's just play out the last minute". But no. They ran into the net, picked up the ball, ran back with the ball and stuck it back down on the centre-spot. They clearly fancied it. So, today, I've no doubt our lads will dig in. I'm certain of that.'

The alternative to Tranmere's qualification for the play-offs is – to independent, impartial eyes, at least – rather irresistible: that later this evening, Braintree, one of the Conference's part-time outfits, would be just three matches from the Football League, from becoming one of the blessed ninety-two. The irony would be that Tranmere would lose out to one of those whose comparative lowliness was sneered at earlier in the season. James Norwood did warn his colleagues months ago that the men from Essex were no pushovers.

Back outside the ground, posters are up for the events that will keep folk flowing into the ground during the summer break. In three weeks' time, the Prenton Park turf will be given over, on consecutive nights, to fans of both Will Young and Status Quo.

Beneath the posters, the Tranmere faithful pay their unstinting respect to Johnny King's statue. For the last few weeks, they've said it with flowers. On the last day of March, on the same morning that Ronnie Corbett's death dominated the news channels, King's demise was also announced. He was the club's Bill Shankly, its Matt Busby. The man who came closest to creating a dynasty at Prenton Park. The man who took Tranmere from the old Fourth Division to being ninety minutes away from the Premier League. Those days seem so distant now. The past is another place entirely. Another planet.

The floral tributes are both plentiful and heartfelt, expressing gratitude for the best years in the life of this club. A white and blue scarf is tied around the neck of the statue, around Johnny King's neck. It would be a churlish person who would ever consider removing it.

It's been an emotional week for Merseyside football. At Goodison Park, the calls for Roberto Martínez's head have been louder than ever while, more poignantly, the verdicts of the Hillsborough inquests were announced a few days ago, finally bringing some sort of resolution to the families of the ninety-six victims, albeit around a quarter of a century too late. Today, there's a minute's applause before the game, followed by a goose-bump-inducing roar that may well have been heard all the way across the water at Anfield.

The dramatic strings that open Frankie Goes To Hollywood's 'Two Tribes' heighten the drama and anticipation in the last few seconds before kick-off, as does a helicopter hovering low overhead. Prenton Park sucks in its breath. Hopeful. Demanding. Expectant. But mainly just hopeful.

A strange mix of emotions is palpable – tense in many quarters, relaxed in others. A beach ball gets batted around the lower reaches of the Kop before a steward confiscates it, to the ire and disgust of the front few rows. Further up the Kop's bank, the diehards appreciate the intervention, demanding everyone give the team their full attention, their full support.

The Tranmere fans can be excused for the poor quality of their opposition-baiting chants this afternoon. They've got other things on their mind. The standard set at Forest Green back in October isn't remotely matched. 'What's it like to smell of fish?' is a time-worn question that probably every club's supporters have posed to the Grimsby fans over the years. 'You're going home in a boat!' is a more surreal offering.

The chorus is quieter today. One eye on the pitch, one eye on the news from Essex. Smartphones are clutched in sweaty palms, itchy fingers hitting the 'refresh' button a little too often than is advisable for their nerves.

Grimsby have elected to rest a fair few first-choice players ahead of their two-legged play-off semi-final. A weakened side isn't necessarily good news for Tranmere. These are second-string players out to impress as the time for contract renewals approaches. Nonetheless, Tranmere take the lead after twenty-four minutes. They're keeping their half of the deal. They need Altrincham to do them a large favour 180 miles away.

Three minutes before half-time, a collective cry of 'Shit!' peels across the rows of the Kop. Braintree have taken the lead. The news spurs the Rovers fans into fuller voice, the stand reverberating to the evergreen chant of 'Super White Army!'. The syllables run into each other, making it sound, as it has done all season, as if they're loudly announcing their appreciation of Gary Numan's old outfit Tubeway Army.

The singing helps paper over the cracks in confidence. Below the surface, the mood is nervous. All the while that just a single goal separates the teams in each game, quick turnarounds could happen in either fixture. Or both. Or neither.

Early in the second half, though, Tranmere's hope goes flat. Smartphones are pushed deep into coat pockets and shoulders shrug in resignation. This is now almost certainly the last forty-five minutes of the season. Braintree have scored a second, meaning that Altrincham have to score three times without response. And if anyone around Prenton Park were unaware of events in Essex, those kindly Grimsby fans at the far end offer their own newsflash. 'Two-nil to the Braintree Town! Two-nil to the Braintree Town!'

A minor consolation for the Tranmere faithful would be to witness one more goal to usher them into summertime, to offer a reason to be cheerful about next season. James Norwood goes close twice, but no joy. Braintree, meanwhile, can't stop. They're now three-up and already making travel arrangements for their play-off semi-final against, fate has decreed, Grimsby.

As the final seconds of Tranmere's season dribble out, the younger members of the home support gather by the side of the pitch, ready to hurdle the advertising boards and charge onto the turf on the final whistle. 'It is illegal to go on the pitch,' says the voice on the PA. 'You are liable to be arrested if you do.'

Three blasts of the whistle and the curtain is pulled across Tranmere's season. The death of all dreams.

There's a strange combination of a chorus of boos and a standing ovation for the home side. The younger fans are the more celebratory ones, having never seen their team win so many matches in a season during their lifetime. Raised on disappointment and stilted ambition, this probably qualifies as a successful season in their book. The older guard, the jaded loyalists who, twelve months ago, were embarrassed by their club's slide into non-league for the first time in nearly a century, are now even more embarrassed by the club's inability to haul itself back out again. The truth hurts. It shames, too.

They take out their frustration on the kids and teenagers currently charging in exuberant fashion around the pitch. 'What the fuck are they celebrating?' one of them calls out to no one in particular. 'We're in this shit league for another season.' There are several hundred on the pitch, many of whom, despite the PA announcer's threats of arrest, have found a ball and are enjoying an impromptu mass kickabout – 50-a-side. The spectacle at least raises a smile on the faces of the more philosophical Tranmere fans. The angrier ones make a swift exit, several days and nights of saloon-bar brooding ahead of them.

Outside, Half Man Half Biscuit's Nigel Blackwell

embarks on the last walk home from Prenton Park this season. Neither Will Young nor Status Quo will have him returning in a hurry. While those around him are either crestfallen or angry, Blackwell, ever the contrarian, is sanguine. For him, this season as a non-league club – and now next season too, of course – hasn't rung too many changes.

'No matter what division the club is in, I'll always go and support them. I still leave the house at the same time, sit with the same people and usually talk all the way through the match about anything other than the football.' As proof, he reveals that this afternoon he wasn't exactly caught up in tracking updates from Braintree, hoping against hope, anxiously chewing fingernails. 'I spent the whole game discussing the famous Julia Wallace murder in 1930s Liverpool. Read up on it. Absolutely fascinating case.'

On the occasions when he's not dissecting the peculiarities of long-gone murder trials, Blackwell does pay some attention to on-the-field matters. 'It's often a stern test of the soul, though,' he drily announces. 'At times I can wholly appreciate how John McCarthy must have felt when he was tied to that radiator.'

The faithful drift out of Prenton Park, saluting Johnny King's statue for the last time for two or three months and surely ashamed that the great man's demise occurred during such a misfiring season. Their despondency is replicated down in the bowels of the stadium.

Backstage, the mood is unsurprisingly subdued and withdrawn. The corner flags are dumped in an alcove, ready for their summer hibernation, while a gaggle of stewards wish each other well now that their Saturday afternoons can be reclaimed.

Along the corridor, the colour scheme of which – white walls, blue woodwork, green carpet – echoes the home team when out on the pitch, Gary Brabin emerges from the dressing room. He walks slowly and silently into a small, narrow room next to the physio's treatment room. The press must still be faced. While the manager's clothes – neat v-necked sweater, pale blue shirt, navy chinos and brown brogues – show little sign of the stress of this afternoon, his face and his body language do. Heavy eyes and hunched shoulders confirm he's been through the wringer.

To the close-fitting herd of local reporters, all padded jackets and laminated passes, Brabin says the expected things. 'Lots of plusses . . . looking at the positives . . . got back to winning ways . . . building process . . . dust ourselves down and look to go again.' He sounds as though on auto-pilot, satisfactorily filling column inches and airtime while his dazed mind is otherwise occupied trying to make sense of the season. 'We had no divine right to go straight back up,' he whispers to me back out in the corridor, 'but I thought the gods were going to shine on us today.'

Beyond Brabin's shoulder, a couple of players are dragging themselves up a flight of stairs, obligated to perform one last meet-and-greet with star-struck, slightly tipsy sponsors in the hospitality suites. Free of any such commitment, the rest of their team-mates make a final, weary shuffle from dressing room to car park, conversation turning to their respective choices of holiday destination. They still dutifully sign autographs and pose for photos en route to their cars, but the signatures are rushed and the smiles are hollow. Dejected, spent, empty.

As the season's top scorer, James Norwood – baseball cap perched backwards on his head – gets the most attention. While annoyed that he didn't score today ('He shouldn't have got to that,' he moans about an effort that Grimsby's keeper managed to tip around the post. 'He was about sixty-five'), this is just a smokescreen, a conversational distraction. That season-long effort, made in recent weeks while carrying a knee injury, is over. The air has gone from the balloon.

'I don't want to feel this way again,' he sighs, a veteran of late-season Conference disappointment after Forest Green's play-off exit twelve months ago. The big time – represented by the words 'Football' and 'League' – remains agonisingly just out of reach for another year. The margin of failure was frustratingly slight. Tranmere fell short by just two points; indeed, their final tally of seventy-eight points would have seen them comfortably qualify for the play-offs last season.

For Norwood, it was too close. Sixth place is the worst place to end up. Sixteenth would be way more bearable. No hopes dashed at the eleventh hour. Failure is failure, after all, wherever you finish. Spare yourself the pain.

The fact that Forest Green, the club Norwood left last May, have a play-off semi-final ahead of them next week makes the pill taste even more bitter. He climbs into his Range Rover and steers it out of the car park. A left turn at the lights at the bottom of road and off to the Mersey Tunnel. Towards Liverpool. Towards home. Towards another season as a non-league footballer.

10

MAY

Forever in our future

A chunky, rusting chain, triple-wrapped around the gate and gatepost at Lakeview, has padlocked away the memories of Bishop Sutton's season. Beyond the gate, beyond the silent gravel of the empty car park, a football ground is entering its summer recess, its fallow period. The time to forgive and to forget.

The hot May sun is scorching the white touchlines into invisibility, while, untouched by the mower, the grass has been allowed to thicken and clump, flecked with the odd brilliant white splash of sun-seeking daisies. The swallows will be back soon, too.

For those non-league clubs untroubled by the play-off process or by imminent cup finals, the season now occupies the past tense. Done, dusted. All is quiet at Lakeview. The only sounds are peripheral, just murmurs in the middle distance. Children in faraway gardens. A tractor in the field beyond the bottom hedge. An airliner taking its human cargo to far-flung climes. Silence hangs in the air of the immediate vicinity, ghostly despite the bright sunshine. The sounds of football have gone. The tannoy announcements, the dugout shouts, the gallows humour, the ripple of ball against net, the foul-mouthed recriminations.

Here at Lakeview, the season couldn't have ended any sooner. That win over Roman Glass St George back in March proved to be the pinnacle, the axis around which the remainder of Bishop Sutton's season revolved. With the club's destiny mapped out early on in the campaign, it was as if avoiding an entire season without a win was the ambition, the only truly realistic objective.

Since that narrow victory, the team reverted to type. The collective foot came off the gas and the hammerings returned: 6-1 to Radstock Town, 8-1 to Keynsham Town, 8-0 to Colin Merrick's old team Wellington. Those defeats were accompanied by the inevitable news – suspected back in August, expected in November – that they could no longer finish anywhere other than the very bottom corner of the Toolstation Western League Division One. It's a position they've made their own all season.

For months, the team has drifted on tides they've been unable to steer against and have finally run aground. Although they survived until the final month of the season before arriving at this point of no return, the lowest ebb in the last twenty-five years of the club's history has been reached.

Unlike last summer – when he was frantically trying to construct a credible squad for whom the obscurity of a mid-table finish would have been an unmitigated success – this year Steve Laker will get a couple of months away from football. Or, at least, away from the game's back end. He can become a spectator again, sinking into his favourite armchair for Euro '16, cold beer and salty snacks to hand. Instead, the devilishly difficult task of recruiting players for a club that finished twenty-two points adrift of anyone else, will fall on the shoulders of Merrick and his assistant, Ian.

This is the time of whispers and tip-offs, of speculative approaches and secret assignations. This is the time when a manager's Machiavellian streak gets tested, trying to spirit players away from under the noses of his brother-hood, of his managerial kin. At this level, the dangled carrot might be nothing more than an offer to pay petrol money on match days, or the guarantee of a lift to Tuesday night training. Here in the cash-light lower leagues, a manager can't make promises any more con-crete than that. All he can do is sell dreams. And he's got to sell these dreams more seductively – and more credibly – than the next man.

For Merrick, the club's final tally of eight points contained the slightest scent of recovery. In among the dark trail of thundering defeats was the dim light of a second home victory, a shallow suggestion that – as long as those 8-0 and 8-1 reverses get swept under the carpet, out of sight and out of mind – the club might be beginning to turn the corner, that happier times are coming into view. That's the dream that needs selling, at least.

Merrick is reliant on half-truths and wild speculation because the truth is cold, hard and unforgiving. Bishop

Sutton have fallen through the relegation trapdoor for the second successive season.

* * *

'There he is, brave as a lion.'

In the bright Saturday morning sun, Peter Beadle – the former journeyman striker best known for his spells at the two Bristol clubs – holds dual positions. He is both umpire and commentator of a light-hearted game of foot tennis, offering sarcastic one-liners whenever the level of commitment of a participant is less than full-throttle, such as the feeble, uncourageous attempt at a diving header we've just witnessed.

Here at this training ground on the outskirts of Hereford, the combination of warm sunshine and unconfined bonhomie wears all the hallmarks of the opening session of pre-season in July, the first day back at school. Or, swap the greener-than-green grass for sand and you'd swear this was a group of old schoolmates messing around on a beach in Kavos or Gran Canaria. Everyone gels with the effortless ease of lifelong pals.

Not quite lifelong, though. The bonhomie obscures the reality. This time last year, barely anyone knew each other; their club didn't actually exist. And that's not all. Nerves and uncertainty should be the order of the day this morning, not ribbing and giggles. Because, in eight days' time, these players will be walking out at Wembley in what will, for most of them, be the biggest game they will ever play in their entire lives.

No one can deny the overpowering romance of Leicester City's extraordinary, brilliant Premier League triumph, a story that has warmed the cockles of any student of modern, open-cheque-book football. But theirs is a tale surely eclipsed by that of Hereford FC who, last August, as the new boys in the Midland Football League, had yet to kick a competitive ball.

Nine months later, they're in a somewhat different position. They're no longer a Midland Football League club, having raced away – under the avuncular rule of manager Beadle – with the title at the first time of asking. forty-two matches, thirty-five wins, 108 points, 138 goals. Not only that, but they've also helped themselves to a couple of other trophies – the Herefordshire County Cup and the Polymac Packaging Midland Football League Cup. And now their eyes are on the prize of a fourth piece of silverware, arguably the most prestigious of all. Next weekend, it's the final of the FA Vase, the FA Cup equivalent for teams at level nine and lower.

It's an extraordinary turnaround from where Hereford – or, at least, the old club Hereford United, on whose remains the new club has been built – found themselves eighteen months ago. Having staved off relegation from the Conference with a last-day victory at Aldershot, six weeks later the club was demoted two divisions to the Southern League Premier for financial irregularities. Paying the wages of their players and staff appeared to have been viewed as an occupational hazard. The new owners, who'd taken over the week before the demotion, appeared to uphold the tradition, missing three deadlines to clear some of the debt and preserve Conference status.

With fans outside the club's famous Edgar Street stadium leading vociferous protests against the incoming regime, the next few months were a steep, inevitable descent for such a historic club. On 19 December 2014, Hereford United were wound up in the High Court. They ceased to be. Met their maker. Joined the choir invisible.

On the sidelines this morning is someone who was at the centre of the club's implosion, right in the eye of the tornado. Jamie Griffiths was the media officer at Hereford United until he walked out after just a few days of working under the new owners.

'I'm not embarrassed to say that, on the day that I left, I went out on the terrace and just cried my eyes out. It was gut-wrenching. When I left, the club was still going, but you could sense it wasn't going in the right direction. I had to get out.

'I hadn't been paid for six months, but it wasn't about the money. It was about the way the club was being run and the attitudes of those people. It was the way they were treating the fans and the employees. Lots of broken promises – "We'll pay everyone tomorrow, tomorrow, next week". It was a horrible time, one I just try to forget. I don't want to be bitter. Up until that point, I'd had thirty years of fantastic memories of following Hereford United up and down the country. Those two weeks were ones I want to forget.'

The loss of a football club to a small city like Hereford was clear to see. The stadium – a slightly ramshackle but

deeply romantic old-style ground that an estate agent
would surely describe as 'pre-loved' – is very conspicuous,
located right on the busiest road cutting straight through
the centre. Along with the cathedral, the four towering floodlights dominate the skyline, iron giants up
above the trees and houses. But these lights went out and
the terraces fell silent.

'It hit the place hard,' explains Griffiths. 'You don't
know what you've got 'til it's gone. Shops and pubs and
restaurants noticed it when there was no football club.
The whole economy of the town missed it.'

But rumours and counter-rumours were circulating,
whispers and hearsay doing the rounds. And the rumours
were that an attempt to resuscitate the club – or, rather,
create another in the image of the original – was afoot.
Certainly, from the mobilisation surrounding the earlier
protests, there was a groundswell of organised activism
that could be drawn from. 'We hadn't been out to kill
Hereford United off,' says Griffiths, defending the boy-
cotts. 'We just weren't happy that they had decided to
effectively relegate the club to the Southern League. That
was their decision by not paying the bills.

'What we, the fans, didn't want was for the club to be
wound up in December and not have a team that following season. That would have been horrendous. So it was
a race against time to get everything set up to prove that
we could have a team ready for the summer.'

The most crucial piece in the puzzle was signing the
lease to reoccupy Edgar Street. Not returning to the
ground where, on the old club's most famous day,

Ronnie Radford hit that screamer against Newcastle, would have been unthinkable. But, with assurances given and documents signed, the main movers and shakers behind the phoenix club were handed the keys to the ground the following June. What they didn't realise was that they were being handed the keys to a mausoleum.

When they opened the doors, Edgar Street was just as it had been left at the time of the club's winding-up the previous December. It was a place trapped in amber, caught in time. Miss Havisham's bedroom, or the lower quarters of the *Mary Celeste*.

In the home dressing room, the detritus of the final training session lay everywhere – muddy shirts, screwed-up socks and mildewing towels. Upstairs in the bar, the beer had been festering in the pipes for six months, while a selection of mince pies lay untouched on a tray. The Christmas decorations were still up. Everything seemed to be waiting for the arrival of a crack forensics team to dust for prints.

The process of renewal had to be swift, but there was a clear template for the new club to copy. For starters, the white and black kit chosen for Hereford FC is extremely close to that of its antecedent. The two clubs share the same nickname (the Bulls). And the motto on the new club's badge states 'Forever United'.

'No one's shying away from that,' says Griffiths. 'We're here because of Hereford United. There would be no Hereford FC otherwise. We still wheel out the giant killers, we still celebrate promotion back to the Football League against Halifax in 2006. And we still sing "Hereford

United, we love you" on the terraces. We wouldn't pretend that this is nothing to do with Hereford United.'

Despite the rich heritage, the fact that Hereford Mk II were starting in the ninth tier, four rungs below where the original club had been little more than a year before, meant that player recruitment wasn't the most straightforward prospect. Peter Beadle has left the rest of today's training session in his coaches' hands and wanders across. In polo shirt, baseball cap and super-baggy shorts, he explains how tricky it was to put together a side that could challenge for promotion.

'It was as difficult as trying to plait soup,' he reveals with a hollow chuckle. 'It was almost impossible. Some of the players we wanted didn't want to drop down to the Midland Football League. It was hard just getting them to come over and look round. We had to sell the club, but there was no club to sell.

'Geographically, Hereford isn't easy to get to and, as much as we want to keep Hereford's talent in Hereford, it had to be the right type of player and the right type of personality. In the end, we've ended up with a fantastic blend of both.

'The team spirit has been the biggest plus for me this year. You can never do anything on your own. The team has to be a family. Sometimes you don't like all your family and you're going to fall out. But the most important thing is that everyone's trying to achieve the same thing. Nothing's ever personal.'

Two crucial signings were those of John Mills and Pablo Haysham, a duo who'd been scoring goals together for fun since schoolboy days in Oxfordshire. The previous season, the pair had notched a large bagful of goals for Didcot Town, one league higher. But they could see the potential at Hereford and wanted to be strapped in on the ride, in the front carriage of the roller coaster.

'They've been magnificent,' says Beadle. 'They travel further than the others, but the rewards have been there for them. They've scored a phenomenal amount of goals this year between them.' Indeed. Of the 200+ goals Hereford have scored in all competitions during this first season, twenty-nine have come from Haysham, while Mills accounts for a full fifty-two.

For the manager, too, the challenge was enticing. After all, Beadle had been the caretaker boss who, over the course of eight games at the tail end of the 2013–14 season, had successfully kept the club in the Conference prior to their demotion (an achievement, incidentally, that didn't seem to merit him being shortlisted for the permanent role when he applied).

At first, though, he was sceptical about the new plans. 'You heard that they'd got the leases back and that these benefactors were going to come in. I'd heard all that before. But once it was all set up, I thought this could be one hell of a project to get involved in. I felt it was unfinished business, having worked so hard for those eight games.'

Despite his Conference credentials, the drop down the leagues to a very part-time role didn't faze Beadle. This is a man who always – very articulately and with rare use of guarded manager-speak – tells it like it is, his footballing heart on his sleeve. 'It wasn't a problem. It was more a case of me getting back into football. Getting back into it is the hardest thing. Hereford wasn't the only job I had my name in for, but it was the one I wanted the most.'

The challenge was made more onerous by the levels of expectation. With around 1,300 season tickets sold in advance of Hereford FC's first competitive game, the pressure had been ratcheted up. 'We were favourites for the Vase before the season had even started. How did they work that out? We were favourites and Salisbury were second favourites – two new clubs who hadn't even kicked a ball. It was crazy.

'There was also expectation from our supporters. I know that if we'd finished second or third this year, it probably wouldn't have been good enough for them. And that expectation is only going to go higher next season. But there are enough people out there who are realistic and who understand that it's small steps.' He glances out across the field to his happy charges. 'Small steps.'

As training breaks up, the exuberance and excitement among the squad is unavoidable. Although they're officially off duty now, a handful of players can't help but put in extra shooting practice, trying to outdo each other's ever more spectacular finishes. Some shots fly into the top corner. Others are wilder, the balls only saved from disappearing into the adjacent housing estate by a row of towering leylandii.

Like an under-11s team that wants to carry on kicking a ball around after a match despite the cajoling of eager-to-leave parents, these players can't and won't stop. Only when the tractor mower is heading straight for them, and when the goal is being wheeled back into storage, do they finally relinquish and head for the showers. No one's sloping off the pitch at the earliest opportunity, their eye on a swift exit. It's an attitude buoyed by both the phenomenal success they've already achieved and the prospect of further silverware next weekend.

Jamie Griffiths – back as media officer at Edgar Street, where he's now getting paid on time – wears a big smile while reflecting on the last eight months. 'People keep saying that a film should be made of this season. But if you wrote the script, you'd throw it out because it would be unbelievable, too far-fetched. My lad's seven and has just started getting into football. He's been going all season and has never seen us not win. I keep telling him "This isn't real. Don't get used to it. Just because you turn up, don't expect us to win every game." I don't know where he can go from here.'

The success has created a slight, but welcome, problem, though. 'We haven't got a trophy cabinet. I think someone's going to knock a few shelves together . . .'

Griffiths is carrying a thick wodge of envelopes as he takes up position in the car park – a car park that's very much that of a lower-end semi-pro club. There are no fancy-dan, high-octane supercars here, just a jumble of Polos and Clios and Fiestas, most of which have seen better days. As the players leave, Griffiths hands the envelopes out. There's one for each of them. The contents are rather special: their ticket allocation for next Sunday's FA Vase final for friends and family. The golden tickets.

Before he heads off with John Mills to drive back to

Oxfordshire (a three-hour round-trip the pair undertake for both training and home matches), I grab Pablo Haysham for a quick chat. I want to understand why a free-scoring player, in whom there'd surely be plenty of interest from higher-ranking clubs, chose to drop down a league rather than trying to catapult himself in the opposite direction.

'I'd had conversations with other clubs at a similar level to Didcot. I'd also been doing pre-season at Oxford City in the Conference South, but I didn't quite get anything there. Once I knew I wasn't going to be staying on at City, this was the place I thought of.

'It was purely and simply because of the club. I had a great time at Didcot and it was a good standard to be playing at, but when the opportunity to play here came, it was something that couldn't be turned down.

'First and foremost, the club is not run in the way you'd expect from a team at this level. You definitely feel like you're playing a few leagues up. I didn't think of it as a big risk at the time, but if it hadn't worked out, it would have been a huge disappointment. But Peter was clear about the ambition of the people involved. There was this feeling that it wasn't going to fail.'

And fail it hasn't. The decisions of both Haysham and Mills have been thoroughly justified. A quick promotion means they're back where they were twelve months ago, emboldened by the memories and goals of a storybook season. But beyond this, the bonding of this new team – with Beadle very much the all-purpose adhesive – has mightily impressed Haysham.

'I've been in a lot of different dressing rooms in the time I've been playing football and this one is truly special. It's close, it's friendly and everyone's ambitious in the right way. We all just love playing football. It takes me back to when I was younger, playing football with my mates. That's why there's success. There's never anyone who gets the hump on in the wrong way. Obviously people get annoyed in training because they're exerting so much energy, but it's truly special when you get a closeness like this. It's fantastic to be a part of.'

And it's been a successful transition from Didcot's Loop Meadow Stadium, with an average gate of little more than 100, to Edgar Street where, for some of the bigger games, the crowd numbered in excess of 4,000 for ninth-tier football. There was no culture shock. 'I've never shied away whenever there's a crowd. It energises me.'

He grips his envelope of tickets a little tighter. 'There are going to be a few more people at Wembley, though . . .'

* * *

The buses left the borderlands before breakfast.

By the time Hereford woke up on this bright, hazy Sunday morning, a third of its inhabitants were halfway to north-west London, scores of supporters' coaches playing tag with each other on the motorway.

The proportion of the population on the roads and on the rails is no exaggeration. It is genuinely a third. Twenty thousand are en route to Wembley for the FA Vase final at lunchtime, the first instalment of the inaugural

Non-League Finals Day, which also includes the final of the FA Trophy. The decision to amalgamate the two was an attempt to prevent showpiece finals rattling around a near-empty Wembley. Indeed, last year's Vase final, between the teams of the faraway towns of Glossop and North Shields, claimed a crowd of just 9,000.

Hereford has whipped itself up into a modest frenzy in the weeks leading up to the third cup final of the season. Outside Waitrose in the shopping complex over the road from Edgar Street, a pop-up club shop has had queues leading out the door every day for weeks, punters eager to snap up Vase-branded memorabilia. Other than that gargantuan cup upset back in 1972, the place has never been gripped by such contagious football fever.

At journey's end, the coaches nudge into their allotted parking spaces before releasing their passengers into the expectant buzz of Wembley. Out on the concourse, the mercury of optimism is reaching into the red, fortified by this season's silverware, goals and extraordinary win ratio. Unprompted, a man with more than a passing resemblance to Tony Blackburn offers his forecast for this afternoon: '4-0! No, 5-0!'

His prediction isn't necessarily the product of the blind – or at least blinkered – faith that comes with unthinking partisanship. The form book suggests it might just be a realistic assessment.

Thirteen-year-old Louis, who travelled down by coach with his younger brother Tom and their grandmother, might be a little more circumspect, but is still expecting a dominant Hereford display. '3-1. John Mills is going to get a hat-trick.' Tom's too busy to offer a prediction; he's otherwise engaged in rooting through his gran's handbag for a mirror so he can inspect the face painting she's just forked out for. 'It's going to be an expensive day,' she mutters, before losing any sympathy onlookers might have for her. 'Do you want me to buy you England shirts later, boys?'

The face-painting concession is doing swift business. With its queue consisting exclusively of Hereford fans, the full palette of colourful paints lies untouched. Every child only wants white and black, the two-tone identity of their club. By the time the Grimsby faithful, in their black and white stripes, arrive later for the FA Trophy portion of the day, stocks may well have run dry.

Hawkers selling flags and scarves out on the pavements surrounding the stadium have wisely skewed their stock in Hereford's favour – perhaps just 10 per cent of their product lines are Morpeth-branded. Nonetheless, despite having bought in bulk, a couple of traders have still sold out by 11 am, more than an hour before the lunchtime kick-off. Such is the invasion of Herefordians on this patch of north-west London. It must resemble a ghost town back home.

Under the concourse, a minibus pulls up and a string of passengers tumble out, unfolding themselves back to their correct heights after several cramped hours on the motorway network. There are fourteen of them, representing three generations of the Carter family, from Grandpa Dave (mid-seventies) to little Eloise (seven and a half). Across the ages, they're all coiled springs.

Dave, a self-confessed 'Edgar Street semi-regular' for

almost seven decades, is thrilled to finally see his precious Hereford at Wembley, while Eloise is looking forward to two things. Firstly, seeing her favourite player, the terrifically gifted Sierra Leonean Mustapha Bundu. Secondly, finding a stall that sells inflatable hammers. (If he plays, today will be Bundu's final match for Hereford, as the terms of his work permit are such that he's disqualified from playing at a level higher than the Midland Football League. I elect not to spoil Eloise's day by breaking this news to her. She might just find a use for that hammer.)

Inside the stadium, each of the four clubs in action this afternoon have been given roughly a quarter of the seats. Hereford will be the only team that will fill its allocation, the only team whose support is of a size that dictates the opening of the top tier. Plenty are taking their places early – and for a particular reason. The Hereford mascot is scheduled to be doing a lap of the pitch an hour or so before kick-off.

While Crystal Palace have a bald eagle making pre-match orbits of Selhurst Park, and French rugby fans are adept at smuggling live cockerels into the Stade de France, Hereford take it to a new level by parading a bull by the name of Hawkesbury Ronaldo. Possibly the only mascot that could top that would be if Millwall liberated a lion from the nearest zoo and kept him on a long lead around The Den.

By the time the teams stride out ten minutes before kick-off, all three tiers of the Hereford end are rammed. Not an empty seat in the house. Full to the rafters. Twenty thousand fans roaring their approval, 20,000 fans with a belief in their team's manifest destiny. It's an astonishing, wholly unnatural number for a ninth-level club. Indeed, it's 6,000 more than the entire population of Morpeth. The Northumbrians' own supporters simply can't be heard.

As he warms up, Pablo Haysham glances up at the massed supporters. For this Madrid boy – he was born, and spent the first eight years of his life, in Spain – this corner of Wembley could be the Bernabéu, a sea of white shirts and a full-voiced chorus of club songs. It's a comparison that carries no hint of exaggeration.

It's an intoxicating sight to be in the middle of – and one thoroughly alien to the little old FA Vase. On the pitch, the Hereford players do nothing to quell and qualify this sense of invincibility. Within seventy-three seconds, they're already one up.

They should be at least two goals to the good by the half-hour mark. Sirdic 'Sid' Grant stings the crossbar with a fierce effort, before Haysham waltzes through the Morpeth defence and fires just wide.

Over on the far touchline, Peter Beadle has today abandoned his trademark baggy shorts in favour of a suit. Initially, he elects to keep the jacket done up, putting its buttons under a little strain. Once play begins, though, the jacket is wisely undone. His faithful old baseball cap makes an appearance, too.

As the first half deepens, Beadle plays with the top of a water bottle. It's his comfort blanket. Screw and unscrew. Screw and unscrew. He's right to be nervous. Honours are even at the break, after Morpeth nick an untidy equaliser.

The Northumbrians' goal has hushed the Hereford supporters somewhat. During the interval, a small party of more senior fans are trying to affect the direction of the second half. 'Lucky' hats, whose good fortune seemed to be increasingly running dry as the first period unfolded, are swapped around. It's a warm day, but the knitwear has come out, too. 'Do you want to wear this scarf from now on? It might do us good.'

Clothing combinations don't legislate for sloppy defending, though, and within seconds of the restart Morpeth score a second. Then they add a third. The reality hits the Hereford massive: their unstoppable march to a fourth trophy is, in fact, perfectly stoppable. What we're hearing now is the sound of silence, of 20,000 people struck dumb.

A fourth goal merely rubber-stamps the defeat, confirming that the North East's stranglehold on the Vase remains. The trophy will be making its seventh trip up the A1(M) in just eight years. Those superstitious Hereford fans in the row behind remain philosophical about Morpeth's victory. 'Well, at least we won our league. They didn't.' A pause. 'Did they . . . ?'

In the back corridors of Wembley, deep down in the stadium's bowels, the walls carry photographs of every significant event that's ever been hosted here. Geoff Hurst's hat-trick. Live Aid. Gazza's thunderbolt of a free-kick against Arsenal. Even Evel Knievel and those thirteen double-decker buses.

One photo has particular resonance today. Taken from directly behind the goal, it shows Alan Shearer putting England ahead against Germany in the Euro '96 semi-final. His goal came with just three minutes on the clock. The nation, already riding a tidal wave of inevitability, went into overdrive. They were going to reach the final. It was a certainty, a given. But they had peaked too soon. A German equaliser and a penalty shoot-out extinguished the dream.

History repeated itself this afternoon. Hereford's first-minute opener convinced its travelling townsfolk that there was no other way the result could possibly go. It made the failure a greater fall, a more painful landing.

In the auditorium that houses post-match press conferences, Peter Beadle sits in the very seat where Roy Hodgson usually suffers the slings and arrows of an impatient, headline-hungry press pack. Today they number less than a dozen and their sympathetic tone suggests they too are commiserating that they won't be reporting on an unparalleled quadruple.

The manager looks drained after a long, exhausting but almost exclusively exhilarating season. Three trophies will have to be sufficient. 'My team have been fantastic for sixty-three games,' he announces, albeit laced with a sigh. 'Maybe today was one game too many. It hurts more because we haven't shown everybody the way we've played all season.'

Down the corridor in the mixed zone, where twenty-four hours earlier Rooney, Rashford, Mata and Martial offered their triumphant post-Cup final thoughts to a battery of cameras and microphones, Morpeth's beaming players recount their own stories to any member of the press who will listen. As they do, Grimsby's players arrive, filing past on their way to the dressing room, hoping that they'll be in that position after the afternoon's second final.

Pablo Haysham is going in the opposite direction. Out and away. His team has done the treble, they've played at Wembley and yet despondency is the emotion of the moment. 'Right now, it's difficult to appreciate it. It's negative. When we look back on it, it'll be something unbelievable. In years to come, we'll have fond memories of a very special day. We're lucky to have had the opportunity. We're privileged.'

What rubs salt into the wounds of the vanquished is that lengthy, contractually obliged climb to receive their losers' medals. At the old Wembley, there were just thirty-nine steps. Now there are 109. 'It's horrible. After you've been running around for ninety minutes, each step is the hardest step ever. They seem endless. Then you take a turn and there are more steps and more steps.'

Only four more steps are left for Haysham's leaden feet to climb. Up onto the team bus to slump into a seat, a time for personal thoughts, for chewing over could-have-beens and should-have-beens. Once everyone's on board, the doors close with a gentle hiss and Hereford FC quietly slip away down the service road under the stadium. There's no trophy on the dashboard, no parade of honking car horns all the way back to the borders. Just quiet reflection and deep sighs.

The fairy tales belong to others this afternoon. The story of Chris Swailes is arguably the most irresistible.

The battle-scarred Morpeth defender scrambled their equaliser earlier, making him, at the age of forty-five, the oldest scorer in a Wembley final. His team-mates call him Uncle Albert.

But there's even more to Swailes. Not only has he got several pieces of metal inserted into various joints and bones, but two years ago he had to have his heart restarted three times after falling ill while playing. Then came four operations on his ticker, including the fitting of a pair of artificial valves to improve his breathing. Unsurprisingly, his smiles are the widest at Wembley this afternoon.

There's another fairy tale in the FA Trophy final, the second match of Non-League Finals Day. Grimsby, promoted to the Football League after their play-off win the previous weekend, are out-thought and outfought by FC Halifax Town, one of four Conference sides who'll play at the tier below next season. While it's modest compensation for being relegated, the ecstasy on the final whistle is loud and absolute. Pablo Haysham found those Wembley steps painful and interminable, but the Halifax players don't even notice them as they collect their winners' medals. They're walking on air.

And yet . . .

Fairy tales can end on a sour note, too. Yesterday, Louis van Gaal led Manchester United to glory here in the FA Cup final. Tomorrow, he will be dismissed from his job. In two days' time, Jim Harvey will endure exactly the same experience, relieved of his duties forty-eight hours after leading Halifax to one of the landmark days in the phoenix club's short history.

Even in the learn-from-past-mistakes world of reborn clubs, it appeared that managers were still not immune to boardroom impatience and myopic short-termism.

* * *

It was expected to be a smooth changing of the guard at Old Trafford in those last few days of May. Out with the Dutchman, straight in with the Portuguese. But the transition was held up by a frankly ludicrous complication. It turned out that the incoming manager's own name – or, at least, the right to stick that name on any old piece of tat and charge top dollar for it – was in the possession of his former employer. To have the words 'José Mourinho' on a mug, a pencil case, a tea towel or a cat litter tray would mean a contribution to Chelsea's coffers. Even more bizarre was the fact that Mourinho himself must have acquiesced to the deal.

A more ridiculous example of the reality-warping world that is football's top table would be difficult to find. Greed and gluttony at every turn. The game's appetite for eating itself was more voracious than ever.

Not everywhere, though. The same morning that the delay in Mourinho's appointment gets explained, the sport's less heralded benevolent side is busy doing the right thing. At six o'clock that morning, as rolls of thick fog engulf the South Downs, two teams take to a football pitch at Lancing College in West Sussex. Their aim is to not leave that pitch, to not stop playing, until teatime the following Monday, a full 108 hours later. If successful, in their possession, along with the inevitable blisters and bruises, strains and sprains, will be the Guinness World Record for the longest continuous football match ever played.

The attempt is being made in the memory of Matt Grimstone and Jacob Schilt, the young Worthing United players who lost their lives in the Shoreham air disaster back in August, and of Matt Chaplain, a local player who died from a heart attack three years ago. With each player sponsored to the hilt, the proceeds of this five-day marathon will be split between a large donation to the British Heart Foundation and a lasting memorial to Matt and Jacob, perhaps in the form of a 3G training pitch or a new hospitality suite at the club, which would bear their names.

It's an undeniably honourable endeavour, a salute to lost young lives, to promise and potential. Two squads of just eighteen players each, many of whom are drawn from Worthing United's ranks, will be running around morning, noon and night until the far side of the Bank Holiday weekend. It's a serious commitment that will test both physical and mental limits, the equivalent of playing two seasons' worth of football in four and a half days.

But what makes the marathon match truly remarkable is its location. Lancing College – an extraordinary gothic building rising from the local landscape like some kind of prototype for Hogwarts – sits just north of the stretch of the A27 where the accident happened. The crash site itself was at the traffic lights at the bottom of the school lane. Not even 300 paces away.

The constant stream of light aircraft taking off from

the airfield just the other side of the dual carriageway is another reminder of that dreadful day. But no one's shying away from that. This is a time to remember. On the opposite side of the pitch stands a double-decker bus, on the side of which are fixed seven-foot-tall posters of the three players in whose memory the event is being held.

By lunchtime on the Saturday, the two teams – one of whom is playing in the pale blue and white stripes of Worthing United – have just nudged beyond the halfway mark of this noble quest. It's something of a noble quest for those keeping a tally of the goals, too. The current score is 517-460.

The tight regulations allow for a five-minute rest period every hour, a time for toilet breaks, substitutions and a new team of match officials to clock on. The players tend to do shifts of between six and eight hours on the pitch and two hours off, during which they head off to the area of tents just behind the touchline for a short kip before the next long shift. On the way, they might have massage or soak their feet in the kids' paddling pool that's been filled for that very purpose.

Wherever they go, it can't be far. The entire 108 hours of the record attempt have to be filmed for the purposes of official verification. This means none of the players can leave the roped-off compound covered by the camera's gaze, a modest area that does at least include the portable loos, the tents and the catering truck. Anyone stepping beyond this boundary could invalidate the entire enterprise.

One of the Worthing players has just been substituted

and, with bandages all the way up both legs, is showing the strain that such an endurance test can have on the human body. His spirit remains strong, though, thanks to the regenerative powers of a can of Red Bull and the fact that he's pretty chuffed with his current tally of fifty-six goals. Also, a muscle-reviving massage awaits him, just as soon as the treatment table becomes free.

One of the opposing players, who's also just been substituted, has a different objective, making a beeline for the catering truck. He returns with a heaped plate of sausage, bacon and beans, all topped by a chocolate cupcake. A shout goes out from the red number ten in the centre circle to the physio in her pitchside marquee. 'Jodie, can I have some painkillers? Two, please.'

The event is a marathon effort from all the support staff, who include the Worthing United chairman Steve Taylor. He's been here, with his fifteen-year-old son Jack, since 5 am. The rain is beginning to fall again and, while Jack puts in an extended – and unsheltered – shift manning the main gate, Steve and I retire to the front seats of his car to get out of the downpour. It's here that he explains just how difficult the last few months have been for everyone involved with the club.

'We started the season very excited and very optimistic. We'd just done the double the previous season, along with five team-of-the-month awards and the team-of-the-season award, so we were optimistic about what we could do in the premier division [of the Southern Combination League]. We knew it would be a hard season but, of course, we didn't realise just how hard it was going to be.'

The rain has quickly become torrential, drumming with intensity on the sunroof. Out on the pitch, players are hastily putting on see-through waterproof ponchos that some kind soul went and bought from the twenty-four-hour Tesco last night at about 4 am.

Steve returns to his recollections. 'I remember a lot about the day. It was 22 August and we were at home to Loxwood. We knew the airshow was on and that there might be some delays as most of the guys come from the Brighton area and so come that way. I remember being really excited because it was a nice sunny day and I was hoping that the lads might come in early for once. It was around quarter past one, but only about four players had arrived. So we started to make phone calls. It would be "Oh, I'm ten minutes behind. I think something's happened at the airshow." By half past, a couple more players had arrived, but others were saying that they didn't think they could make kick-off.

'Nigel [Geary, the manager] gave Matt and Jacob a call. Absolutely nothing. These two are the most reliable guys you can ever imagine. They come to training every week and they'd be very apologetic if they were ever just a minute late. They're both that sort of person.' Steve Taylor's occasional lapses into the present tense are poignant and telling.

'We knew they were travelling from that direction. We just thought that if an accident had happened, cellphones might be off in that area. Or that they were in the tunnel that's quite close to Shoreham. It was getting close to two o'clock now, so we told the referee there might be a delay.

By half past, there were a few anxious people. Some of us were getting worried. The officials made a good call and decided to call the game off. Loxwood were amazing and totally understood.

'We came into the clubhouse and started watching the pictures on TV. People started looking on their phones because footage had been uploaded to YouTube. Then someone said they thought they'd seen the car Matt and Jacob were driving.' Unofficial reports were also coming in from members of the emergency services who said they'd seen Worthing United bags in the back of one of the cars caught up in the crash.

'We dispersed at around six o'clock, but there was still no information. I got home about seven. Two police officers at the door. They came in and told me. It was unofficial at the time because they still needed to get the phone numbers of the families. I had these at the club, but I gave the keys to the police to get them. I wasn't in a state to drive.'

The following morning, Steve, Nigel and the club's vice-chairman Mike Sanderson went to the club, where they encountered crews from every major news outlet. 'We were thrust into this media circus. We couldn't say anything because we didn't have confirmation, but they were trying to get everything out of us. At that point, though, Matt and Jacob were two missing people who were hopefully going to come through that door at any minute.'

The rain has ceased and we head back pitchside. Nigel the manager has now arrived, a gaggle of patient and quiet kids at his ankles. He too recalls that media scrum on the Sunday morning. 'It was mayhem. We had every newspaper, every TV channel contacting us. Wild accusations were being said in an attempt to get the story. We're not used to that. I'm used to dealing with the local paper and talking about football.'

The two players' deaths were officially confirmed by mid-afternoon. Then began the grieving process, with Steve and Nigel acting as the protective shield for the players. Counselling was offered to all the team. In particular need of such support could be those who'd been six or seven cars back from Matt and Jacob at the traffic lights that afternoon. Unbeknownst to them at the time, they had just witnessed their team-mates being killed.

Brighton & Hove Albion, for whom Matt was on the ground staff, were an absolute crutch for the club to lean on. They provided counselling, laid on buses to the funerals and hosted the wakes. When the time came for Worthing United to play that first post-accident match, they offered use of their Amex Stadium, as well as printing programmes, manufacturing scarves and providing stewards, all free of charge.

The offer of use of the stadium was politely declined. 'We wanted to stay on our pitch and try to get back to normal,' explains Steve. 'After about three weeks, we knew we'd have to get back into it. Talking to the families, we know that both Matt and Jacob were players who hated football-free weekends. Absolutely hated them.

'All the players wanted to play. But the one thing they all said was that they didn't want to see the number one and number eleven shirts.' Football associations and leagues are often notorious for their unbending adherence to the rulebook, but the authorities had no hesitation in permitting Matt and Jacob's numbers to be retired.

With the club used to an average gate of sixty, the first match back – at home to East Preston in the FA Vase – attracted a crowd of more than 1,000. The non-league football family showed its solidarity and sympathy in good numbers. For Nigel, the crowd helped his match preparation.

'To play in front of that many people was brilliant. That got them going. No team talk was needed. That was just as well. Just as I started talking, I welled up. I had to get out of there. We had a minute's applause and I was bawling my eyes out, but the players were absolutely fantastic.

'It was a strange atmosphere. It was very quiet because people didn't know how to act in that situation. People weren't there to watch Worthing United. They were there to pay their respects to Jacob and Matt. But the first goal went in and everyone was lifted because we were winning. Then they equalised and it went silent. The best roar was when we scored again and got the win.'

As healing as that first match – and the rest of the season, when they matched their highest-ever league finish – was, Nigel Geary still carries the pain. 'I've never lost anyone close to me. I've still got all my nans and granddads. So I don't know if I've finished dealing with it. It's still so much in the public eye. The first anniversary is coming up, the reports are coming out soon and then there's the police investigation. It will all keep dragging it up.

'I'm from round here and I've used that stretch of the A27 all my life. Three or four times a day sometimes. I can't go past without thinking about what happened on that day.' Gone but never, ever forgotten.

'They'll be forever in our future.'

The sun has returned to the fields of Lancing College, prompting players to not only dispense with their waterproof ponchos, but to also remove insulating layers of foil from under their shirts. Sun cream is being thickly applied, like war paint, while a tray of ice pops is being offered around.

As if playing for 108 hours isn't a sufficiently stern test of character and resolve, the weather gods have made their own contribution to the cause. Fog, sunburn and near-sub-zero nights have all had to be endured so far, while the lightning from a dramatic thunderstorm on the second night enhanced the output of the temporary floodlights.

The rise in temperature this afternoon would usually slow down the match, but the pace has suddenly quickened, with goalkeepers and defenders noticeably more attentive and strikers more fleet of foot. There's a reason. The total has reached 999 goals and a bottle of champagne awaits the scorer of the 1,000th. It turns out to be the longest period of the game without a goal.

To keep minds focused and spirits buoyant, throughout the hours and days the players have been devising a few mini-games to be played within the big match.

During one period of play, they can only score with their left foot. During another, they have to try to score in off the post. For an hour or two this afternoon, they're only permitted to shoot from outside the eighteen-yard box (although this is primarily to allow the soggy penalty area to dry out. There are still more than two whole days left to play, after all).

A Sainsbury's home-delivery truck rumbles across the grass to donate a few crates of complimentary groceries to the cause. Hopefully there's plenty there to satisfy the diet of the chairman's son. After the accident, Jack Taylor offered up his own tribute to the deceased. Matt Grimstone had been a vegetarian so, in his honour, the teenager elected to give up meat. It's a tribute that will last a lifetime.

Jack's gesture is a touching one, a reflection of a cause that's all about honour, integrity and solidarity. Never mind image rights or official partners or Chinese take-overs or FIFA backhanders. These are mere sideshows to the main attraction of football itself. And one moment in particular today tells you all you need to know about the sport.

Matt's brother Paul is one of the valiant thirty-six players. With legs comparatively fresh from a restorative spell in goal, he collects the ball in the inside-left posi-tion, dips his shoulder and curls it into the far top corner. It's the most glorious strike of the day.

He looks across to the double-decker bus and raises an arm in salute to the giant pictures of Matt and Jacob.

* * *

An unexpected postscript.

Chairman George is on the line. Chairman George sounds happier than he's been all season. Chairman George has some news.

The drawbridge has been raised on the membership of next season's Toolstation Western League Division One and, remarkably, Bishop Sutton have made the cut. While two new teams are joining – Wiltshire side Malmesbury Victoria and Bishops Lydeard from Somerset – the division is also expanding. But, with no other promotion-seeking county-level clubs having the requisite standard of facilities for level-ten football, no team needs to make room for them by being relegated. Bishop Sutton can stay just where they are.

It's a delicious irony. The club that had to turn down promotion to the Southern League three years ago because of the unaffordable improvements needed to Lakeview have earned a reprieve based on others' grounds not being up to scratch. Good karma has finally arrived in this pocket of south-west England.

Had they been forced to drop down, the future would have been beyond bleak for Bishop Sutton. It would have been uncertain whether Chairman George would have had the spirit or energy to continue, forty years after converting that cow field. But, what's crystal-clear, from the chipper tone of his voice down the phone line, is that his spirit and energy remains.

Another season awaits. Another adventure ready to unfold. Another attempt to escape the bottom corner.

Epilogue

After we met at Heathrow, **Rob Gier** never played another game of competitive football, either for Ascot United or for the Philippines national team. A long-standing knee injury forced his retirement, the healing process suffering from the lack of round-the-clock physio care he would have received at a full-time club. Gier's time is now filled running soccer tours to the UK and Spain for Filipino youngsters and working towards his UEFA 'A' coaching licence, the latter with a possible eye on becoming the Philippines' boss at some far point. It will never match playing, though. 'I miss the sense of belonging and the team spirit the most. I am no longer a footballer.'

Sam Bangura's first season playing men's football in the lower leagues went well. Although Marlow struggled to maintain a presence in the top half of the table, Bangura himself was named the club's player of the season. He's now looking forward to a pre-season divided between three league clubs, one of which could offer a passage back to the Premier League. And should a professional contract be forthcoming from any of the three, the resurrection of an international career is surely back on the agenda.

It turned out to be a topsy-turvy season for **Adam Priestley**, who had to be content with a mixture of first-team starts and substitute appearances. As Shaw Lane Aquaforce pushed for a third successive promotion that was ultimately denied them, he hit a rich vein of scoring, finishing on eighteen for the season – not a bad tally for someone in and out of the side. Then, two days before the start of the new season, Priestley made the move that might just snag the attention of the Gibraltar boss, climbing two non-league tiers to sign for Alfreton Town of the Conference North.

After eleven harmonious years, **FC United of Manchester** experienced its most turbulent season yet. Although their status in the Conference North was maintained despite a mid-season flirtation with the relegation zone, all was not happy behind the scenes. Not only did the influential general manager Andy Walsh announce his intention to stand down, but the *Guardian* reported that the backdrop was one of 'legal action, resignations, protests, gagging orders and the overall feeling that FC are locked in an identity crisis'. Choppy waters are lapping on the shores of Utopia.

As if to prove his iconoclast tendencies, towards the end of Forest Green's season, **Dale Vince** took an unparalleled decision, one that bemused almost every single onlooker. With one game of the season left, he sacked manager Ady Pennock, despite the club's highest-ever finish – second in the Conference. Vince based his decision on a hunch that Pennock wasn't the man to lead them to play-off success. The team had endured poor form in the last few games of the regular season, but the counter-argument was that – with second place secure and no hope of catching ultimate champions Cheltenham – this was down to Pennock deliberately resting players in advance of the play-offs. With a caretaker manager in charge, they did indeed reach Wembley, but were ultimately denied by Grimsby.

The adventures keep coming for **Barry Hayles**. After FA Cup glory and a mediocre league season with Chesham United, he jumped on a jet plane to spend June representing England Veterans at the Seniors World Cup in Thailand. At the age of forty-four, Hayles is now in possession of a World Cup winner's medal.

After the stoppage-time draw with Leiston before Christmas, **Lewes** saw a distinct upturn in their form. Of particular note were their last ten games of the season, of which they only lost one. However, eight of those were draws, not enough to stave off the inevitable. Next season they will be reacquainting themselves with life in the Ryman League Division One South.

John Kyte finished the season officiating his 4,758th match when he took charge of the Jim Blower Memorial Cup final between Azaard Sports and Whitmore Reans. The whistle's not going into retirement just yet. 'I'll be continuing next season,' he smiles defiantly. 'God willing . . .'

The Birkenhead Premier Inn didn't have the pleasure of **Lasse Larsen**'s business again this season. After the Halifax trip, he didn't make it to another Tranmere match. However, his optimism levels are high for the next campaign, fuelled by a couple of sharp signings by Gary Brabin shortly after the season finished. While his desire to visit Grimsby's Blundell Park has had to be put on hold (with the Mariners returning to the Football League), Larsen has new destinations in his sights, including trips to just-relegated York City and Dagenham & Redbridge.

From his first season as boss, **Chris Todd** has collected more memories than most managers take a decade to gather. While his Eastleigh side couldn't quite dump Bolton out of the cup, they couldn't quite squeeze into the Conference play-offs either. Still in the mix on the last day, they managed a very creditable seventh in what was only their second season in the fifth tier, finishing just one place below Tranmere.

Just as last season, **Salford City** timed their promotion push perfectly, going up into the Conference North via the play-offs having finished third in the table. After his sacking by Valencia and resignation from the position of England assistant manager, Gary Neville will have more time to be hands-on again at Moor Lane, although the club and **Gareth Seddon** parted ways at the end of the season. He's now with his hometown team Ramsbottom United, 'literally thirty seconds from my house. I'll hopefully bang in a few more goals after spending five months out injured last season. I will miss those cameras, though. Who's going to capture my thirty-yarders now?!'

Johnnie Walker completed yet another season on Hackney Marshes, all his league's fixtures being fulfilled on time 'without any nasty dramas'. While neither World War III nor the marital bedpost were responsible, he did miss one Sunday, though; a spell in hospital with pneumonia was to blame. He's all fixed now. 'Would I think of jacking it in? If I ever did say that, it would have been in a moment of madness.' Meanwhile, **Bow Badgers** avoided finishing bottom of the bottom division of the Hackney & Leyton Football League. They hauled themselves into penultimate place by the tiniest of margins, their goal difference of -41 just pipping Eastway Olympia's -42.

By season's end, **Chris Freer** had reached ground number 702, having notched up eighty-one new grounds since August. But he remains a strict self-adjudicator. 'I turned down one tick, as I considered the ground to be just a park pitch. Groundhopping snobbery!'

At **Dulwich Hamlet**, it was déjà vu for the Rabble. Not only was it the third consecutive season that the club had topped the Ryman Premier table at Christmas before falling away, they also experienced a second successive play-off failure. Still, the club did win the Football Foundation Community Club of the Year gong at the National Game Awards, where lifetime supporter Mishi Morath collected the cut-glass decanter.

Ken Ryder was one game away from his job changing quite dramatically – to being head of recruitment for a Premier League club. In the end, Sheffield Wednesday couldn't get over the line in the Championship play-off final, so another year in the second tier beckons instead. It means that non-league remains very much on his scouting radar, even if he's cautious about the prospects. 'It's getting harder to find a jewel in that class of football,' he notes. Not that he won't keep trying, though. More wet Tuesday nights, more miles on the Nissan's clock.

While on his holidays, **Ashley Flynn** did indeed make up his mind about where he was going to play next season, deciding to sign up with ... AFC Emley. Having previously admitted he'd be 'silly' or 'stupid' not to move up to a higher league, Flynn feels that, in the wake of that play-off penalty shoot-out, he has unfinished business at the club. Whether honourable or misguided, he's elected to stay on to achieve the promotion so narrowly missed. It was a decision aided by the club – rather smartly, objective eyes might think – signing up a couple of Flynn's pals. Ambition deferred. For now ...

At 6 pm on Bank Holiday Monday at Lancing College, tears and cheers greeted the final whistle at **Worthing United's** record attempt. The valiant thirty-six players had notched up 108 hours on the pitch, a new world record for a continuous 11-a-side football match. While the final fundraising figure wouldn't be known for a while, the final score was an impressive one: 1,009-872.

Finally, down at Lakeview, Bishop Sutton's theatre of dreams, the near-empty touchlines will no longer echo with the barked instructions of **Colin Merrick** and **Steve Laker**. Merrick has left the club by mutual consent, while Laker has taken a new coaching role one division higher – and it's with Street, the team responsible for shattering his FA Cup dreams way back in August.

Acknowledgements

Firstly, enormous thanks to all the interviewees who were generously tolerant in having their time and personal space invaded by a nosy author and his note-pad. Your knowledge and opinions greatly helped to colour my own thinking over the season. You are the stars of this book. Keep dreaming.

Their voices might not be heard, but for being fixers in the field, or for offering leads and suggestions, thanks to Kenny Amor, Jon Bauckham, Ian Burke, Geoff Davies, Colin Docherty, Craig Elliott, Phil Fifield, Dave Goat, Dave Jeffrey, Richard Joyce, Ray Murphy, Andrew Painten, Jeremy Pound, Nick Ramsland, Phil Reade, Tony Ritter, Tim Roberts, Tom Rowland, Terry Staines, Andy Walker and Mark Whittle. And thanks to my occasional co-driver James 'Eyes On The Pies' Witts for being an amiable, if cartographically illiterate, travelling companion.

Big thanks for big favours are due to Barry Davies, Stuart Maconie and David Bauckham. David took the cover image and is the non-league world's finest photojournalist – check out his excellent work at dbauck-ham.exposure.co.

Throughout the season, the forensically compiled pages of *The Non-League Paper* were an invaluable guide, while the insight provided by Caroline Barker's (now-silent) *Non-League Show* on BBC Radio Five Live was equal parts illumination and entertainment.

Among all the backslapping, an apology has to go to Nigel Blackwell for the deplorable and wholesale lifting of one of his (many) great lines halfway through Chapter Five. I've no excuse.

At Yellow Jersey, Frances Jessop has been a tremendous editor, her enthusiasm matched by her sharp pen and judicious suggestions. Elsewhere at YJ HQ, Matt Broughton, Anna Redman, Nick Skidmore, Josh Ireland and Richard Collins each get a grateful tip of the hat.

Kevin Pocklington might be the most laid-back literary agent around, but he hit the bullseye with his very first dart. Eternal thanks, Agent K.

Finally, to home. To Jane goes endless love and gratitude for patiently tolerating the absences and the long hours that I was chained to the computer. Your support is appreciated every second of every day. And hugs to Finn and Ned for whom, throughout the season, I was too often either a grumpy presence behind a closed office door or sloping off to yet another match. I'm ready for that kickabout in the garden now, boys. Three and in?

penguin.co.uk/vintage

NIGE TASSELL

Nige Tassell writes about sport and music, and his work has appeared in the pages of *FourFourTwo*, the *Guardian*, the *Sunday Times*, *Esquire*, *New Statesman*, *Q* and *The Word*. He is also the author of *Mr Gig: One Man's Search For the Soul of Live Music*. He lives in the hill country of Somerset with his wife and two prospective future non-league players.

ALSO BY NIGE TASSELL

Mr Gig: One Man's Search for the Soul of Live Music
Three Weeks, Eight Seconds: The Epic Tour de
France of 1989